Dixie's Daughters

NEW PERSPECTIVES ON THE HISTORY OF THE SOUTH

Florida A&M University, Tallahassee
Florida Atlantic University, Boca Raton
Florida Gulf Coast University, Ft. Myers
Florida International University, Miami
Florida State University, Tallahassee
University of Central Florida, Orlando
University of Florida, Gainesville
University of North Florida, Jacksonville
University of South Florida, Tampa
University of West Florida, Pensacola

NEW PERSPECTIVES ON THE HISTORY OF THE SOUTH
Edited by John David Smith

"In the Country of the Enemy": The Civil War Reports of a Massachusetts Corporal,
edited by William C. Harris (1999)
The Wild East: A Biography of the Great Smoky Mountains,
by Margaret L. Brown (2000; first paperback edition, 2001)
Crime, Sexual Violence, and Clemency: Florida's Pardon Board and Penal System
in the Progressive Era, by Vivien M. L. Miller (2000)
The New South's New Frontier: A Social History of Economic Development
in Southwestern North Carolina, by Stephen Wallace Taylor (2001)
Redefining the Color Line: Black Activism in Little Rock, Arkansas, 1940–1970,
by John A. Kirk (2002)
The Southern Dream of a Caribbean Empire, 1854–1861, by Robert E. May (2002)
Forging a Common Bond: Labor and Environmental Activism during the BASF Lockout,
by Timothy J. Minchin (2003)
Dixie's Daughters: The United Daughters of the Confederacy and the Preservation
of Confederate Culture, by Karen L. Cox (2003)

Dixie's Daughters

THE UNITED DAUGHTERS OF THE CONFEDERACY
AND THE PRESERVATION OF CONFEDERATE CULTURE

Karen L. Cox

Foreword by John David Smith, Series Editor

UNIVERSITY PRESS OF FLORIDA

Gainesville · Tallahassee · Tampa · Boca Raton · Pensacola · Orlando · Miami · Jacksonville · Ft. Myers

First cloth printing, 2003
First paperback printing, 2004

Library of Congress Cataloging-in-Publication Data
Cox, Karen L., 1962–
Dixie's daughters: the United Daughters of the Confederacy and the preservation
of Confederate culture / Karen L. Cox; foreword by John David Smith.
p. cm. — (New perspectives on the history of the South)
Includes bibliographical references and index.
ISBN 0-8130-2625-3 (alk. paper)
ISBN 0-8130-2812-4 (pbk.)
1. United Daughters of the Confederacy—History. 2. Southern States—
Civilization. 3. Popular culture—Southern States. 4. Southern States—Politics
and government—1865–1950. 5. Political culture—Southern States.
6. United States—History—Civil War, 1861–1865—Influence.
I. Title. II. Series.
E483.5 C68 2003
369'.17—dc21   2002040904

The University Press of Florida is the scholarly publishing agency
for the State University System of Florida, comprising Florida A&M
University, Florida Atlantic University, Florida Gulf Coast University, Florida
International University, Florida State University, University of Central Florida,
University of Florida, University of North Florida, University
of South Florida, and University of West Florida.

University Press of Florida
15 Northwest 15th Street
Gainesville, FL 32611–2079
http://www.upf.com

For Hilda Brody

Contents

List of Illustrations   ix

Foreword by John David Smith, series editor   xi

Preface   xv

Note on Sources and Evidence   xix

List of Abbreviations   xx

1. Journey into the Lost Cause   1

2. The Sacred Trust   8

3. The Rise of the UDC   28

4. The Monument Builders   49

5. Confederate Progressives   73

6. Combating "Wicked Falsehoods"   93

7. Confederate Motherhood   118

8. Vindication and Reconciliation   141

Epilogue   159

Notes   165

Bibliography   195

Index   207

Illustrations

2.1. Winnie Davis 15

2.2. Caroline Meriwether Goodlett and Anna Davenport Raines 17

3.1. Virginia McSherry 31

3.2. Rassie White 33

3.3. Cornelia Stone 36

3.4. Mildred Rutherford 40

3.5. Elizabeth Lumpkin 42

4.1. Confederate monument in Augusta, Georgia 50

4.2. Advertisement from marble company 51

4.3. Moses Ezekiel 55

4.4. Katie Behan 57

4.5. Confederate souvenir spoon 58

4.6. Monument unveiling, Lebanon, Tennessee 60

4.7. Richmond children with Jefferson Davis monument 61

4.8. Monument unveiling, Dallas, Texas 62

4.9. En route to monument unveiling 63

4.10. Young girls representing the Confederate states 64

4.11. A "living" flag in New Orleans 65

4.12. A "living" flag in Richmond 66

4.13. The Confederate monument at Arlington National Cemetery 69

4.14. Daisy Stevens presents the Arlington monument to President
Woodrow Wilson 71

5.1. Beauvoir, Mississippi's soldiers' home 79

5.2. Caroline Helen Plane 81

5.3. The Virginia Daughters 83

5.4. Lizzie George Henderson 88

5.5. Varina Davis 89

5.6. Carr-Burdette College advertisement 92

6.1. Adelia Dunovant 94

6.2. The White House of the Confederacy 99

6.3. Laura Martin Rose 108

6.4. Advertisement for Rose's primer for children 109

6.5. Leonora Schuyler 113

7.1. "Little" Laura Galt 119

7.2. Baby with Confederate flags 120

7.3. A young girl in Confederate dress 121

7.4. Portrait of Jefferson Davis 132

7.5. Children of the Confederacy in Tennessee 134

7.6. Decca Lamar West 138

8.1. Daisy McLaurin Stevens 151

8.2. Cordelia Powell Odenheimer 154

Foreword

Writing in 1941, Wilbur J. Cash described the South as a "tree with many age rings, with its limbs and trunk bent and twisted by all the winds of the years, but with its tap root in the Old South." Late-nineteenth-century southern white polemicists, determined to venerate and vindicate their antebellum and Confederate "tap root," crafted the Lost Cause myth. This integrated set of ideas argued that differing interpretations of states' rights, not slavery, caused the Civil War and that the right of secession stood deeply embedded in American constitutional history. Lost Cause spokesmen sketched an idealized portrait of the antebellum South, one that romanticized white paternalism and African American slavery and glorified the valor of Confederate soldiers. They contrasted the supposedly faithful, contented, and productive slaves of the Old South with their allegedly disloyal, troublesome, and inefficient descendants, the freedmen and freedwomen of the New South.

In her timely, well-researched, and insightful analysis of the United Daughters of the Confederacy (UDC), Karen L. Cox, who teaches at the University of North Carolina at Charlotte, argues that elite southern women, not men, led the way in constructing the Lost Cause image. The first scholar to underscore the role of gender in commemorating and preserving the ideals of the Old South, Cox writes persuasively that women provided sustained leadership in fashioning the Lost Cause. From the 1890s through World War I, the women of the UDC expanded woman's sphere by playing prominent roles in southern public life, championing the region's conservative social and racial values, and celebrating the role of Confederate women during the Civil War. Within a decade of its founding, the UDC emerged as "one of the most socially and politically effective organizations in the region."

The movement to celebrate the Confederate past began soon after Appomattox, when Ladies' Memorial Associations commenced honoring and memorializing the slain Confederates by sponsoring Confederate memorial days. "Across the South," Cox writes, these organizations "helped to extend women's domestic role as caretakers into the public sphere as they memorialized dead fathers, brothers, and sons buried in Confederate cemeteries." The UDC, established in 1894, built upon this foundation and functioned as a benevolent, historical, educational, and social organization that vindicated Confederate veterans. "Daughters" (as they were known throughout the region) "raised the stakes of the Lost Cause by making it a movement about vindication, as well as memorialization." They defended the South's actions in seceding and fighting the Federal government. Much like the Confederates themselves, UDC members asserted that their ancestors, not those of northerners, were the "true" interpreters and inheritors of the Founding Fathers' revolutionary legacy and the U.S. Constitution. Transforming Confederate "defeat into a political and cultural victory," Cox explains, the Daughters preserved and transmitted what she terms "Confederate culture."

"Confederate culture" dominated America's historical memory of the Old South and the Confederacy for decades and was not dislodged until the rise of the modern Civil Rights movement. Ironically, the UDC accomplished in peacetime what their Confederate forebears had failed to achieve during war. The Daughters did so by memorializing dead Confederate soldiers and the society that they had fought to preserve. UDC members rewrote history by transforming the Confederates from traitors into patriots. They raised funds to support homes for aging and indigent Confederate veterans and their widows. They erected monuments to the Confederate dead at courthouses and town squares throughout the South. And they distributed Confederate flags and library books to public schools for white children. As Cox makes clear, the UDC made a concerted effort to use these symbols to educate white children in the alleged glories and venerable traditions of the Old South.

The Daughters recognized the importance of weaving Confederate traditions into the "true" history of the Civil War in textbooks and public culture on the state, local, and national levels. Determined to document and interpret history "impartially" (which for them meant from a decidedly southern perspective), the Daughters played instrumental roles in establishing cultural institutions in the South, including the Museum of the Confederacy, the Alabama State Department of Archives and History, and the North Carolina Museum of History. To advance its cause, the UDC sponsored essay contests and offered college scholarships for needy white men and women, descendants of Confederate veterans. "The UDC left no stone unturned," Cox concludes, "to insure that the next generation was motivated to honor and uphold the values of the Confederate generation as they had."

The UDC's success in honoring the sacrifices of the Confederate generation perpetuated the traditions and values of the Old South, including white supremacy and racial segregation. Later generations of women and men exposed the intolerance and racism that had always lain at the "tap root" of Confederate culture.

John David Smith
Series Editor

Preface

In the late 1980s, when I was working at the Museum of the Cape Fear in Fayetteville, North Carolina, my colleague Rob Siewers asked if I could help him with some research. Rob does traditional woodworking (without power tools), and when he sells handmade items, he includes information on the history of the materials used. This day, he came to my office because he was making benches from wood salvaged from the North Carolina Confederate Woman's Home that had once stood in Fayetteville. His request for information on the home set me on a journey, both figurative and literal, that has lasted several years. For what I learned about this Confederate woman's home opened a window into an entire world that was dominated by Confederate culture. Moreover, I learned, it was a culture in which women assumed prominent roles of leadership—particularly those women in the United Daughters of the Confederacy (UDC). *Dixie's Daughters* is the culmination of my interest and research whose genesis is a piece of wood.

Throughout the writing of my dissertation, from which this book is drawn, I received generous financial support from the University of Southern Mississippi (USM). The USM Committee on Services and Resources for Women provided a research grant during the initial stages of the project, and the Department of History's McCain Dissertation Fellowship enabled me to travel and conduct research throughout the South for the better part of a year. In addition, a Mellon Fellowship from the Virginia Historical Society allowed me to gather important research on the UDC from the society's collections. I also wish to thank Mary Jane

Boswell, whose support allowed me to make major revisions to the manuscript during the summer of 2000.

Many people have played a role in bringing this project to fruition, not the least of which are archivists and librarians. John Coski, at the Museum of the Confederacy, provided invaluable assistance, which is genuinely appreciated by those of us who use the museum's collections. I am particularly indebted to the reference librarians at the University of Southern Mississippi's McCain Library, who were always gracious about having to haul out yet another volume of the *Confederate Veteran* and photocopy the pages I requested.

Marjorie Spruill headed my dissertation committee, which included Neil McMillen, Charles Bolton, Tom Richardson, and Kay Edwards. Each reader brought a unique perspective and expertise to this topic of women and the Lost Cause, challenging me to press certain arguments further and offering constant reminders of the larger contexts. Marjorie Spruill, in particular, has championed my work and pushed me to revise the dissertation for publication. Her enthusiasm for my scholarship has made me the envy of several of my peers who recognize what a rarity it is to find such support from a dissertation advisor.

Peers, friends, and family also made this journey worthwhile. While I was writing, Jason Dawsey, Steve Parris, and Greg Mattson provided friendship and a regular social outlet, as we all believed that hard work was to be rewarded with a beer now and then. Joan Johnson, Rebecca Montgomery, Chrissy Cortina, and I met as graduate students during meetings of the Southern Association for Women Historians. I have greatly appreciated the friendship and support of these fine scholars over the years; they are all history divas. My mother, Flora Miller, and friends Helen Aikman, Sheri Rawls, Tracey Yost, Lucy Gutman, and many others have all encouraged me in one way or another, motivating me to complete the revisions so that this book would see the light of day.

Véronique LaCapra pressed me to make the final revisions to the manuscript even when I felt I had no more energy to do so. Her support and willingness to read parts of the manuscript were instrumental in my completing the revisions that led to this publication.

Finally, I wish to thank Hilda Brody, to whom this book is dedicated. I met her as an undergraduate when I came to volunteer at the Alamance

County Historical Museum in Burlington, North Carolina. Her belief in my abilities, as a human being and as a historian, gave me confidence when I had none. Her friendship has been steadfast, and her wisdom and counsel have been of enormous value to me. It is with gratitude that I make this dedication.

Note on Sources and Evidence

The primary sources for this study include the publications of UDC members, the minutes of state and general conventions, pamphlets and speeches by members, and the *Confederate Veteran*, a periodical that faithfully covered the activities of the UDC. One of the ironies of an organization that placed a premium on preserving history is that former UDC presidents, whose correspondence was no doubt voluminous, did not deposit their correspondence in public repositories. Biographical information proved to be sparse; however, numerous manuscript collections across the South contain information from which some personal portraits can be created. Those manuscripts also offer insights on the inner workings of the UDC and are included in this study.

The Museum of the Confederacy in Richmond, Virginia, founded by the Confederate Literary Memorial Society in 1896, has the best collection of primary source material on the UDC. Even there, presidential correspondence is meager; however, the museum does house the scrapbooks of former historian-general Mildred Rutherford. A native of Georgia who often appeared in 1860s attire, complete with hoop skirts and Spaniel curls, Rutherford zealously perpetuated the "truth" about the South and compiled more than seventy scrapbooks that offer valuable information on the organization's membership and history.

Finally, I have conducted several interviews with women whose long-time association with the Daughters began when they joined the Children of the Confederacy (CofC)—the UDC's official auxiliary—in the 1920s and 1930s. These oral histories provide valuable insights into the personality of the early organization and the ways in which children were involved in the Confederate tradition. These interviews also serve as evidence of the longevity of Lost Cause ideology.

Abbreviations

CMLS Confederate Memorial Literary Society
CofC Children of the Confederacy
CSMA Confederated Southern Memorial Association
DAR Daughters of the American Revolution
DOC Daughters of the Confederacy
LMA Ladies' Memorial Association
SCV Sons of Confederate Veterans
UCV United Confederate Veterans
UDC United Daughters of the Confederacy

Journey into the Lost Cause

Do not fail to realize that we [the Daughters] are no accidental thing.
God has brought us into existence for specific purposes.

Lizzie George Henderson, president-general,
UDC General Convention, Norfolk, Virginia, 1907

In this study of the United Daughters of the Confederacy (UDC), its leadership within the Confederate tradition, and the vital role its members played in shaping the social and political culture of the New South, I argue that women were longtime leaders in the movement to memorialize the Confederacy, commonly referred to as the "Lost Cause," and were active participants in debates over what would constitute a "new" South. I also argue that the Daughters, as UDC members were known, raised the stakes of the Lost Cause by making it a movement about vindication, as well as memorialization. They erected monuments, monitored history for "truthfulness," and sought to educate coming generations of white southerners about an idyllic Old South and a just cause—states' rights. They did so not simply to pay homage to the Confederate dead. Rather, UDC members aspired to transform military defeat into a political and cultural victory, where states' rights and white supremacy remained intact. By preserving and transmitting these ideals through what I call "Confederate culture," UDC members believed they could vindicate their Confederate ancestors.

The term *Confederate culture* is used to describe those ideas and symbols that Lost Cause devotees associated with the former Confederacy. The images and beliefs are based on a hierarchy of race and class and often reflect the patrician outlook of Lost Cause leaders. Confederate culture, to be sure, is based on the historical memory of its believers and is often racist. The Old South is idealized as a place where a benevolent planter class worked in harmony with its faithful and contented labor force. Within this culture, women remain wedded to their traditionally prescribed roles. Confederate soldiers are remembered as heroes in spite of military defeat, because they fought to defend states' rights. Consequently, they were also heroes for fighting to sustain white supremacy.[1]

The most visible symbols of Confederate culture are monuments and flags, both of which were considered important to the edification of southern youth. After the UDC was founded, the majority of monuments erected to the Confederacy were placed in public settings such as courthouse lawns or town squares, where, it was reasoned, they could be observed by children. Likewise, the Daughters successfully placed Confederate flags in nearly every white public school in the South. The flags accompanied portraits of Confederate heroes, particularly Robert E. Lee, for the purpose of reminding children of just causes like states' rights and, correspondingly, the defense of white supremacy. Monuments and flags were significant in transmitting Confederate ideals to white southern children, because they were vivid symbols of the lessons the Daughters vehemently believed should be learned.

It can be argued that women founded the Confederate tradition. The first southerners to engage in activities associated with the Lost Cause were women, specifically Ladies' Memorial Associations (LMAs). LMAs were essential to sustaining the Lost Cause tradition from 1865 to 1890, even though their work was primarily memorial. Beginning in 1890, many elite white southern women organized into groups and called themselves "Daughters of the Confederacy" (DOC). These groups saw the need to extend their work and influence beyond memorializing the past and sought ways to preserve Confederate culture for future generations. Then, on September 10, 1894, the UDC was founded, thus bringing thousands of southern women together in a quest to honor and vindicate their Confederate ancestors. Significantly, they also sought to instill in white children a reverence for the political, social, and cultural traditions of the former Confederacy.[2]

UDC founders cast a wide net when establishing objectives for the organization. Those objectives were formally referred to as memorial, benevolent, historical, educational, and social. They translated into building monuments, caring for indigent Confederate veterans and widows, promoting and publishing pro-southern textbooks, and forming chapters of the Children of the Confederacy. There was a regional consistency in the types of activities in which the Daughters engaged because the objectives were dictated by the general organization. Thus, UDC members from Virginia to Texas built monuments and published pro-southern histories; the differences essentially boiled down to which local and state heroes should be memorialized.

The organization's overarching objective, though not officially stated in its constitution, was vindication for the Confederate generation. It is important to understand that vindication motivated the Daughters and was key to their effectiveness, because the people they sought to vindicate were their parents and grandparents. Their pursuit of this all-important goal is critical to understanding the Lost Cause and its impact on the creation of a "new" South. The enormous success of the UDC in achieving its goals makes its history a useful lens through which to view issues of race, class, and gender; women's political power; the South's distinctive form of progressivism; sectional reconciliation; and, most important, the role of women in the preservation and transmission of Confederate culture. Moreover, the long-term significance of the Lost Cause for the New South becomes much more obvious.[3]

This study also seeks to reinterpret the Lost Cause by paying close attention to the implications of gender. Numerous historians have examined the Lost Cause, its philosophy, and its social and cultural implications. Most have focused almost exclusively on the activities of male participants. While these historians suggest that women, particularly the UDC, were important to the Confederate tradition, they have neglected to fully describe or analyze the role of women in shaping the Lost Cause. In their failure to fully integrate women's activity into their studies, historians have also underestimated the long-term significance of the Lost Cause for the South. Building on more recent scholarship on women and the Lost Cause, this study challenges previous assumptions about what constitutes "leadership" in the Confederate tradition. In fact, an examination of the history of the Lost Cause and the forms it took makes it clear that women had long held positions of leadership in commemorating and preserving the southern past.[4]

The Evolution of the Lost Cause

The phenomenon known as the Lost Cause developed in the South immediately after the Civil War, as a response to Confederate defeat. It has been described by historians as a regional "myth," a "cult," a "civil religion," the "Confederate tradition," and a "celebration." Many of these terms are used interchangeably, but they all refer to a conservative movement steeped in the agrarian tradition that complicated efforts to create a "New South." Among Lost Cause believers, even the term *New South* was repugnant because it implied there was something wrong with the Old South and, by association, Confederate men and women. In contrast, they upheld the values of the former Confederacy and the agrarian past and intended to honor the region's heroes and heroines by preserving a history of the war that viewed white southerners as defenders of the U.S. Constitution, specifically the Tenth Amendment, supporting states' rights.[5]

This belief was particularly useful for sustaining white southerners during Reconstruction. In these years, they held annual observances of Confederate Memorial Day, a movement begun by LMAs immediately after the war. Memorial days were held across the South, generally on either April 26, the day of General Joseph E. Johnston's surrender, or May 10, the day General Thomas "Stonewall" Jackson died. On memorial day white southerners—men, women, and children—went to their community's Confederate cemetery, gathered around the Confederate monument built with funds raised by women, listened to speeches about the heroic deeds of southern soldiers, and placed flowers and flags on the graves of the Confederate dead.[6]

Once the period of Federal intervention ended and southern conservatives resumed control of their state governments, regional enthusiasm for the Lost Cause increased. The Confederate tradition then focused less on bereavement and became a celebration of the region and patrician values. During the late 1870s and into the 1880s, many southerners began writing and revising the history of the Civil War; the movement to build monuments expanded; and Confederate organizations multiplied.[7]

The Confederate celebration expanded in the 1890s, as the region became a fertile breeding ground for the foundation of new Confederate organizations for both men and women. White political supremacy was being sanctioned by every southern state legislature, and states' rights appeared secure. Moreover, northern whites, troubled by an ever-increasing ethnic diversity in their region, expressed both sympathy and admiration for southern whites, adopting a conciliatory tone on the subject of southern race relations. This "cult of Anglo-Saxonism," as historian Nina Silber describes it, provided a supportive climate for a movement that celebrated white heroes.[8]

During the 1890s the Lost Cause also experienced significant change as the UDC came to dominate the leadership of the movement and made vindication the goal. In addition to honoring the Confederacy and its heroes, these women placed critical importance on preserving and transmitting Confederate culture. Reclaiming Civil War history and providing it with a pro-southern interpretation became a primary objective of Lost Cause devotees. Southern white women had long shared the stage with their men in promoting this form of "revisionist" history, but beginning in the 1890s, UDC members became the most visible and vocal proponents of "true" history. Although the Sons of Confederate Veterans (SCV) was founded in 1896 with similar objectives, most "New Men" were more committed to their own business and political success than to the success of the Confederate tradition. Moreover, a new generation of women—daughters of the first generation—came to the fore with an even greater devotion to Confederate ideals and provided the driving force behind the leading Lost Cause organization—the UDC. These women, I argue, are primarily responsible for the impact that the Lost Cause had on the South in the twentieth century.[9]

Throughout the book, members of the UDC are frequently referred to as elite. If the UDC leadership is representative, and I argue they are, then many members of the organization were, at the very least, social elites. Judging by the officers of the organization, the Daughters married well—to merchants, lawyers, judges, and members of state legislatures. Many were also descendants of planter families, whose fathers were Confederate officers. Still others were related by blood or marriage to governors and U.S. senators. Most received a formal education, at private female seminaries and women's colleges. The organization actually restricted membership during the period of this study, wary that someone "not to the manor born" might join its exclusive ranks.[10]

Presidents Theodore Roosevelt, William Howard Taft, and Woodrow

Wilson each hosted a UDC president at the White House to discuss ways in which the federal government could assist the organization in achieving its goals of memorializing the Confederacy at Arlington National Cemetery—further evidence of the status and influence of the organization. When the UDC held its annual meeting in Washington, D.C., in 1912, the *Washington Post* reported that the group's opening reception was one of the highlights of the city's social season and provided detailed descriptions of the women's gowns. The UDC, to be sure, was an elite organization.[11]

This study does not address the response of African-American organizations to the activities of the UDC. Certainly, the UDC did not operate in a vacuum, and its activities had serious repercussions. The Daughters' idealization of white supremacy as an Old South custom that should remain intact is critical to understanding the racist implications of their work. African Americans clearly understood the negative implications of the Lost Cause on race relations, as historians Joan Johnson and David Blight ably prove. Indeed, Johnson argues, in the case of black women's clubs, it "would be a mistake" to assume that because they repudiated the Lost Cause, they were simply being reactive. Rather, they sought to tell their own history by stressing the contributions of African Americans to the nation. There were also higher priorities, among them improved health care, education, and campaigns to prevent lynchings. Finally, and perhaps most important, African Americans in the region understood the serious repercussions of publicly criticizing white women in the Jim Crow South. They could criticize the message, but not the messengers.[12]

Several chapters of this study correspond loosely to the UDC's organizational objectives. I first examine the years leading up to the founding of the UDC and then document its rapid rise between 1894 and World War I. I also explore the cultural significance of monument building; the Daughters' efforts to care for needy and indigent Confederate men and women, in what I describe as Confederate progressivism; the Daughters' drive to preserve historical "truth"; the crucial role the UDC played in transmitting Confederate culture to children; and, finally, the ways in which the organization's insistence on promoting Confederate social and political values hampered the process of sectional reconciliation until World War I.

After 1918 the UDC never again exerted the public influence it had prior to and during the Great War. The organization had achieved many of its objectives—monuments dotted the landscape of the region; pro-Confederate textbooks were adopted by the South's public schools; and care for the remaining members of the Confederate generation had been provided. Perhaps more important, members of the first generation of the UDC, women who had experienced the Civil War firsthand or had grown up in its aftermath, were being replaced by a new generation of Lost Cause women. These new Daughters, while committed in theory to the ideals of the first generation, did not have the same emotional commitment to preserving Confederate culture. Moreover, the majority of Confederate men and women on whom the first generation of the UDC had relied to provide the vivid details of a heroic past were dead. Nevertheless, in the years between 1894 and 1919, the Daughters' success served notice that the values they held dear remained important to the creation of a New South.

The Sacred Trust

Who bears the long suspense of war? . . .
When from the bloody battlefield they bring
Them home? And who must comfort, who restore
Men's shattered hopes—who must extract the sting
When victory has passed them by? . . . We know
Whose task this is. . . . It has been woman's part in war.

Mary H. Southworth Kimbrough, "Woman's Part in War"

Annie Kyle was an upper-class young woman living in Fayetteville, North Carolina, when her state seceded from the Union in 1861, and, like many of her female contemporaries across the South, she helped organize her town's soldiers' aid society. In addition to collecting and distributing materials to make shirts for soldiers, she tended to the sick and wounded in the army hospital throughout the war. "I went every morning at nine o'clock and staid until one, and I always went late in the afternoon to see the wants of the patients were attended to during the night," she wrote.[1]

Kyle's hometown of Fayetteville was the site of a Confederate arsenal and consequently was a target of Gen. William T. Sherman's troops as they marched through the Carolinas in the spring of 1865. Sherman's army leveled the Fayetteville arsenal, burned the town's five cotton factories to the ground, and ransacked homes, including Kyle's. Within days of Sherman's departure, and despite her own loss, she returned to work at the hospital. There she learned that six men had died and were buried three to one grave; a seventh was about to be added to one of them. Upset by the way these Confederate soldiers had been buried, Kyle began to raise money in order to buy coffins and have new graves dug. She organized the grisly task of disinterring bodies buried in the hospital yard and others buried "where they camped." She wanted the deceased to be placed in individual graves, in the town cemetery, and in a space reserved specifically for the Confederate dead. Her goal was realized, and, Kyle recalled, there was a space where a monument could be placed.[2]

Like soldiers' aid societies in other towns, Kyle's group became a Ladies' Memorial Association after the war. They continued their service to the Confederacy by having the bodies of soldiers disinterred from battlefield graves and reburied in designated cemeteries; later they honored the memory of those soldiers with monuments. Members of Fayetteville's LMA made a quilt and raffled it to raise money to erect a Confederate monument in the cemetery. Unveiled in May 1868, it was one of the first built as a result of women's fund-raising efforts.[3]

The memorial activity of LMAs in the post–Civil War South marked the beginning of women's involvement in the Lost Cause. As early as 1865, an elite corps of southern white women who, like Annie Kyle, had been members of wartime soldiers' aid societies, became leaders in a movement to memorialize Confederate men. Initially, their work consisted of disinterring the bodies of Confederate soldiers from mass graves on battlefields and removing them to individual ones in Confederate cemeteries. In these cemeteries, the LMAs erected monuments to the Confederate dead—an activity with which they became identified. Each spring, on Memorial Day, members led their communities in paying homage to the Confederate dead by placing flowers on their graves.[4]

Between 1865 and 1890 memorializing Confederate men had become part of what historian LeeAnn Whites has described as "the politics of domestic loss." With the decline of men's public position in the face of Confederate defeat, the responsibility of rehabilitating them became a primary activity of southern women. The LMAs' memorial activities enabled elite southern women to play a significant role in the creation of the New South. They became influential public figures, but did so under the guise of preserving the integrity and honor of their men. Even as women's participation in the Lost Cause translated into an expanded public role for elite women, they continued to define themselves and their work as rooted in tradition. It was the source of their strength as public women in a region that was historically reluctant to accept changes in traditional gender patterns.[5]

In many ways, women's wartime experiences had prepared them to assume the task of rehabilitating Confederate men through their memorial activity. The creation of a larger public role for southern white women in the post–Civil War era had been accelerated by their wartime activity. Confederate women's experience as nurses, laborers in munitions factories, and members of soldiers' aid societies gave them the necessary skills and confidence to meet the social and cultural needs of the region in the war's aftermath. What historian Drew Faust has described as a "general breakdown in paternalism" also made a greater public role for women possible. Having failed in their role as defenders of the hearth, southern men also lost the social authority that accompanied that responsibility. Florence Barlow, editor of the *Lost Cause* magazine, was succinct on this point. Without women's assistance, she asserted, "the rehabilitation . . . of the Southern States would have been impossible." What this change meant for women, especially in the postwar period, was an expansion of their social power and increased autonomy.[6]

The work of ladies' memorial associations represented well the interplay of traditional definitions of womanhood with the new expanded public role of southern white women. Memorializing Confederate men did not threaten prescribed gender patterns and was generally accepted as an extension of women's domestic role as caretakers. Members of LMAs were simply traditional women, promoting traditional virtues associated with the Confederacy. Consequently, little stood in the way of their success.

This expansion of women's public activity in the postwar era occurred successfully because the prevailing ideology of the Lost Cause sanctioned such a change. Among other things, this class-based narrative held elite white women in high esteem and suggested that their wartime sacrifices afforded them a place of honor in the postwar South. Confederate women were believed to have been the last southerners to admit defeat. Southern men were particularly indebted to these women, such that memorial associations, and later the UDC, were free to pursue a central and leading public role within the postwar Confederate tradition.

During Reconstruction, a time when Confederate veterans were further emasculated, members of LMAs controlled memorial activities. Despite a depressed economy, they were successful in raising funds to build monuments, in part because of their elite status. Confederate Memorial Day, a female invention, also received wide popular support during this period. This day, described by some as "the Sabbath of the South," was enlivened by the LMAs. These women, claimed the president of the Confederated Southern Memorial Association (CSMA) in 1919, were "like Mary and Martha of old, last at the cross and first at the grave." Such biblical imagery was a common feature of the Lost Cause narrative; like Mary and Martha, whose faith never wavered and who paid homage to Jesus at his tomb, southern women had remained faithful to the Confederacy and were the first to pay homage to soldiers who died for what they considered to be a sacred cause.[7]

The women in the LMAs were undaunted in their efforts to memorialize men, even in the face of Federal control. A female journalist in North Carolina noted that during Radical Reconstruction, Memorial Day processions were not allowed in her state unless the United States flag was carried. Although several years passed "before the ladies were so much 'reconstructed' as to march under this [United States] flag," she boasted, the event nevertheless continued. Memorial activities were important to southern whites during this period of social upheaval and, as Gaines Foster asserts, "helped the South assimilate the fact of defeat without repudiating the defeated."[8]

The end of political Reconstruction and the advent of Democratic control over state and local governments changed the southern political structure, and Redemption had implications for the Lost Cause movement as well. The reestablishment of southern "home rule" paved the way for the next phase of the Lost Cause. Memorial Day continued to be observed, and monuments were raised and unveiled; however, these activities were now conducted in a region controlled by former Confederates and free from Federal troops. Under these conditions, the Lost Cause focused less on bereavement and more on celebrating the virtues of the Confederacy.[9]

Support for the Lost Cause strengthened during the years following Reconstruction. The celebration attracted more participants and proved to be a strong impediment to efforts at building a New South based on manufacturing and industry. Confederate celebrants lauded the agrarian past and abhorred the very term *New South,* because it implied that there might have been something wrong with the Old South. As one woman put it, "This is no 'New South.' The term is repugnant. Away with it! We are the same people, have the same instincts, the same chivalry, and the same patriotism." *Atlanta Constitution* editor Henry Grady, the well-known New South spokesman, felt obligated to pay deference to the traditions of the Old South even as he promoted southern industry. Indeed, the new order Grady envisioned required that the Confederate dead hold a place of honor. Accordingly, followers of the "New South creed," about which historian Paul Gaston has written, "had to adjust to the mythology of the Old South."[10]

Lost Cause myths not only gave white southerners a sense of regional pride; such myths also provided a story line in which men and women, black and white each played a significant role. The leading characters in this fiction were elite, white, and wealthy, the planters and plantation mistresses. The Old South was recalled as a region led by benevolent masters who were supported by genteel women, both of whom were rewarded by the faithfulness of slaves. In this narrative the South fought the war not in order to preserve slavery, but rather to preserve the Constitution, specifically the Tenth Amendment, protecting states' rights. And through this narrative, men and women of the Lost Cause invented a version of the southern past based on a belief in the superiority of their race and class. While they understood that the Old South could not be resurrected through this narrative, they nonetheless attempted to restore the culture associated with the prewar South, even under the changed economic and social conditions in which they lived.[11]

As the Lost Cause entered its celebratory phase, the accompanying ideology was important to the role women played in its development. Women of the Old South elite were a visible element in the LMAs of the postwar South. Their work building Confederate monuments and caring for the graves of the Confederate dead made them important public figures. Indeed, their efforts to memorialize men became an important source of their own social power. Even as the Lost Cause evolved to include new ways of celebrating the Confederacy—writing and publishing history, forming Confederate organizations, and building regional monuments—southern women assumed a leading role.

The movement to erect a monument to the South's best-loved hero,

Robert E. Lee, illustrates women's influence in the early stages of the Lost Cause celebration. In the 1870s Confederate Virginians sought to place in Richmond a monument to Lee, their state's, and the Confederacy's, most illustrious leader. Richmond's women raised the majority of the money for the project, and because they controlled the much-needed funds, they also exerted control over the project. In fact, they delayed the enterprise because of differences in opinion over the monument design. In 1886 Virginia Governor Fitzhugh Lee finally negotiated an agreement to create the Lee Monument Association, which included women representatives. The proposed design for the monument, however, became a point of contention between Janet Randolph, who represented the women's association and was a leading figure in Richmond Confederate circles, and Jubal Early, leader of the male Confederate coalition in Virginia. Early's efforts to pressure Randolph into accepting the recommendation of the coalition failed; the design committee selected a revised version of Randolph's choice. Randolph and the women she represented held not only the purse strings, but also the power that came with it. This scenario was to be repeated again and again, as the overwhelming majority of funds for Confederate monuments was raised by southern women, giving them a great deal of control over design, cost, dimensions, and placement.[12]

Throughout the 1880s, enthusiasm for the Lost Cause celebration continued to build. The Southern Historical Society, founded in New Orleans in 1869, published essays in which contributors debated the war and defended the actions taken by Confederate leaders. Southern men organized groups of Confederate veterans into camps and held annual veterans' reunions. In June 1889 those camps became official members of the the United Confederate Veterans (UCV). The South also called upon Jefferson Davis for the purposes of the Lost Cause celebration, and he presided over several monument unveilings. His death in 1889 only heightened his status among former Confederates, as he became the most visible martyr to the Lost Cause.[13]

Women of the Lost Cause became increasingly visible during the decade of the 1880s. They joined any number of organizations founded to commemorate the Confederacy. These included LMAs, monument associations, auxiliaries to Confederate soldiers' homes, and auxiliaries to the camps of Confederate veterans. By 1890 southern women who wanted to support Confederate men, the living as well as the dead, had several options.[14]

As the South entered the 1890s, political changes occurred that, though not directly related to the Lost Cause, sanctioned the movement and its goal to honor those who fought to preserve the southern way of life. Beginning with Mississippi in 1890, southern states reaffirmed white supremacy by passing laws that removed what political power remained in the hands of black men. Aside from the obvious political benefits white men saw in disfranchising black men, there were social and psychological ones as well. They were able, in some measure, to restore their status as protectors of southern white women and, consequently, redeem their manhood from the specter of defeat that had hovered over them since the Civil War.[15]

In many ways the Confederate celebration in the 1890s was a celebration of white supremacy being expressed nationally. Elite white men, especially elected officials, implemented those ideals that were being honored—namely, states' rights and white supremacy. Southern white women perpetuated these same values through their effort to honor and memorialize Confederate men. By removing black men from the public spaces where politics was conducted, southern legislators in the 1890s paved the path for southern women to assert their own political influence. While women shunned any reference to their Lost Cause work as political, the success of Confederate women's organizations was fostered by their willingness to become politically involved when Confederate memory was at stake.[16]

While the Confederate celebration was enhanced by Jim Crow politics and provided a cultural outlet for honoring states' rights and white supremacy, the primary activity of the movement was to honor veterans, especially former Confederate leaders. Chief among them were Robert E. Lee and Jefferson Davis. Indeed, during the 1880s Davis became the leading cult figure within the Lost Cause celebration. The glorification of Jefferson Davis spread to his family, particularly his daughter Winnie, whose claim to celebrity was justified by her birth in the White House of the Confederacy during the middle of the war. On April 30, 1886, as she stood on a train platform in West Point, Georgia, General John B. Gordon of the UCV introduced her to the crowd gathered to greet her as the "Daughter of the Confederacy." Thereafter, at each of her public appear-

Fig. 2.1. Winnie Davis, "The Daughter of the Confederacy."

ances, Winnie Davis was similarly introduced, so that she soon became identified with that title.

Southern women who had banded together for Confederate work idolized Winnie, and the Davis family generally, and many of them renamed their organizations "Daughters of the Confederacy" beginning in 1890.[17] Although Winnie Davis did not earn this title through wartime sacrifices, her popularity as the daughter of the revered Jefferson Davis lent prestige to the women who adopted the title for their local organizations. Her death in 1898, while still a young woman, only cemented her status as a Confederate icon.[18]

Ironically, the first group of women to call themselves "Daughters of the Confederacy" was organized in a non-Confederate state, Missouri, in 1890. The Daughters of the Confederacy in St. Louis, led by Mrs. A. C. Cassidy, organized for the purpose of assisting the Ex-Confederate Association that wanted to build a home for disabled veterans. The men's association purchased the land with the intention of building the home, yet had struggled to complete their project. They solicited the assistance of Missouri women to help them build and furnish the home. Through fund-raisers that included a strawberry and ice cream festival, picnics, and Confederate balls, the women of Missouri raised the money to build the home within three years of being organized. By comparison, the Ex-Confederate Association had labored nine years without success. Women across the South repeated the Missouri DOC's efforts as they stepped in to complete projects that men had begun, but had failed to finish.[19]

The Missouri DOC's involvement in providing for a soldiers' home was evidence that change was occurring in the Lost Cause celebration. For twenty-five years, southern women had cared for the graves of the Confederate dead, erected monuments in those same cemeteries, and perpetuated the rituals of Confederate Memorial Day. In so doing, they provided a strong foundation upon which the next generation of Lost Cause women, literally daughters of the Confederate generation, created their own legacy. The activity of LMAs across the South and the resulting network of women involved in memorializing the Confederacy paved the way for a Lost Cause women's organization that was to become national in scope.

The work of memorial associations, monument associations, ladies' auxiliaries to soldiers' homes, and auxiliaries to camps of Confederate veterans and the formation of DOC chapters opened doors for the next generation of middle- and upper-class southern women, a generation who came to perpetuate and redefine the Confederate tradition. Looking back on the work of southern memorial associations, the president of the CSMA, Katie Behan of New Orleans, wrote that the LMAs had "left a priceless heritage to the 'Daughters of the Confederacy,' in whom they feel a mother's pride, and rejoiced to find that the spirit lives within their hearts to continue the work begun by their mothers and grandmothers."[20]

Chapters of Daughters of the Confederacy multiplied in the early 1890s, and the work of women in the LMAs, as well as ladies' auxiliaries to the UCV, continued. Then, in the spring of 1894, two women, Caroline Meriwether Goodlett of Nashville, Tennessee, and Anna Davenport Raines of Savannah, Georgia, began a correspondence that would significantly alter women's role in the Lost Cause. Their exchange eventu-

Fig. 2.2. UDC cofounders Caroline Meriwether Goodlett (*left*)
and Anna Davenport Raines.

ally led to a September 1894 meeting of Confederate women in Nashville to discuss a federation of Confederate women's organizations.[21]

Caroline Meriwether Goodlett, a native Kentuckian, was one of the "noble women of the sixties" recognized for their service to the Confederacy. She participated in a wartime soldiers' aid society and had, since the war's end, participated in memorial work. She was a charter member of the Monument Association in Nashville, which was reorganized as the Ladies' Auxiliary to the Tennessee Confederate Soldiers' Home in 1890. She served as president of the auxiliary and continued to head the organization when, in 1892, it instituted another name change to "Daughters of the Confederacy."[22]

Anna Davenport Raines, the daughter of a Confederate officer, was secretary of the Ladies' Auxiliary to the Confederate Veterans' Association in Savannah. After reading a newspaper article about the DOC in Tennessee, she wrote to Goodlett about using the same name for her group in Savannah. Raines recognized that when the remaining veterans died, the purpose of the veterans' association ceased to exist; thus, she hoped to redefine the work of the women's organization. She formed a DOC chapter independent of the one in Nashville, but in her letters to Goodlett, she expressed a desire to create a "federation of all Southern Women's Auxiliary, Memorial, and Soldiers' Aid Societies into one grand united society."[23]

Anna Raines's initial inquiry sparked a flurry of correspondence beginning in April 1894, in which the two shared their ideas for forming a general organization. "The Ladies of the South ought to organize . . . [into] one broad Sisterhood," Goodlett wrote, and "exclude all persons and their descendants who were not loyal to the South in her hour of need." Through their exchange, they sketched out the objectives of the new organization. Goodlett wrote about the need to continue caring for aging veterans and to collect and preserve the "history and homelife of Southern women." Raines concurred, further arguing that southern women should "use their might" to protect children from the "falsehoods" evident in history texts. Both agreed that the organization should perpetuate the memory of Confederate soldiers, and Raines felt there was but "one way" to do so: "by unity of action and influencing our legislatures."[24]

Eventually, Goodlett and Raines decided to call a meeting of "representative southern women" to create an umbrella organization for all Confederate women's groups. Through advertisements that appeared in leading southern newspapers, southern women with an interest in "perpetuating the memories of the South" were invited to Nashville on September 10, 1894, to assist in creating what was described as a "national" society. The actual meeting, however, was primarily attended by women from Tennessee. Other representatives included Mrs. J. C. Myers from Dallas, Texas, and Anna Raines from Georgia. Raines traveled to Nashville by train and was greeted by Goodlett, and the two began work on a constitution for the organization that was loosely based on the UCV constitution.[25]

On September 10 the women who had responded to the invitation met at the Frank Cheatham Bivouac in Nashville to discuss the proposed organization and its constitution. Southern white women were then using the term *Daughters of the Confederacy* to describe all types of women's work in the Lost Cause. Those who met in Nashville wanted to join all Daughters into an organization that was "national in its scope" with the authority to "charter sub-organizations [i.e., chapters and divisions] in all parts of the United States." Women devoted to memorializing the Confederacy realized their goal that day, as the National Association of the Daughters of the Confederacy (NDOC) was born.

Caroline Goodlett was elected president, and Anna Raines was made first vice president. Another vice presidency was assigned to Katie Cabell Currie, then president of the Texas DOC, when it was discovered that Mrs. J. C. Myers, the Texas representative in attendance, was married to a "Union man." Currie, by contrast, had married a southerner, and even her wedding decorations were in "Confederate colors, predominately red and white with red roses and white carnations." Regarding the replacement of Myers, Goodlett wrote, "this ought to be a lesson to us . . . to be very careful to investigate everybody's credentials," indicating that membership in this new organization was to be selective.[26]

The NDOC constitution charted new territory in the Lost Cause celebration. Generational differences between the LMAs and the DOCs were evident, and yet the two came together to form the NDOC. Cofounders Caroline Goodlett and Anna Raines provide an excellent example of this union of the Confederate and postwar generations. Goodlett was sixty-one when she helped found the NDOC in 1894. An active member and president of Nashville-area Confederate women's organizations for more than thirty years, she brought valuable administrative experience and status to the new organization. Anna Raines, who at forty-one became the NDOC's first vice president, represented a generation of women relatively new to the cause, but nonetheless enthusiastic. Members of her generation joined women's organizations in droves, hoping to use their educations to benefit their communities. Indeed, the ambitious goals of the new organization seemed to require such youthful energy, though the NDOC certainly benefited from the experience and wisdom of its older members.[27]

The Daughters established five primary objectives to define their responsibility within the Confederate celebration: memorial, historical, benevolent, educational, and social. They retained the Confederate memorial tradition as established by the LMAs and planned to continue building monuments. As history had the potential of vindicating the war generation, the Daughters also had a keen interest in what was being written and published about the Confederacy. The new organization was also concerned about the care of the surviving Confederate veterans and their widows and vigorously pursued plans to ensure the well-being of their aging and indigent Confederate fathers and mothers. Most of the Daughters' activities also had some social component, such as a gathering held at the home of one of their members.[28]

The educational objectives of the Daughters, however, distinguished their work from that of other Confederate organizations. Lost Cause women believed that it was their duty "to instruct and instill into the descendants of the people of the South a proper respect for . . . the deeds of their forefathers." Lost Cause men and women wrote tomes about the importance of teaching the younger generation the "true history" of the Confederacy; the NDOC constitution implied that the Daughters intended to take further steps to actively "instruct and instill" in future generations of southern white children the values of Confederate culture.[29]

The new organization, now clearly defined in the NDOC constitution, reflected traditional gender patterns within the Confederate celebration, while also indicating that further changes in women's role were taking place. Men have been recognized as the leaders in the Lost Cause by historians, in large part because of their public visibility as ministers, heads of veterans' organizations, and authors. Yet these same men had always shared the spotlight with southern women during Memorial Day ceremonies, at monument unveilings, and even at veterans' reunions. Indeed, a more accurate reading of the Lost Cause finds that women were the movement's leaders, that monuments were built as a result of their fund-raising efforts, and that it was through their insistence on honoring Confederate memory that Memorial Day became a springtime ritual throughout the South.[30]

Women's involvement in the Lost Cause added another dimension to the movement, as they desired to preserve and perpetuate the values of the Lost Cause for future generations. Women used their education and leadership skills to take a public and, if needed, political stance to achieve their goals. Using their social power to accomplish their sacred task was exactly what the Daughters were all about.

The increased leadership role of women within the Confederate celebration had always been tempered by a definition of their role as helpmeet. However, the formation of a national organization of Lost Cause women indicated that women saw themselves as the natural leaders of a tradition whose focus was on vindicating the Confederate generation. Like other national organizations in which women expanded the definition of moral guardianship, the UDC allowed southern women to expand their own traditional sphere as they took an active, and very public, role on behalf of their Confederate ancestors.

The 1894 constitution guided the NDOC through its first year, as twenty new chapters were chartered. The constitution was significant to the success of this emerging organization, and over the course of the first year, a committee on bylaws was at work to revise the document and eliminate language that might make some southern white women ineligible for membership. Eliza Nutt Parsley of Wilmington, North Carolina, served on that committee, and her correspondence with Anna Raines and Caroline Goodlett reveals the critical importance of the constitution to the success of the national organization.

Parsley, later known as the "mother" of the North Carolina UDC, chartered the first chapter of the Daughters in her state. Though she was not in attendance in Nashville, her revisions of the original constitution helped shape the organization in its early years. Parsley's work as a member of the bylaws committee eventually led to changes in the 1894 constitution that addressed the concerns of the first generation of Lost Cause women, the LMAs, as well as the younger generation of women expected to join.

The preamble of the original constitution, which stated that the purpose of the NDOC was to establish a "general Federation . . . uniting under one Constitution all organized bodies of 'Daughters of the Confederacy' throughout the United States of America," concerned the women in the older LMAs. They feared losing their status by being absorbed into the larger organization. Parsley wrote to Raines, "we will probably meet with some opposition on the part of the older ladies from a sentiment in regard to the original organization." She later wrote Raines that efforts to charter a DOC chapter in Wilmington included a plan "to retain the Memorial Association which already has a charter as a branch of the Daughters." Parsley felt that LMAs deserved the NDOC's respect because they "were among the first organized . . . erected the first monument to the Confederate dead in this state . . . [and] held the first memorial celebration while the city was under martial law and the state under carpetbag rule." In short, the memorial association was "very dear to them." Raines agreed that LMAs should remain intact but insisted that their continued existence did not prevent them from being members of the NDOC "unless of course they are not [eligible]."[31]

Eligibility requirements in the new NDOC became an important topic of discussion. The founders tried to ensure that their fledgling organization commanded respect, which is why they dismissed one of the founding officers for having married a "Union man." The 1894 constitution stated that membership was open to women who were descendants of men who served honorably in the Confederate army or navy. Another measure of eligibility was based on social standing, as the new NDOC gave chapters permission to reject an applicant who received "three black balls" when voted upon by the members. The original constitution's requirements for eligibility reflected Raines's influence and became the focus of an exchange with Parsley.[32]

Parsley worried that many women might be left out if only the descendants of soldiers were eligible. "Does this exclude those who . . . 'endured' the war themselves?" she asked. Pointing to the fact that her local memorial association had members who were "daughters of men undoubtedly loyal to the Southern Cause but [for] one reason or another were not in active service." Clearly, Raines wanted to restrict membership primarily to exclude northern women who had married southern men since the war. Such women, she replied, might be "in sympathy with us and make admirable workers. Still [they] are not to the manor born and cannot be a Daughter."[33]

Caroline Goodlett was more concerned that harmony within the new organization be preserved. "I don't think that there is any danger of getting any wolves in our field," she wrote Parsley in 1895. "I think we have a great deal more to fear from misunderstandings among ourselves," she continued, "than we have from any one getting in that is not [entitled] to join us." Goodlett was also troubled that Raines might damage the organization's reputation by creating membership restrictions. "It does no good to be kicking at every step that is taken," she wrote in reference to Raines. "It will only keep other people from joining and eventually break up the National Association and make us the subject of ridicule (especially to Northern people)." Her reference to "Northern" ridicule was telling, since the failure of the new organization was tantamount to another Confederate defeat.[34]

Raines persisted with her agenda to restrict membership. Writing to Parsley in 1896, she insisted that "anyone joining must have the endorsement or be 'recommended'" by a charter member. "This is simply done to keep out an [objectionable] character," she explained, "who might by their *war record* be eligible to membership, yet their daily record will bear questioning and it might prove detrimental to the society." Raines obviously saw the NDOC as representing the interests of Confederate descendants and the interests of her class. She was not alone in her concern, as the issue of eligibility continued to be raised as the organization grew in size and influence.[35]

Aside from her concerns about membership, North Carolina's Parsley was interested in preserving state authority within the new national organization. In her suggestions to the NDOC, Parsley explained, "the life and work of the Daughters of the Confederacy is in the State Division." Thus, as representative of the North Carolina Division, she recommended that "all amendments to and changes in the Constitution be made from this point of view." Parsley's assertion was consistent with her support of states' rights. Just as the rights of states were protected by the U.S. Constitution, the rights of state divisions of the UDC should be reflected in the new NDOC constitution.[36]

When the NDOC met again in Atlanta in November 1895, the revised constitution included significant changes, the most important being the name change from the "National Association of the Daughters of the Confederacy" to the "United Daughters of the Confederacy." The section on blackballing had been replaced with "the mode of electing and admitting members may [vary] with each Division." Furthermore, in the new constitution each state, rather than the national association, chartered chapters. The new constitution added the claim that action taken by the UDC be "without any political signification whatever." Although the UDC as an organization officially rejected any involvement in formal politics, on some level this disavowal was a rhetorical rejection, as the Daughters, both individually and collectively, became savvy politicians in pursuing the organization's goals.[37]

One subject on which all the Daughters agreed was that their female Confederate ancestors, "the women of the sixties," were equally deserving of the reverence previously reserved for Confederate men. In fact, a woman became a UDC member based on her relation to either a male or female Confederate ancestor. The Daughters recognized that Confederate women shared in the "dangers, sufferings, and privations" that accompanied the Civil War. Moreover, the UDC firmly held that it was the Daughters' responsibility "to record the part taken [in the war] by Southern women" as well as to honor Confederate men. The Daughters' insistence helped establish gender parity in the cultural memory of the war and further distinguished the work of the UDC from its male counterparts in the Lost Cause celebration.[38]

The joy of helping to form this highly successful women's organization soon dissipated for Anna Raines, as a controversy erupted between her and Caroline Goodlett over who had founded the UDC. Goodlett was celebrated as the founder of the organization in the pages of the *Confederate Veteran*. Yet Raines and her supporters in Georgia felt as if the honor belonged to her. Raines's claim was fostered in part by her anger toward what she saw as the "ruling [power] in Tennessee." Writing to Virginian Janet Randolph as early as 1895, she declared, "I am done with the National as far as I am personally concerned. . . . They seem to think the local Daughters in Nashville have power to make and unmake laws to suit themselves." Nevertheless, Raines did not give up on the national organization, as she and her supporters in Georgia continued to press for her recognition as the UDC founder. The issue was finally resolved in 1901.[39]

The conflict between Raines and Goodlett was more than petty infighting. The UDC was fast becoming a prominent women's organization, and its members were heralded as representing the best of southern womanhood. Positions of leadership within the UDC were prized, as state and national officeholders were often held in high esteem both in and out of Confederate circles. Thus, the question of who should be credited with organizing the Daughters was a serious one indeed, especially among women of their class, whose accolades often came through their volunteer work.

In 1901 President-General Julia Weed of Florida had the unenviable task of appointing a committee to put an end to what she described as "an unhappy wrangle in regard to who conceived the plan of organization." The committee itself was made up of six women—three representing the interests of Goodlett and three representing the interests of Raines. The group met during the UDC's 1901 general convention, held in Wilmington, North Carolina. The women examined documentary evidence submitted by both parties, especially the Raines-Goodlett correspondence from 1894. Goodlett had written Weed that Raines had several opportunities to make her claim, including at the original meeting and at the early conventions, "but such a thought never entered her brain."[40]

Anna Raines's role in founding the UDC appeared in print, infuriating Goodlett and drawing Sumner Cunningham, editor of the *Confederate Veteran,* into the debate. He begged Raines not to continue her conflict with Goodlett, who was extremely offended. "There is not enough in the conception of a name to justify an acrimonious controversy," Cunningham wrote, "and such a one as I am sure will follow if this be kept up." The bitterness did indeed continue. In a letter written to Raines on New Year's Eve, Goodlett expressed outrage. Calling Raines's claims of helping to found the organization "absurd," Goodlett asked, "Do you suppose that after spending years in trying to bring the women of the South in touch by effecting this organization . . . that I would permit you to take the credit of it from me?"[41]

Much of Caroline Goodlett's anger stemmed from what she considered a breach of southern honor, which she clearly believed should guide the actions of both women and men. She refers to honor three times in her letter, once in reference to Raines, once in reference to herself, and a third time in reference to Raines's husband: "I cannot understand how an honorable woman can claim to have done something she did not do." Then later, "my honor is dearer to me than anything else and I shall vindicate it, no matter what it costs." And finally, "I would like to know what your husband, who is a Southern man (and doubtless understands the code of honor that regulates Southern hospitality) thinks." Goodlett's admonishments also offer evidence that she expected deference from Raines, who was twenty years her junior.[42]

Goodlett also felt rebuked by the women who backed Raines, complaining that their criticisms were an affront to her honor. "I organized the UDC for the good of the South, not myself," she wrote, "but no unworthy person shall have the credit of what I have done." The committee eventually decided in favor of Caroline Goodlett by a vote of four to two. The report, which was read and approved by delegates to the 1901 Wilmington general convention, finally ended the debate.[43]

The founding of the UDC in 1894 signaled a change in the Lost Cause celebration and in the public lives of thousands of the region's elite women. Membership in the UDC allowed these southern women to apply their education and leadership skills without fear of being criticized as "unfeminine." The UDC also brought together two generations of Lost Cause women, ensuring that the goals of Lost Cause devotees survived at least another generation.

The new organization was built upon a twofold legacy that in many ways defined the UDC and contributed to its success in the years leading up to World War I. One part of this legacy was the tradition of public service to the Lost Cause begun by the LMAs at the close of the Civil War. Through their work of memorializing Confederate men, LMAs carved a niche in the public life of the region in which elite southern women were vital participants. The UDC was a product of this tradition and built upon it, expanding a public role for women as the organization entered the twentieth century.

The second part of this legacy was the preservation of traditional definitions of womanhood. Across the South, LMAs helped to extend women's domestic role as caretakers into the public sphere as they memorialized dead fathers, brothers, and sons buried in Confederate cemeteries. LMAs did not overtly threaten traditional gender relations with their work, and neither did the UDC. The generation that had come of age since the Civil War sought to emulate Confederate women, whose example of womanhood blended self-sacrifice with stamina and fortitude.

As the organization grew, the Daughters further expanded the scope of women's time-honored responsibilities. In this, they were part of a national trend by women to create new public roles for themselves through their own organizations. The founding of the Women's Christian Temperance Union (1874) and the General Federation of Women's Clubs (1890), among others, fostered women's involvement in public education and progressive reform. Southern women joined these organizations, too. Rhetorically speaking, it was an extension of their role as moral guardians of society. The reality, however, was that these "New Women" had created a venue, thinly veiled by tradition, in which to express themselves politically.[44]

The UDC allowed southern women to pursue a public agenda and still receive the accolades accorded to women for being "ladies." Becoming a Daughter, moreover, gave them cachet in a region that valued its pre–Civil War traditions. UDC members continued to serve as public caretakers of the Confederate dead, but they also maintained a watchful eye over the indigent and aging generation of the 1860s—placing the care of that generation on the agenda of southern state legislatures. Additionally, the UDC pledged to monitor history and committed itself to preserving and perpetuating the values of Confederate culture for future generations of white southerners. Building on the legacy of the LMAs, the Daughters paved the way for women to use their education and influence—and, indeed, to have careers—within a movement that perpetuated tradition. They developed leadership skills and became professional fund-raisers, writers, publishers, speakers, and political lobbyists—all in the name of vindicating the Confederacy. The result was a woman's organization that became one of the most influential of its time.

→ 3 ←

The Rise of the UDC

I want the UDC to work like a well-regulated army. . . . If we would do that,
we would very soon be the most influential association in this country. . . .
God has not allowed us to grow so rapidly and so well for a small purpose.

President-General Lizzie George Henderson, 1907

The society may well be likened unto some monster machine that is carefully
inspected as to its hundreds of tiny separate mechanisms, each of which has
its allotted part to play in the workings of the whole; then it is carefully oiled
and set in motion by the engineer. It is in this manner that the president-
general of the United Daughters of the Confederacy sets moving the mighty
machinery of her great army of willing workers.

Anna Bland, Chattanooga Times, *1913*

When President-General Lizzie George Henderson attributed the UDC's
rapid growth to God's influence, she was able to point to membership
rolls for proof of what she regarded as divine assistance. The UDC filled
a void in the lives of thousands of southern women eager to join a voluntary organization whose goals were, by definition, conservative. Attracted by the organization's mission, they responded by joining in large
numbers. One year after the UDC was formed, 20 chapters were chartered, representing women in Tennessee, Georgia, North Carolina, South
Carolina, Virginia, Maryland, Texas, Kentucky, and Washington, D.C.
Within two years, there were 89 chapters, and by the third year, 138 chapters were actively pursuing the organization's goals. The UDC's growth
was so phenomenal that within a few years railroad companies offered
the Daughters discounted travel to their conventions. The small group of
women who met in Nashville in the fall of 1894 to organize the UDC had

grown to nearly 30,000 women, a remarkable rise, in just ten years. The Texas Division alone reported nearly 5,000 members in 1902, and by the end of World War I, the organization claimed a membership of nearly 100,000 women.[1]

Southern women joined other organizations as well, but they joined the Daughters in greater numbers. In 1902, when the UDC had close to 30,000 members, the total membership in the southern state federations of the General Federation of Women's Clubs was less than half that number.[2] Southern state memberships in the Women's Christian Temperance Union in 1900, the last time the organization kept such records, was less than 6,500.[3] The UDC, like other organizations, offered women a social and cultural outlet and the opportunity to engage in progressive reform. UDC membership, however, also offered southern women something unique—the opportunity to vindicate the Confederate generation and simultaneously uphold the values of their race and class. Ironically, it also gave them respectability within the traditionally male sphere of politics—cachet they often used to their advantage.

The UDC was active at the local, state, and national levels. It was primarily an urban voluntary organization; chapters were organized in small towns and cities and were required to have a minimum of seven members. When three chapters formed within a state, a state division was created, with officers elected at annual conventions. While most of the membership of the UDC was drawn from the South, chapters were organized wherever seven white female descendants of Confederate ancestors banded together. During the early twentieth century, the Daughters were represented in several states outside of the region—in California, New York, and Illinois, to name a few. Thus, the UDC's claim that it was a national organization was legitimate.[4]

Southern women were attracted to the UDC for many reasons. Prestige and elite social status accompanied membership in the organization. Women were able to command considerable influence through the UDC, as they perpetuated a conservative ideology and agenda consistent with the politics of white supremacy. Southern women who lived outside the region—in places like Ohio, Montana, and Pennsylvania—joined the organization despite living in what they described as a "hostile atmosphere." According to the UDC, the organization had such a stronghold in San Francisco that "women of Northern birth" were in a desperate search for a relative "whose services to the Confederate cause might render them eligible" for membership.[5]

The UDC's initial success was certainly helped by the natural constituency provided by the LMAs. Cofounder Anna Davenport Raines insisted that members of memorial associations join the UDC. Katie Cabell Currie of Texas, an early officer and later president-general of the general organization, sent a message to the 1898 Alabama state convention, urging memorial associations "to merge into the Daughters of the Confederacy." Two years later, Mississippi's president, Josie Frazee Cappleman, noted that members of memorial associations, as well as their daughters and granddaughters, were "gradually falling into the new order of [UDC]." At the 1903 meeting of the Georgia UDC, state historian Mildred Lewis Rutherford reiterated the plea of her fellow Georgian Anna Davenport Raines that "the members of one general body should be the members of the other."[6]

Kate Mason Rowland, who served as the general organization's corresponding secretary in 1896 and 1897, encouraged women to join the UDC, expressing great confidence in the Daughters' mission. A frequent contributor to the *Confederate Veteran,* she contacted numerous individuals, often women of prominence in their local communities, to organize a UDC chapter. "We are the latest of the hereditary societies," Rowland wrote one woman, "but we do not wish to be the smallest." In a letter to the head of a UCV camp, imploring him to encourage members of its auxiliary to join the UDC, she bragged that "if it is considered an honor now to have descent to a Revolutionary Patriot, we esteem it equally glorious to belong to the families of those who fought in a cause so holy and as just in 1861–65."[7]

Most of the women who joined the UDC within the first decade of its founding belonged to the second generation of women active in the Lost Cause. Their mothers had belonged to memorial associations, and now they wished to assume their places within the new order. Several others were new to the work of the Lost Cause, particularly northern women who had married southern men and were accepted into the organization based on the biblical principle that "the twain shall be one flesh." As the organization grew, however, the leadership became increasingly concerned that not all southern women were worthy of becoming Daughters. Aware of the drawing power of an organization perceived as elite,

Fig. 3.1. President-General Virginia McSherry (1909–1911) of West Virginia.

UDC leaders were intent upon preserving the UDC's exclusive reputation. Leading Daughters wanted the organization to grow but also wanted a membership that exemplified upper-class or patrician values. Cofounder Anna Raines argued that voluntary associations were not "compelled to receive as a member one who is morally or otherwise objectionable."[8]

The extraordinary growth experienced by the UDC during its first two decades actually alarmed leaders, who subsequently recommended restrictions on membership. In her report to the general convention of 1911, President-General Virginia McSherry of West Virginia proposed that chapters were "not obliged to accept as a member one who is not personally acceptable to the chapter." In 1912 her successor, Rassie Hoskins White of Tennessee, recommended precautionary measures to further limit eligibility. "As the organization grows in strength, popularity and prominence," she asserted, "membership in it becomes more desirable, and therefore should be hedged about and protected by more stringent rules." White knew something about status, as she had married a banker in her hometown of Paris, Tennessee, and was regarded as one of its prominent residents.[9]

Though women were attracted to the UDC because of social status, clearly the organization's success rested on an active membership with the desire and ability to accomplish broad objectives intended to vindicate Confederate men and preserve Confederate culture for future generations. Many women joined the organization out of a real sense of duty and responsibility to honor the Confederate generation and to instill the values of those men and women among future generations of white southerners. Mississippian Virginia Redditt Price referred to the work of the Daughters as fulfilling a "sacred obligation." Indeed, vindication of the Confederate generation was "the promise you virtually make when you become a UDC." Price treasured her membership in the organization and proclaimed that because she had been born and reared in the South, she valued her membership in the UDC above her membership in other women's organizations. Caroline Goodlett, cofounder of the organization, concurred. After repeated requests to join the DAR in the early 1890s, Goodlett proclaimed "I am prouder to be known as a Daughter of the Confederacy."[10]

Membership in the UDC also seemed to touch an emotional chord with southern women. Addressing the 1913 UDC convention in New Orleans, President-General Rassie White reflected upon the importance of the UDC to its members. "Long ago I discovered it was not a hobby with any of us, but is and has been from the very beginning, a serious work," she told those in attendance. White felt that defending the Confederate past gripped "the very hearts of Southern women." Indeed, the Daughters were personally motivated to defend the actions of their mothers and fathers, and their membership in the UDC had become central to their lives. As White's daughter remarked accusingly to her mother, "if you are not talking 'Daughters' you are thinking 'Daughters.'"[11]

The UDC swiftly became a powerful and influential women's organization in the early twentieth century, not only in terms of its numbers, but also in its ability to accomplish goals on behalf of Confederate causes. It was an organization that allowed southern women to assert their influence as public figures and at the same time maintain their image as traditional women. As President-General Rassie Hoskins White put it, "I love the United Daughters of the Confederacy because they have demonstrated that Southern women may organize themselves into

Fig. 3.2. President-General Rassie White (1911–1913)
of Tennessee directed the Shiloh monument campaign.

a nationwide body without losing womanly dignity, sweetness, or graciousness."[12]

As the UDC grew in numbers and influence, the fact that its members behaved like "southern ladies" gave the organization respectability
while also serving as the source of its power. "We are not a body of dis-
contented suffragists thirsting for oratorical honors," Anna Raines reminded members in 1897, even though several members participated in
the suffrage movement. Instead, they considered themselves a "sisterhood of earnest, womanly women." Ten years later, when the UDC held
its convention in Norfolk, within a short distance of the Jamestown Exposition, President-General Lizzie Henderson reminded delegates that
people from around the world who had come for the exposition were
interested in how southern women "conduct their conventions." She
advised delegates to keep the scrutiny of "hypercritical eyes" in mind
and urged each delegate to uphold the reputation of southern women as
"high-toned, courteous, gentle-mannered ladies."[13]

Women who joined the UDC between 1894 and 1919 were, in many respects, a diverse group. Daughters belonged to a variety of women's organizations, including hereditary societies such as the Daughters of the American Revolution (DAR), Colonial Dames, the Daughters of 1812, and, in the West, the Daughters of the Republic of Texas.[14] UDC members also belonged to the Women's Christian Temperance Union (WCTU), the Young Women's Christian Association (YWCA), and the King's Daughters, a Christian organization of single women whose work often benefited community hospitals. Some Daughters were suffragists, while others were virulent anti-suffragists. The UDC was active in cities as dissimilar as Savannah, Georgia, and Tacoma, Washington. Its membership included Episcopalians, Presbyterians, Methodists, Baptists, Jews, and Catholics. The diversity within the UDC, however, was balanced by those factors that made these women similar: gender, race, class, and a common Confederate heritage.

Comparisons between the UDC and other women's organizations prove difficult when there was such a cross-pollination of membership. The goals of one were often the goals of another; education and reform were central to the agenda of many women's organizations. Many women's groups also had a similar organizational structure, in which the real work was being done at the state level. What made the UDC different was its emphasis on Confederate culture, with its goal of preserving the race and class values held by its members.

The oldest members of the UDC, those born between 1820 and 1850, had experienced the Civil War as adults. In many cases, at least one male relative died in battle. When the war was over, these women became members of their local LMA. In fact, they had engaged in considerable Confederate memorial activity by the time the UDC was founded. Becoming a member of the Daughters was just another stage in their evolution as Lost Cause women. Finally, their activity as public women extended beyond the celebration of the Lost Cause, as they joined numerous women's organizations, many of which were reform-oriented.

UDC cofounder Caroline Meriwether Goodlett is representative of this older generation. Born in 1833 in Todd County, Kentucky, she was in her late twenties when the war broke out. Her brother was killed during the first year of the conflict, and throughout the war she helped sew uniforms, roll bandages, and care for wounded soldiers. She became active in memorial work immediately after the war. In 1866 she joined a benevolent society that raised money for artificial limbs for Confederate veterans. Goodlett also belonged to the Monument Association in Nashville and headed the Ladies' Auxiliary to the Tennessee Soldiers' Home. In many respects, Goodlett's role in the creation of the UDC was the culmination of her experience as an active participant in the Confederate tradition.

After her term as the first UDC president, Goodlett turned her attention to reform in her own state. She served on the board of managers of the Protestant Orphan Asylum and Mission Home, was vice president of the Humane Society of Nashville, and was a member of the Ladies' Auxiliary to the Masonic Widows' and Orphans' Home. Goodlett explained to a later president of the UDC that she did not seek fame for her Confederate work. "I am known in my own State," she wrote, "as a woman who is interested in all measures proposed for the good of the people of the State." In fact, she lobbied her legislators to pass a bill raising the age of consent from sixteen to eighteen years. She proposed a bill to build a home for "feeble-minded children" and urged the state legislature to "abolish whipping women in the Penitentiary." Goodlett obviously saw her work on behalf of Confederate veterans as one among her many reform interests.[15]

Cornelia Branch Stone, a contemporary of Goodlett, offers an instructive example of women whose experiences in other voluntary organizations prepared them for UDC's top office. A resident of Galveston, Texas, Stone was born in 1840 and became president-general of the UDC in 1908. She also belonged to the CSMA, the Daughters of the Republic of Texas, Colonial Dames, and the DAR. Serving as president-general of a state division was regarded as critical experience before ascending to the UDC presidency, and Stone's case was no exception. Her leadership in other organizations, moreover, was typical of women who served as president-general of the UDC in the first two decades of the organization. By the time Stone came to head the UDC, she had served as president of the Texas Woman's Press Association, as first vice president of the Texas Federation of Women's Clubs (TXFWC), and as corresponding secretary for the Colonial Dames.[16]

A position of leadership in the UDC was regarded by many as a significant public achievement. Election to the organization's highest office,

Fig. 3.3. President-General Cornelia Stone (1907–1909)
of Texas was a leader in several women's organizations.

president-general, meant election to one of the most powerful political
positions a southern woman could hold in the late nineteenth and early
twentieth centuries. The president-general of the UDC wielded considerable power, as she summoned the support of literally thousands of
southern women when it suited her cause. Moreover, as the UDC grew
in size and influence, the president-general was invited to represent the
organization at veterans' reunions, monument unveilings, and meetings
of other women's organizations. Presidents Theodore Roosevelt, William Howard Taft, and Woodrow Wilson all hosted a UDC president-
general at the White House.[17]

Many UDC members, like Goodlett and Stone, engaged in some aspect of progressive reform. Virginia Clay Clopton, a member from Alabama who was once married to U.S. Senator Clement C. Clay Jr. and later to a judge, belonged to the Equal Suffrage League for more than twenty years. Rebecca Latimer Felton of Georgia, the wealthy widow of former U.S. Congressman Dr. W. H. Felton, supported women's suffrage and worked to reform education for the uplift of rural white women. While with the TXFWC, Cornelia Stone, described by a contemporary as "one of the bright and brainy women of the Southland," chaired a committee that lobbied for an amendment to better enforce her state's poll tax law to increase funds to public schools. Historian Judith McArthur argues that southern women increasingly participated in reform even though they faced criticism for their public activity. UDC members, however, were able to avoid much of this criticism because of their dedication to rehabilitating the image of Confederate men.[18]

Most of the women who joined the UDC between 1894 and 1919 were born after 1850. Of the fifteen women elected president-general of the UDC between 1894 and 1919, more than half were born after 1850. They were literally daughters of the Confederacy, and often they were daughters of Confederate officers. Some of them were children during the Civil War and had memories of its devastating impact on their families. Those women born during or soon after the war experienced Reconstruction as children or teenagers and had participated in Memorial Day exercises as young girls. Their opinions about the war were largely shaped by Confederate men and women whose loss was transformed into bitterness, particularly during the era of Reconstruction. Like nearly all whites in the region, they regarded Reconstruction as the South's tragic era, an insult added to injury. Carpetbaggers, scalawags, and "ignorant" freedmen, they believed, had forced change on an unwilling South. Not surprisingly, they regarded the Ku Klux Klan (KKK) of Reconstruction as the South's redeemer.[19]

UDC members born after 1850, therefore, developed their perceptions about the Old South based on their parents' memories. Nevertheless, this generation of southern women was moved to defend the patrician culture of the Old South and seek vindication for their parents. Images of plantations and faithful slaves held more appeal than the "dark days" of Reconstruction, in which they had grown to maturity. The agrarian past, moreover, provided a stark contrast to the problems of industrialization they associated with plans for a "New South"—a term that was an expletive in their vocabulary. By the time this younger generation of women reached adulthood, the Old South had been idealized through the narrative of the Lost Cause. So too had the women of the Old South, who were portrayed as models of femininity to be both celebrated and emulated. For this generation, myth had replaced reality.[20]

UDC members had much invested in preserving the social structure and culture of the Old South. Clearly, they shared the privileges that accompanied membership in their race and class. And while information on the rank and file of the UDC has not been preserved, an examination of the presidents-general in the period between 1894 and 1919 suggests an organization led by social elites who were related by blood or marriage to men of power and influence in the region.

Ellen Foule Lee (president-general, 1897–1899) was married to Robert E. Lee's nephew Fitzhugh Lee, governor of Virginia in the late 1880s. Lizzie George Henderson (president-general, 1905–1907) attended Fair Lawn Institute in Jackson, Mississippi, described as "a young ladies' school of the Old South." She was the daughter of U.S. Senator James Z. George, author of the Mississippi Plan, which included the infamous disfranchisement clause adopted by southern state governments to sidestep the Fifteenth Amendment. Daisy McLaurin Stevens (president-general, 1913–1915), another Mississippian, was the daughter of Anselm J. McLaurin, who served as that state's governor and, later, U.S. senator. She was educated locally at the Brandon Female Seminary and was married to a state judge. Virginia Faulkner McSherry (president-general, 1909–1911) of West Virginia was the daughter of Charles J. Faulkner, a U.S. congressman and later minister to France before becoming a member of General Thomas "Stonewall" Jackson's staff. Cordelia Powell Odenheimer (president-general, 1915–1917) of Maryland was the daughter of a Confederate captain. Mary Poppenheim (president-general, 1917–1918) graduated in 1888 from Vassar, where she was vice president of the student body. Her father was a sergeant in the Confederate army.[21]

These presidents-general were not atypical of the membership. They initially joined the UDC as members of the rank and file and made their way to the organization's senior position by first holding local and state offices. Of the fifteen women who served as president-general between 1894 and 1919, seven (46 percent) of them were under the age of fifty when they were elected. Among the eight remaining presidents-general, one-half of them were less than sixty years old. The oldest woman to assume the post of president-general, Cornelia Branch Stone, was sixty-seven when elected. The youngest woman, Hallie Alexander Rounsaville of Georgia, was just thirty-seven when she assumed the UDC's highest office. Rounsaville was also one of the founding members of the DAR at the age of twenty-seven. On the whole, the Daughters were women who had the youthful energy required to meet the organization's objectives. They were not, as has been assumed, the "gray-haired friends" of the UCV.[22] And though these younger representatives may not have experienced the war firsthand, their quest to vindicate Confederate men and women was extremely personal. Indeed, the men and women they wished to honor were their parents and grandparents.

Mildred Lewis Rutherford, probably the best-known member of the UDC, is representative of the generation of Daughters who had grown up in a defeated region. Born in Athens, Georgia, in 1851, Rutherford needed to look no further than her own backyard for evidence of war's destruction. She was educated locally at the Lucy Cobb Institute and later became its president. In 1888, at the age of thirty-seven, she was elected president of the Athens Ladies' Memorial Association—a post she held the rest of her life. Between 1901 and 1903 she served as president of the Georgia Division of the UDC and in 1905 was appointed historian-general for life in her state. She eventually became historian-general for the general organization, a post she held for five years, during which time she became a celebrity within Lost Cause circles.[23]

Rutherford crusaded for "truthful" histories of the Civil War, often appearing in 1860s costume, her hair in Spaniel curls. All Daughters considered "true history" to be a primary means of achieving vindication. Rutherford used her position of leadership to promote a pro-southern view of events, and she defended traditional roles for men and women as well as the preservation of white supremacy. She believed that women of the Old South—plantation mistresses, to be exact—represented a feminine ideal worthy of preservation. For Rutherford true men were chivalrous, and true women were genteel and deferential to their men. African Americans, moreover, should remain faithful to their former masters if the New South were to resemble the Old South she longed for.[24]

Fig. 3.4. Mildred Rutherford, UDC historian-general (1910–1915), crusaded for "true" history.

Rutherford's stance on the question of woman suffrage reveals the influence that tradition and the Lost Cause had on her life. A member of the Georgia Association Opposed to Woman Suffrage, Rutherford vociferously condemned woman suffrage, believing that many of the South's traditions were under attack. Not only were states' rights in jeopardy, but so were traditional gender roles. In expressing her "violent" opposition to suffrage for women, she personally addressed the Georgia House of Representatives committee that dealt with the question of women's suffrage. The irony of this action was apparently lost on her.[25]

Rutherford opposed the amendment by summoning images of the Old South. "[Go] back to your ideals of manhood," she scolded committee members, and "remember chivalry of old, yours by inheritance." She believed that women should also look to the past, "back to the home and those God-given rights." Like other Lost Cause women, she celebrated female role models of the Old South and admonished her female peers to "turn backward in loving emulation to the ideals set by the mothers and grandmothers of yesterday."[26]

Though unique among UDC women, Rutherford was typical of the Daughters in many respects. For while she worked to preserve tradition and the values associated with Confederate culture, she did so by taking advantage of the public forum created in part by Lost Cause women, but also by social change. Advancements in education and progressive reform, and women's increased participation in voluntary organizations, opened new doors for southern women, creating a dilemma for women like Rutherford who sought to remake the New South in the image of the Old. At the same time, the politics of Jim Crow supported her expression of conservative values and racist beliefs.[27]

In many ways Rutherford and members of the UDC stood at the crossroads of the Old and New South. They were very much a product of the Lost Cause and romanticized the Old South, yet they were visibly caught up in the changes occurring in the New South, particularly those affecting women. Many members of the UDC were engaged in reform, and several were active in the suffrage movement. Yet, as historian Marjorie Spruill Wheeler argues, southern suffragists understood that their activities as "New Women" were often tempered by the fact that these same southern women were also "hostage" to the Lost Cause and its traditional definitions of womanhood.[28]

A public role for UDC members was certainly enhanced by Lost Cause sentiment. The Daughters, continuing in the footsteps of the LMAs, intended to resurrect southern men from the doldrums of defeat by reassuring them that the cause they fought for was just and that women were willing, if only rhetorically, to reassume a primarily domestic role. And even though the Daughters had become influential public women, they continued to present their work as that of helpmeet.

More than any other single UDC member, Elizabeth Lumpkin, a favorite speaker at veterans' reunions, eloquently expressed these sentiments. Born in Georgia in 1880 to former planter elite, Lumpkin was well educated and had grown up listening to her father's stories about the Confederacy. Like many young women of her generation, she came to admire white womanhood in the Old South, as characterized by the

Fig. 3.5. Elizabeth Lumpkin, a favorite speaker at veterans' reunions.

southern lady. Referring to that feminine ideal, she told a group of Georgia veterans in 1904, "I would rather be a woman than a man. . . . What woman would not, if she could be a Southern woman and be loved by Southern men?"[29]

Lumpkin's speeches were purposefully crafted for the moral uplift of aging Confederate men. When she addressed throngs of veterans, she regaled them with stories of their youth, when, according to the Lost Cause fiction in which they all believed, southern men were real men. Then she returned to the present, proclaiming how much the women of her day envied Confederate women. "We can work with tireless fingers, we can run with tireless feet for these men; but they [Confederate women] could love and marry Confederate soldiers!"[30]

The local press hailed Elizabeth Lumpkin's gifts as an orator wherever she spoke. The *Confederate Veteran* remarked that her speaking ability was not exaggerated and that her oration at the Louisville reunion was "thrilling and penetrating." Dr. F. L. Powell, another speaker at the reunion, described her sway over the audience by proclaiming that "you could put a flag in her hands and conquer the world."[31] Lumpkin was the Confederate woman reincarnated, but for the purposes of the Lost Cause. According to legend, southern women were the last to give up the fight. Similarly, Lumpkin had a never-say-die attitude regarding the agrarian past; in fact, it became a central theme in her speeches. "If we say that the glory of the Old South is dead," she dramatically told veterans, "skeleton hands will rise again and fold the old flag in loving embrace, socketless eyes will blaze again with the glory of that dear past, and skeleton teeth will chatter again the old Rebel yell." It is no wonder that Lumpkin's speeches were often interrupted by "thunderous applause."[32]

The image of womanhood Lumpkin projected was based in tradition, yet it was tradition personified by the public activity of women in a New South. Lumpkin was an enormously popular public figure in the Lost Cause because she represented traditional womanhood—cultivation, refinement, and gentility. Yet in significant ways she was a "New Woman." She was well educated and skilled in oration. She was able to step outside the bounds of domesticity, stand atop the speakers' platform at a veterans' reunion, and still be admired for typifying tradition. This blending of Old and New South identities worked well for Lumpkin and was the formula for success for thousands of women who participated in the Lost Cause in the early twentieth century.

One of the most striking aspects of this extraordinary group of southern women in the UDC was that they had, to a degree, been emboldened and empowered by the women they admired: the women of the 1860s. Confederate women, according to the Lost Cause narrative, had one foot planted in the domestic sphere and one in the public sphere. On the one hand, women of the "old regime" were described as "the finest types of true womanhood; refined, cultivated, gentle; devoted wives, good mothers, kind mistresses, and splendid homemakers." Yet they were also lauded for being more patriotic than southern men, for being "Spartan women," or women who demonstrated "Spartan endurance." Indeed, Lost Cause literature often portrayed Confederate women as maintaining the virtues of domesticity even as they rose to face the public challenges of war. To the extent that their Confederate mothers had been liberated by the gender upheaval caused by the experience of war, women of the Lost Cause had also been liberated—but only to that extent.[33]

The same terms used by Lost Cause devotees to characterize Confederate women were often invoked to describe the Daughters. UDC members were often portrayed as powerful yet genteel women. Kate Litton Hickman, a founding member of the UDC, was described by a friend as "a Josephine in diplomatic power and a Marie Antoinette in graciousness and in the power of winning hearts."[34] Such characterizations indicate how the Daughters managed to maintain their image as traditional yet public-minded women.

While the Daughters existed to honor tradition, much of their activity, collectively and individually, also placed them in the category historians describe as "New Women." Certainly, the Daughters carved a niche for themselves in the political culture of the New South as preservers of tradition. The source of their power, in fact, lay in their ability to employ their influence as southern ladies in order to gain access to politicians, as well as to maintain control over the public celebration of the Lost Cause. They also drew power from the example set by women of the 1860s. Just as women had played a critical public role in the interest of the Confederate cause, the Daughters had a critical public role to play in the vindication of the Confederate generation. It was the Daughters' charge, Florence Barlow asserted as editor of the *Lost Cause*, to come to the "defense of Southern integrity."[35]

Tradition was important to the Lost Cause because it not only defined the role women were to play; it defined the role of men as well. Within the Confederate tradition, both women and men accepted a particular set of traits as typical of southern womanhood and southern manhood. Such ideas were largely derived from the Lost Cause narrative, a class-based fiction in which such ideals were represented by the elites of the Old South. The Lost Cause narrative generally ignored poor whites, and former slaves were little more than racist caricatures of devoted "uncles" and "mammies." Moreover, the term "faithful slaves" grouped males and females together, disregarding their individuality.[36]

The men and women who constituted the generation of the 1860s, therefore, were the men and women whom the Daughters chose as role models for their own generation. Mildred Rutherford argued as much as late as 1912, when she said that "the men of today and the women of today are adjusting themselves to the Old South remade." While the Daughters sought to emulate southern womanhood of the 1860s, however, their male contemporaries were often criticized for their lagging interest in the ways of the Old South. UDC members, in fact, often prodded or made excuses for the South's "New Men," who were uninterested in emulating their Confederate fathers, and for good reason.[37]

The South's New Men were markedly different from their Confederate fathers. In the Old South men had earned their living in a plantation economy, while New Men were often self-made businessmen who helped build the towns and cities of the New South. These younger men were less interested in preserving their Confederate heritage than in creating a concrete foundation for their own power, based on their business interests.[38]

The South's New Men also operated in a world that had changed considerably since the Civil War. Many of these young men had fought in the U.S. Army, rather than against it, in the Spanish-American War. Their military service, according to historian Nina Silber, was accepted by northerners as proof of southern manliness as well as patriotism. Southern men held views consistent with men who lived outside the region. They employed the language of empire, a language in accord with racial theory in the 1890s. Anglo-Saxonism and the belief in the superiority of "white civilization" were, to be sure, consistent with the goals of southern politicians. In the late nineteenth and early twentieth centuries white supremacy, politically sanctioned in the South, had become integral to the new emphasis on American nationalism.[39]

The world and the self-image of New Men, therefore, stood in stark contrast to the provincial world of their fathers. While Old South patricians had lived in a region that relied solely on agriculture, New South men lived in a region that offered them economic diversity and many business opportunities. In addition to agriculture, men engaged in mining, manufacturing textiles, and building railroads. The business interests of the region, however, spurred discussion that pitted the values of this New South against the agrarian values of the Old. The Daughters blamed New Men for the trend of abandoning the agrarian past, and Confederate veterans joined in the criticism. New Men, according to UDC and UCV members, were more concerned with making money than with honoring their ancestors.

To be sure, New Men were much less likely than their female contemporaries to see their Confederate fathers, the defeated, as role models. They regarded themselves as more powerful and successful, eager to shed the burden of defeat. The South's New Men, Glenda Gilmore explains in *Gender and Jim Crow,* "had ample evidence that the older generation of men had mistreated white women by failing to provide for them after the Civil War." They believed that they had proven themselves better able to provide for southern women. Certainly they made a point of proclaiming their allegiance to the patrician ideals of the Old South. And they regarded disfranchisement and their success in reestablishing white supremacy as evidence of their chivalry and ability to protect white women. Yet they were clearly focused on the region's future, and their interests were linked to the new business ventures of the era.[40]

New Men may have been reluctant to take an active role in the Confederate celebration, but they were willing to assist the Daughters as businessmen and as elected public officials. Indeed, as UDC petitions for monument funds came before local and state governments, men often granted the Daughters the financial support they sought. Though appreciative of receiving financial assistance, the Daughters nevertheless believed that these same men should join them in the campaign to honor the generation of the 1860s.

Members of the UDC and UCV lamented the poor enthusiasm displayed by the new generation of leading southern men. "Our younger men," wrote a member of the UDC in 1911, "are sordidly forgetting the past in the getting of a dollar." Speaking to a meeting of the UDC in Nashville, Judge J. M. Dickinson complained that "at times Southern men . . . seem lethargic if not indifferent" to the commemoration of their heritage. An article in the *Confederate Veteran* went further, claiming that the SCV "had in many respects become a hindrance rather than a blessing to the cause for which it was created." New Men, in other words, appeared to eschew a role in the Confederate celebration, choosing instead to devote their attention to business and industry.[41] By the turn of the twentieth century, southern men had deferred to southern women as "the sole protectors of the honor of ancestors."[42] Still, women continued to criticize them for their conspicuous absence from the Confederate celebration.

The founding of the SCV in 1896 did not do much to change women's minds about what they viewed as apathy. "It is good for women to do their part," a South Carolina Daughter wrote in 1897, but "we cannot make healthy manhood by standing in its place and assuming its obligations."[43] She was not alone in her belief that young men, both in and out of the SCV, had an obligatory role to play in continuing the celebration, nor was she alone in her awareness that responsibility for the Lost Cause celebration had been shifted entirely to women. One veteran complained of the complacency of the SCV membership, noting that the majority of its members had left the duty of preserving Confederate culture "to the willing Daughters." He pleaded with the SCV not to allow "commercialism" to affect their duty to this important work, arguing that "there is no excuse for man allowing money to dwarf exalting memories."[44]

UDC members were clearly frustrated by this lack of interest in the Lost Cause. In their view, young men ignored the fact that they were morally and politically indebted to their Confederate ancestors. Yet according to historian Donald Doyle, many of these men, though sons of Confederate veterans, were not descended from planter families and, therefore, were not personally motivated to preserve agrarian traditions.[45] Thus, the Daughters' continued reverence for their forebears, many of whom were of the planter class, set them apart from New Men whose fathers had been common soldiers. Still, women's dedication in the face of men's indifference served as a powerful bargaining chip for the UDC. New Men may have been unwilling to join women in the Confederate celebration, but they resolved to support UDC objectives financially, through allocations from local and state budgets, and private donations. Indeed, the UDC demanded that male descendants of Confederate veterans participate in the effort to preserve Confederate culture, even if they only provided financial support.[46]

By the end of the first decade of the twentieth century, the Daughters had toned down their criticism of New Men and began to make excuses for what they had once regarded as apathy. They agreed instead to accept men's financial participation in the Lost Cause, which was considerable. President-General Lizzie Henderson offered her own explanation about why the SCV did not share equally the responsibility for preserving southern heritage. After all, they, too, were lineal descendants of Confederate veterans. The Sons, she told the Daughters, "are the busy men of today. . . . They do not have time for these things." A few years later, in 1913, President-General Rassie White also excused SCV members by stating that they were "active business men with little time to give to this work." If the SCV did not have the time, the UDC was still committed to honoring the generation of the 1860s. Indeed, the Daughters accepted the task as their very own, maintaining their dedication to honor the Confederate dead and to serve those still living.[47]

From its beginning in 1894, the UDC saw its role as defender and preserver of Confederate culture as similar to the role played by southern women of the Confederacy. Tapping into the wellspring of sentiment for the Confederate generation, and following the example set by the women of the 1860s in active support of a cause, the UDC steadily grew in numbers and influence. "As the women of the South in the past were steadfast, true, and loyal," Elizabeth Lumpkin reminded Georgia veterans, "so the women of the South in the future will be loyal and true forever." The Daughters abided by this model of loyalty and made a conscious attempt to conform to the image of the "Southern lady." That southern men often referred to UDC members as the finest examples of womanhood is a testament to their success in living up to the ideal.[48]

The Daughters played a prominent role in the public life of the South from the 1890s through World War I. They reaffirmed the region's conservative traditions, even as they expanded woman's sphere. The extent of their influence provides ample evidence that traditional methods of feminine power were effective, particularly when used in support of conservative goals. Yet this era was also a time when increasing numbers of southern women went to college, engaged in occupations outside the home, and attacked the evils of society as organized reformers. UDC members were part of this new tradition too. They achieved enormous success because they were able to draw upon both traditions. The most visible of their accomplishments, of course, are the hundreds of monuments that mark the southern landscape. Yet even these stone testimonials barely hint at what the Daughters accomplished in their campaign to vindicate Confederate veterans.

The Monument Builders

When the historian comes to count the monuments [built] to perpetuate
the memories of heroes of the Confederate States, he will pause and
question if his figures be really correct.

Confederate Veteran, *August 1914*

"Scarcely a month takes its place on the calendar" President-General
Rassie Hoskins White remarked in 1913, "but a new Confederate monument is outlined against the sky." White's comments to the UDC delegates assembled in New Orleans were no exaggeration. For nearly
twenty years, the Daughters successfully campaigned to build monuments in almost every city, town, and state of the former Confederacy.
When White claimed that "hundreds and hundreds of monuments dot
the entire South," it was a legitimate claim. Monuments were central to
the UDC's campaign to vindicate Confederate men, just as they were
part of an overall effort to preserve the values still revered by white
southerners. The stone soldiers who stand sentinel in southern towns
pay homage to white heroes who were revered as both loyal southerners
and American patriots, for their defense of states' rights. Significantly,
southern blacks, who had no stake in celebrating the Confederacy, had to
share a cultural landscape that did.[1]

From its founding in 1894, the UDC was committed to perpetuating
the tradition of monument building begun by Ladies' Memorial Associations. Many UDC members were also longtime members of memorial associations and remained active in both groups. Even after the
founding of the Confederated Southern Memorial Association (CSMA)
in 1900, the UDC actively participated in Memorial Day commemora-

Fig. 4.1. The most common Confederate monuments built by the UDC are those that appear in town squares, like this one in Augusta, Georgia.

tions and raised money for monuments. Although the UDC was the larger and more influential association, it remained committed to the goals and activism that began with LMAs—a tradition of activism that had opened doors for southern women to become public women.[2]

It is no coincidence that Confederate monuments appeared on the southern urban landscape at the same time that the UDC was growing in numbers and influence. According to historical geographer John Winberry, 93 percent of the monuments erected on the urban landscape were built after 1895. One-half of them were unveiled between 1903 and 1912. Concurrently, the UDC grew from a membership of approximately 35,000 in 1903 to nearly 80,000 in 1912. The Daughters were the white

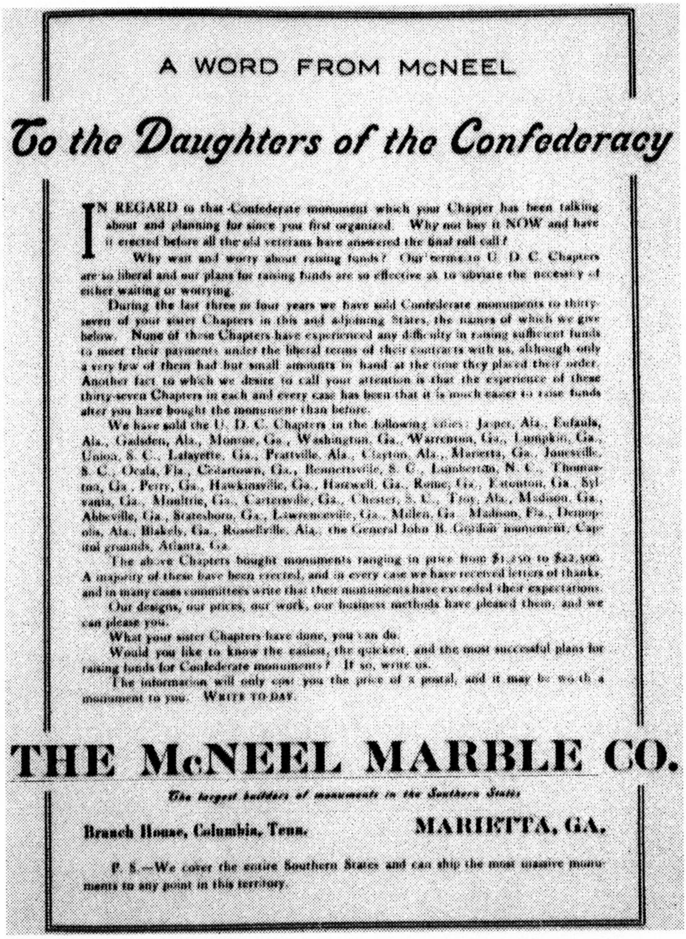

Fig. 4.2. Marble companies actively marketed to the UDC.

southerners most committed to monument building; the UDC's growth, therefore, provides a key explanation for the marked increase in monument building in the region.[3]

Most frequently, monument campaigns were conducted at the local level. In nearly every city and town across the South, the local chapter of the UDC led the fund-raising effort to erect a monument to Confederate soldiers, usually in the form of the lone foot soldier standing sentinel atop a pedestal. The success of Daughters at the local level was evidence of their standing in the community, as UDC members drew on their power and influence as elite women to raise money and monuments.

The UDC was also very successful in building state and regional monuments, projects that required substantial sums of money. Despite the costs, the Daughters were known for completing their projects free of debt. They were such effective fund-raisers that their white male counterparts, the United Confederate Veterans and the Sons of Confederate Veterans, generally played only minor roles as advisors. The campaign to build the monument to Jefferson Davis in the capitol of the Confederacy illustrates how, only a few years after its founding, the UDC had become the leading Lost Cause organization.

Within a few years after Jefferson Davis's death, there was much discussion among Confederate organizations that a monument to their former president was needed. Responsibility for raising money for the project originated with the UCV, which established the Jefferson Davis Monument Association (JDMA). By 1899 the veterans had raised more than $20,000 for the monument, which was to be built in Richmond. The amount raised, while quite substantial, was not nearly sufficient to pay for the monument they envisioned. Fearing that the UCV might "never achieve success" unless it enlisted the assistance of the "noble women of the South," JDMA chairman General W. L. Cabell proposed handing the project over to the UDC, an organization then just five years old.[4]

The United Confederate Veterans, by a unanimous vote, passed a resolution to request that the Daughters "undertake the patriotic task of building the monument to President Jefferson Davis at Richmond." The veterans promised to give the women the funds they had raised, as well as their continued assistance. General Cabell believed that success was almost assured in the hands of the UDC. "When the Daughters [get] to work something would be done," he claimed. Besides, the general continued, "all the good" that was being accomplished in the South was through "women's work anyway."[5]

The timing of the UCV's offer was significant, since General Cabell's daughter, Katie Cabell Currie, was the current UDC president-general. When her organization held its general convention in 1899, the proposal was almost assured of success. As expected, the Daughters "took charge of the movement," and leadership in the JDMA was transferred to the UDC. The Daughters created a committee to handle the project and appointed Janet Randolph of Richmond, Virginia, as chair. Directors were also appointed from each state division to assist in a regional campaign.[6]

The newly formed UDC committee acted immediately, as Randolph issued an appeal to Confederate organizations to assist the UDC in building the Davis monument. Randolph, who had been instrumental in the effort to erect a monument to Robert E. Lee in Richmond, was distressed that the South had not similarly honored the Confederate president. Southern women, she proclaimed, were "sworn to wipe out this disgrace at once." In fact, both the Daughters and the region's memorial associations worked together for this common goal.[7]

The Davis monument was the first of three large-scale monuments that the UDC committed to build prior to World War I. Discussion of a fourth monument, to be carved into the side of Stone Mountain in Georgia, was put on hold for several years while two other projects were completed: a monument to Confederate soldiers buried at Arlington National Cemetery and one to Confederate soldiers on the grounds of the Shiloh battlefield. The Daughters estimated the cost of the monuments to be $50,000 each—no small sum for any voluntary organization. The UDC, however, had proven to be a fund-raising powerhouse, and, more importantly, the Daughters regarded monument building as part of their responsibility to the Confederate generation. The fact that they made such large financial commitments in 1906 and 1907 to build monuments at Shiloh and at Arlington suggests that the UDC was fully conscious of its power and influence as an organization.[8]

Confederate organizations in the District of Columbia had begun the campaign to build a monument in Arlington National Cemetery. On June 6, 1900, at the urging of Confederate veterans, Congress passed a law allowing the bodies of 267 Confederate soldiers buried on northern battlefields to be disinterred and then reburied in Arlington National Cemetery. Talk of building a monument on the grounds began almost immediately. Mrs. Magnus Thompson, president of the District of Columbia Division of the UDC, called a meeting of Confederate organizations in the city on November 6, 1906. The meeting resulted in the formation of the Arlington Confederate Monument Association (ACMA).[9]

The Arlington association, whose members included local Daughters and veterans, wasted little time in seeking the assistance of the entire UDC. Colonel Hilary Herbert, a UCV member and acting chair of the committee, attended the Daughters' Norfolk Convention in 1907 to seek the group's aid on behalf of the ACMA. Herbert emphasized the significance of building a Confederate monument close to the nation's capitol and urged the Daughters to assume responsibility for its completion. He recommended that delegates from UDC chapters in Washington manage the project and that an advisory board of men provide financial guidance. Convention delegates unanimously agreed to accept responsibility for the monument "without conditions." In other words, the male advisory board was to have no formal control over the Arlington monument campaign.[10]

Once the Daughters took charge of the project, they established an executive committee headed by the president-general, who appointed a board of directors composed of one representative from each state division. State directors were responsible for rallying their members to raise the funds needed to complete the Arlington monument. Hilary Herbert remained as acting chairman, and a local committee in Washington, D.C., oversaw local preparations.[11]

Now controlled by the Daughters, the Arlington committee's first act was to obtain permission to build a monument in the national cemetery. Mrs. Magnus Thompson, assisted by U.S. Senator John Sharp Williams of Mississippi, sought permission from Secretary of War William Howard Taft to erect the monument. Taft granted the group's request, after which the fund-raising campaign began in earnest. "Do not let this be an ordinary monument," Herbert appealed to the UDC in 1909, asking that the memorial fully demonstrate the South's love and admiration for its Confederate dead. To be sure, the UDC did not desire to build anything "ordinary," particularly in a cemetery carved from land once owned by the South's best-loved hero, Robert E. Lee.[12]

As arrangements were under way for the Arlington monument, the Daughters also turned their attention to Shiloh National Park, where no Confederate monuments had been built. Like Arlington, Shiloh's landscape was also sacred to the UDC, because it marked the site where so many Confederate soldiers had lost their lives in a particularly bloody Civil War battle. In 1900 women who lived near the battlefield organized the Shiloh Chapter of the UDC, whose purpose was to raise a monument at the park. The chapter sent out circulars and appealed for funds for several years without much success. The Tennessee Division even created a committee to pressure its state legislature for appropriations and was promised support from veterans. Finally, the chapter went before the general convention of the UDC.[13]

Fig. 4.3. Moses Ezekiel, sculptor of the Confederate monument
in Arlington National Cemetery.

The Tennessee Daughters made their first appeal for the Shiloh monument during the 1905 UDC general convention in San Francisco, California. The general organization officially endorsed the plan, and the following year the Shiloh Monument Committee (SMC) was created. President-General Lizzie Henderson appointed state directors and a director-general, Rassie Hoskins White of Paris, Tennessee. White, who became the UDC's president-general in 1911, headed the Shiloh committee until the $50,000 monument was unveiled in 1917–eleven years after the project was initiated.[14]

The Daughters expected a monument that would be worthy of the time and energy they expended to build regional monuments. Design, therefore, was an important aspect of monument building. While most small communities could afford only the mass-produced monuments showing a Confederate soldier on a pedestal, state and regional monuments were significantly more detailed. For those monuments the Daughters were careful in their choice of sculptors and designs. Moses Ezekiel, a Confederate veteran and prize-winning artist who worked in Rome, Italy, was chosen to create the Arlington monument. A design committee worked with Ezekiel to develop the monument's theme, which they agreed should be "peace for the living and honor to the dead." Ezekiel's design includes a heroic-sized figure of a woman, who represents the South, with an olive wreath in one hand. In relief on the circular pedestal below her figure are images that he said typified "the heroism and devotion of men, women and children, and soldiers of the South."[15]

Chicagoan Frederick Hibbard, a pupil of acclaimed sculptor Lorado Taft, was chosen to design the Shiloh monument. Hibbard's design represented his conception of the events of the two-day battle. The central grouping, which he called "A Defeated Victory," includes three figures. The potential for Confederate victory is represented by one figure; a second symbolizes the death of the Confederate commander-in-chief at Shiloh, Albert Sydney Johnston; the final figure depicts "the advent of night, which brought reinforcements to the Federals."[16]

The cost of hiring well-regarded artists, and the materials used to build these monuments, required a great deal of capital. The local monuments, generally of an individual Confederate soldier, ranged in price from $1,000 to $4,000. Larger monuments found on the grounds of state capitols generally cost between $10,000 and $20,000. Some were even more expensive. The state monument in Montgomery, Alabama, unveiled in 1899, cost $43,000. It took several years for the Daughters to raise money for their most ambitious projects. The Jefferson Davis Monument in Richmond cost $70,000; the final tally for the Arlington Monument was approximately $64,000; and expenditures for the Shiloh Monument reached $50,000. By today's standards, the South spent millions of dollars to build Confederate monuments.[17]

Fund-raising at the local level often involved hundreds of people in the white community. UDC members spearheaded the drive, but drew men and children into the effort. Women raised funds for the Confederate monument in Franklin, Tennessee, for example, by holding ice cream suppers, cakewalks, and concerts. The San Antonio Daughters raised money for their local monument by sponsoring teas, dances, concerts, and quilting bees. In 1900 the UDC chapter in Nashville benefited from the performances of two operettas, *The Mikado* and *Olivette*. Afterward, *Confederate Veteran* editor Sumner Cunningham boasted that the Nashville Daughters were "hard to beat in providing for their soldier veterans."[18]

Fig. 4.4. Katie Behan, president of the
Confederated Southern Memorial Association.

Large monuments required more money than the small sums raised
by social events, and the Daughters were not reticent about going to their
political representatives. Local and state appropriations for monuments
were common, because the UDC willingly used its power and influence.
The Mississippi Division reported to the general organization in 1906
that its state legislators had passed an act empowering local boards of
supervisors and aldermen to appropriate funds to erect monuments to
the Confederate dead buried in their respective counties. Mississippi
Division President Helen Bell reported that five counties had indeed appropriated funds totaling close to $9,000. The Monumental Association
in Raleigh, North Carolina, a group that included UDC members and
was headed by women, received money from private citizens for its state
monument. However, when more money was needed, the North Carolina state legislature appropriated $20,000.[19]

Fund-raising for the grandest monuments required the greatest
amount of capital. The Confederated Southern Memorial Association,
which assisted the UDC in raising money for the monument to Jefferson Davis in Richmond, employed traditional methods of raising
money, such as sending circulars to Confederate organizations. Katie
Behan, longtime president of the CSMA, appealed to the commander of

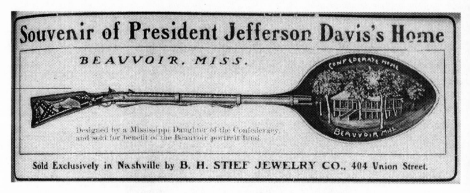

Fig. 4.5. Sales of Confederate souvenirs helped to fund monuments.

the UCV, Major-General John B. Gordon, to encourage veterans' camps to assist women in this project as promised. "If you will add a few words of approval," Behan told Gordon, "it will make the appeal much more effective." The committee responsible for the Davis monument also sent "thousands of envelopes" with requests for a contribution of at least one dollar.[20]

The Daughters also engaged in commercial ventures to help raise funds for their largest projects. They endorsed items, from which they received a share of the profits when sold. The UDC sold Confederate calendars, while the Shiloh committee sold postcards showing the Bloody Pond, "with historic facts printed on them," as well as lithographs of Lee and his generals. They reasoned that engravings of Robert E. Lee would sell well because UDC chapters needed them to place in public schools. Not all proposed items were considered tasteful, however, and the Daughters rejected the suggestion of placing images of Confederate heroes on belt buckles. "These men are idols of the South," claimed one Daughter, "and it would seem to cheapen their sacred memory to sell over counters of stores articles bearing their pictures."[21]

In 1910 the UDC hit upon the "scheme," as President-General Virginia McSherry put it, of selling Confederate Christmas seals. Pointing to the success of the American Red Cross in the sale of its stamps, McSherry believed that the Daughters could conceivably raise $35,000 in eighteen months. A UDC member from Florence, Alabama, created and copyrighted her design for the seals, which were to be sold for the Arlington Monument. The Daughters hoped to replicate the success of the Red Cross and printed "several million" Confederate Christmas seals for purchase, though it is not clear how many were actually sold.[22]

Kentucky businessman and former Confederate Captain J. H. Reed of Lexington proposed one of the more unusual moneymaking ideas to the UDC. Reed owned a soft drink company that developed a soda called "Celery-Phos." To promote the sale of the drink, Reed offered 10 percent of the net profits from the beverage to the UDC. "Celery-Phos" was described as a "wholesome soft drink" that contained "no 'dope,' caffeine, morphine, or any other ingredient deleterious or detrimental to health." How much the UDC profited from the sale of Celery-Phos is uncertain; however, Reed automatically increased his potential for profit through his connection with the region's most influential women's organization.[23]

In early 1903 the committee responsible for the Jefferson Davis monument devised a plan to raise a large sum of money in a short period of time. Janet Randolph, committee chairwoman, announced that Richmond would host a "Confederate Bazaar" between April 15 and May 1, 1903. In addition to the ordinary bake sales and concerts, the committee planned to sell Confederate relics. Randolph was frustrated that only $8,000 had been raised in the four years since the UDC had taken charge of building the monument. "I have appealed personally at Confederate reunions, through the medium of the press, and circulars, without accomplishing my object," she noted with disappointment. She hoped that the two-week event would raise the money needed to build a memorial worthy of Jefferson Davis, whom Randolph called a "martyr [of] the 'Lost Cause.'" The Confederate bazaar was indeed a huge success, adding $20,000 to the JDMA coffers.[24]

The Daughters never failed in raising money for monuments once they accepted responsibility, partly because they insisted that men contribute to the cause. Frequently, their tactic was to shame men into contributing to a monument fund. Janet Randolph, who headed the fundraising for the Davis monument, constantly reminded veterans of their failure to build a monument to the Confederate president, after they had promised their assistance. From time to time, she authored appeals to men on behalf of the monument. In March 1902, for example, she asked rhetorically, "Have you fulfilled your promise?" Then answering her own question, she scolded, "If you had, we would have already

Fig. 4.6. Monument unveiling, Lebanon, Tennessee.

commenced the actual erection of this monument. You have not done your duty." Two months later Randolph commented in another of her appeals that "it is a shame that we have had so often to remind you of your duty."[25]

Ultimately, failure to raise money for monuments was simply not an option, since such public symbols were critical elements in the campaign to vindicate Confederate men. The monuments were intended to serve as a record of the South's devotion to patriotic principles, principles white southerners believed they shared with the nation, including the defense of states' rights. Moreover, monuments were a reflection on the women of the UDC, whose commitment to honor veterans and the Confederacy was steadfast. Even when informed in 1913 that there were not enough funds on hand to complete the Arlington monument, sculptor Moses Ezekiel remained confident. "Any promise by the UDC is good enough for me," he said.[26]

Whenever one of their monuments was unveiled, the Daughters were rewarded for being dutiful to the Confederate generation. On the day of the unveiling, they were accorded honors for emulating the women of the 1860s. Just like those self-sacrificing women who supported the Confederate cause, UDC members had been equally vigorous in their campaign to build monuments. A monument unveiling, therefore, was not simply about memorializing veterans. It was a ritual in which

Fig. 4.7. Richmond children pulling the Jefferson Davis monument
to its final resting place, 1907.

women were honored for maintaining, if only symbolically, the traditions of their gender. It was also a ritual gathering of the entire white
community—men, women, and children—to honor the nation that
never was.

The Daughters made sure that a monument unveiling was celebrated
as an important moment in the history of the community. The town was
decorated with the colors of the Confederacy—red and white streamers,
bunting, and flowers. Occasionally, a dance was held the evening before.
On the day of the unveiling, the appointed speakers and leading members of the UDC arrived at the monument site in carriages adorned
with red and white flowers and ribbons. There was the parade, led by
surviving Confederate veterans; those who had lost legs during the war
hobbled on crutches, adding to the drama of the procession. Members of
the UDC followed them. After the Daughters came the white children of
the community, who occasionally had the added responsibility of pulling
ropes that brought the monument—stationed on a wheeled platform—
to its final resting place. Once at the site of the unveiling, the day's speakers, political dignitaries, and UDC members all took their places on the
platform built next to the monument, and the main ceremony began.

The monument unveiling in Dallas, Texas, in 1898 offers an instructive example. Confederate veterans and their wives "from every town in
Texas" attended what was described as a "love-feast" in their honor. The

Fig. 4.8. Monument unveiling, Dallas, Texas, 1898.

governor was there, as were members of the Texas legislature, which had "closed its doors, that her lawmakers might come." The city of Dallas was decorated with American and Confederate flags; private homes were adorned with red and white bunting and Confederate flags; and a ball was held the night before the unveiling. Distinguished guests included Margaret Davis Hayes, eldest daughter of Jefferson Davis, and Mary Anna Jackson, widow of General Stonewall Jackson. Hayes's children and Jackson's grandchildren were also honored guests.[27]

Descendants and relatives of some of the South's most acclaimed heroes were accorded places of honor at the more celebrated unveilings. Stonewall Jackson's wife and Jefferson Davis's daughter, for example, were also special guests at the unveiling of the J.E.B. Stuart monument in Richmond in 1907. Mary Lee, the daughter of Robert E. Lee, attended the same unveiling, as did Ellen Lee, the UDC president-general and the wife of one-time Virginia governor Fitzhugh Lee. The children and grandchildren of Confederate heroes also played an important role during these celebrations, as they were chosen to pull the cords to reveal the monument.[28]

The Dallas monument was unique, containing a central figure of a Confederate soldier, at the four corners of which stood life-sized figures of Jefferson Davis, Robert E. Lee, Stonewall Jackson, and Albert Sydney Johnston. Jefferson Hayes Davis, grandson of the Confederate president, was chosen to pull the cord that revealed the figure of Jefferson Davis.

Fig. 4.9. Young girls on their way to unveil a Confederate monument.

Lucy Hayes, another of Davis's grandchildren, pulled the rope that revealed Lee's likeness. Stonewall Jackson's grandson unveiled the statue of Jackson, while his granddaughter revealed that of Johnston. Young women from the community, UDC members, and veterans unveiled the remaining central figure of a Confederate soldier.[29]

Children always played a central role in monument ceremonies. At every unveiling, a young girl or boy was chosen to pull the cord that revealed the monument. This was an important part of the ritual, because the Daughters envisioned each monument as a gift that connected past generations with future generations. It was culturally significant, therefore, that a child symbolically open the gift. Students were also released from school for the ceremonies and usually dressed in the colors—red and white—of the Confederacy.

Commonly, thirteen young girls were chosen to represent the states of the former Confederacy; the UDC included Kentucky and Missouri in this number. The girls wore white dresses with sashes bearing the name of the state they represented. For example, at the monument unveiling in Montgomery, Alabama, in June 1899, thirteen young girls dressed in "Confederate colors" were central to the ceremony. In 1905, when the monument in Huntsville, Alabama, was unveiled, "thirteen beautiful

Fig. 4.10. Thirteen young girls, representing the former states of the Confederacy, are present for the unveiling of this Mississippi monument.

girls, representing the Confederate States by appropriate banners," were chosen to decorate the monument's pedestal. A few years later, in Mt. Pleasant, Tennessee, thirteen "maidens" representing the Confederate States of America unveiled the monument there.[30]

Children also formed choirs and performed patriotic songs for the occasion. "Dixie" was, of course, a crowd favorite, and it was usually accompanied by the singing of "America." In one of the more unusual spectacles of monument unveilings, children formed their choir into a "living" Confederate flag. At the unveiling of the Jefferson Davis monument in New Orleans, "576 pupils formed a 'living' Confederate flag" to sing "Dixie" and "America." The children who lived in and around the

Fig. 4.11. More than 500 students from New Orleans public schools were assembled to form a "living" flag during the unveiling of that city's monument to Jefferson Davis.

city of Huntsville, Alabama, also formed a living Confederate flag as they sang "America." Since they generally assembled into a likeness of the battle flag of the Army of Northern Virginia, the children who represented the stars wore white hats.[31]

The role of children during Confederate monument unveilings was a symbolic endeavor by the UDC to transmit the values of the Confederate generation to future generations of white southerners. The UDC made children a central part of the ritual in an effort to immerse them in the spirit of the Lost Cause. Pulling the cord to unveil a monument, dressing in the colors of the Confederacy, forming a living Confederate flag, and singing "Dixie" were all part of a calculated attempt to impress children with the Lost Cause message of reverence for the southern past.

The singing of "America" and the display of the U.S. flag were evidence of the air of American patriotism surrounding monument unveilings. The Daughters wanted to vindicate their ancestors by celebrating them as patriots, not only of the region, but of the nation as well. For white southerners, monument unveilings were at once a public expression of regional devotion and a means of reclaiming their identity as patriotic Americans. They genuinely believed that southern patriotism was synonymous with American patriotism; therefore, they saw no contradiction in singing "America" along with "Dixie," or waving the flags of the Confederacy with that of the United States.

Fig. 4.12. A "living" Confederate battle flag in front of the monument
to Robert E. Lee in Richmond, Virginia.

Confederate monuments have always been imbued with some larger
meaning. Initially, monuments served the region as symbols of mourn-
ing. The earliest monuments, erected in the aftermath of the Civil War,
were placed in cemeteries, overlooking the graves of the Confederate
dead, and became the focal point of Memorial Day rituals. Beginning in
the mid-1880s and continuing through World War I, the meaning and
purpose of Confederate memorialization changed. The restoration of
home rule in the South set the stage for building monuments that celebrated, rather than mourned, the former Confederacy and its heroes.
Statues of soldiers now appeared in civic spaces, such as town squares
and on the grounds surrounding courthouses.

No longer hidden away in cemeteries, the monuments became part of
the political landscape, marking an important change in their cultural

significance. Confederate monuments were not simply about honoring the past; they had come to serve as symbols of the present, helping to ensure a continuity of values held by the generation that had instituted Jim Crow. They served notice that the political and cultural values of the former Confederacy were important to the creation of a New South. The Daughters also hoped that these stone memorials served the higher purpose of inspiring future generations of white southerners to maintain and defend the values of the Confederate generation.[32]

Between 1890 and World War I, the cultural significance of monument building in the South became more complex. In a search for meaning, scholars have suggested several reasons for the marked increase in monument building between 1895 and World War I. One explanation is that Confederate monuments helped to ease white southerners into the New South by honoring the values of the Old South. Another interpretation suggests that southerners hastened to build the monuments so that the men white southerners celebrated, Confederate soldiers, would be honored before death claimed all of the survivors. Scholars have also concluded that monuments were built to recognize the South as a distinct, yet equal, part of the nation. While each of these arguments has validity, historians have neglected one very significant explanation for the increase in monument building between the 1890s and World War I: the rise of the UDC.[33]

In time, Confederate monuments also became permanent symbols of devotion to patriotic principles as southerners understood them. They helped to illustrate the part of the Lost Cause narrative which maintained that the South had fought the Civil War to defend the Tenth Amendment to the Constitution, which protected the rights of states. Thus monuments recognized Confederate heroes as American heroes. This was a critical point to be made if these men were to be redeemed from their national reputation as traitors.

The Daughters undoubtedly wanted to make a public statement by placing imposing monuments on landscapes of national significance. As director-general of the Shiloh Monument Committee, Rassie White was keenly aware that the park attracted "many, many visitors" from the North. To raise awareness for the need to build a Confederate memorial, White noted how the North had spent "more than $200,000 at Shiloh" for monuments to its dead. "Is not the vanquished as worthy as the victor?" she asked. White appealed to the UDC to build a Confederate monument to "eclipse any monument erected there to the Federal side, since this one is for all the South." She also insisted that the Shiloh monument had to impress children by showing them that Confederate soldiers were not "cowards . . . unworthy of remembrance."[34]

Placing monuments at Arlington National Cemetery and Shiloh had special meaning for white southerners. To be sure, the memorials at these particular locations honored the Confederate dead. Yet they were also symbols of defiance, justifying the South's actions on landscapes visited by thousands of northerners. The Arlington committee report to the UDC in 1913 reflected its sense of accomplishment in building a monument in the "capitol of the country where all our people and visitors from all nations may see it." Rassie Hoskins White made similar comments when she gave the Shiloh committee's annual report: "Do not think you will be placing this monument in an obscure place or that it will not be seen." While these monuments were intended to honor Confederate soldiers, it is clear that the UDC also wanted them to be seen by northerners who made annual pilgrimages to these sites.[35]

The desire to impress northerners, while important to the UDC, was not the primary motivation for building monuments, especially those intended to honor local heroes. The Daughters in Franklin, Tennessee, stated plainly that monuments were not built for "strangers" but for southern youth. "We teach our children patriotism," the Franklin UDC explained, "to love, honor, and defend the government under which we live." In fact, the Franklin chapter built its monument in the town square so children "might know by daily observation of this monument" the cause for which their ancestors fought. Similarly, the UDC chapter in West Point, Georgia, took pride in the fact that the Confederate monument stood in a place where children from all the public schools had to pass.[36]

The Confederate monument at Arlington National Cemetery, more than any other built by the UDC, symbolized the South's longing to be recognized as patriotic by the rest of the nation. This monument, they believed, would serve notice that the region's defense of states' rights was not a defense of slavery, but rather evidence of a commitment to constitutional principle. It was also intended to serve as a token of reconciliation with the North. For the Daughters, reconciliation could occur only

Fig. 4.13. The Confederate monument at Arlington National Cemetery.

when Confederate men had been vindicated. The federal government had, for all intents and purposes, met the Daughters' conditions for reconciliation when it allowed the burial of Confederate soldiers in the cemetery and gave the UDC permission to build a monument to honor those soldiers.

The significance of placing a memorial to the Confederacy within sight of the nation's capitol was not lost on the UDC. The location was also important because the monument was to be built on land that surrounded Arlington House, Robert E. Lee's former home. When the monument was unveiled on June 4, 1914, the day was one of celebration for the Daughters. Not only had they fulfilled their duty to honor Confederate soldiers, they felt that they had made an important step toward vindicating them as well.

The Arlington monument unveiling was unique because northerners and southerners came together to admire and validate what Confederate organizations heralded as a grand symbol of peace and sectional reconciliation. General Washington Gardner, commander-in-chief of the Grand Army of the Republic, was a featured speaker, as was General Bennett Young, the commander-in-chief of the UCV, and Colonel Robert E. Lee, grandson of the Confederate general. Veterans from both Union and Confederate armies were present, as were leading members of the DAR and the UDC. Moreover, Washingtonians were asked by the president of the chamber of commerce to decorate their homes and places of business in honor of the unveiling.[37]

The ceremonies were attended by more than 4,000 people. They arrived in a "swarm of motors" and mingled with veterans who had "made weary pilgrimages from the far South and North to join once more in the fraternal spirit of the great Gettysburg reunion," a reference to the fiftieth anniversary of the Blue and Gray that had taken place the year before. Speaker after speaker commented on the spirit of fraternity and brotherhood that marked the occasion, until the time finally arrived for the unveiling. At that moment, a child walked over and jerked the cord to reveal the monument. Then, Mississippian Daisy McLaurin Stevens, the president-general of the UDC, approached the speaker's stand to present the monument as a "gift" to the United States, which was accepted by President Woodrow Wilson.[38]

Stevens, a respected orator, first paid homage to the Confederate soldiers buried at Arlington. She spoke of self-government, but also included themes of reunification. The U.S. flag that flew that day did not "wave above their [Confederate soldiers'] dust in cheering triumph, but in loving protection," she remarked. Stevens also found it meaningful that "a President Southern by birth and breeding and Northern by choice of residence and training" was there to accept this gift from the Daughters. She concluded her remarks by asserting her firm belief that the monument was important to all boys and girls because it inspired reverence and reminded them to be thankful that they were Americans.[39]

The theme of self-government was most appropriate, as Stevens presented the monument to Woodrow Wilson, a champion of self-determination on the world stage. In accepting the monument on behalf of the United States, he acknowledged the UDC's effort to present to the nation

Fig. 4.14. UDC President-General Daisy Stevens presents the Arlington monument to President Woodrow Wilson (*left*) as a "gift to the nation."

"a memorial of their dead," yet he was quick to note that the U.S. government had played a major role in its creation. The idea was proposed by President William McKinley; Congress authorized it; and another president, William Howard Taft, oversaw the laying of the cornerstone. Wilson, therefore, saw his part in this chain of events as fitting, and he expressed pride in being able to participate in a ceremony that drew northerners and southerners together. Before he finished, a fierce thunderstorm forced the large crowd to quickly disperse in search of shelter. The full text of his speech, however, made clear that Wilson saw the monument as a celebration of a united country.[40]

At the time of the unveiling, most members of the UDC did not honestly believe that reconciliation had occurred between the North and the South. The Daughters, in particular, were loath to speak of reconciliation as long as northerners regarded southerners as traitors. Members of Confederate organizations had long railed against the "biased" interpretations of the Civil War by northern historians. The Arlington monument, however, looks like a three-dimensional pro-Confederate text, or, as one contemporary observer put it, "history in bronze." Indeed, the plinth is marked by scenes inspired by the Lost Cause narrative, including images of heroic men, self-sacrificing women, and faithful slaves.

For white southerners, the Arlington monument was a success, because it represented reconciliation in terms they found acceptable. It offered no compromises in its interpretation of the Civil War, and its place in the nation's cemetery honors Confederate soldiers as American patriots.[41]

Monuments, to be sure, are the most vivid expressions of Confederate culture and were central in the UDC's campaign of vindication. Thus, choosing the type of monument, deciding where it was placed, raising the money to build it, and then organizing the celebration surrounding the unveiling all became part of the ritual. The Daughters were chiefly responsible for the movement to honor the Confederate generation, and their role as shapers of public memory cannot be overemphasized. The monuments that cover the southern urban landscape and sites of national significance are central to an understanding of the Lost Cause as a movement about vindication and the preservation of conservative values. Monuments also help to gauge the degree to which the New South was really new, as the Daughters demanded that the sacrifices of the Confederate generation be honored. Paying homage, as state legislatures discovered, was costly, because the UDC was not content to honor the "generation of the sixties" with monuments. They also wanted southern states to provide for aging and indigent veterans and their widows. To do less, they believed, was sacrilege.

Confederate Progressives

Let our mission be to comfort and solace the remaining few short
years that are left to the gallant men who fought so bravely for
"wife, children, and friends."

Caroline Meriwether Goodlett, UDC cofounder, 1894[1]

"Our interest is not confined to just one line of work, like monument
building," Rassie Hoskins White told the New Orleans convention of the
United Daughters of the Confederacy in 1913, "but branches out in many
directions for the uplift of the South."[2] White, who served the organization as president-general from 1911 to 1913, understood that the UDC
had earned a reputation for erecting monuments to Confederate heroes,
yet her statement also reflects the fact that the Daughters' activities were
not limited to changing the southern landscape. Certainly town squares
provide ample evidence of the UDC's success as monument builders,
but the organization also had historical, educational, social, and benevolent objectives.[3]

The least-known of the UDC's objectives—benevolence—reflects the
influence of progressivism within the organization, as the Daughters
sought to assist the Confederate generation and its descendants. The
Daughters were strongly committed to providing for the aging and indigent veterans and widows still in their midst, and the soldiers' and widows' homes they supported are evidence of this commitment. They also
sought to provide educational assistance to young men and women of
Confederate descent, so that they might serve the region as teachers.
Helping these young southerners receive a college education was more

than an act of benevolence. It furthered the UDC's objective of instill-ing respect for the Confederate cause among coming generations of white southerners. The organization's progressivism, therefore, was in-fluenced by its commitment to Lost Cause ideals.[4]

The Daughters' benevolent activity fits into the larger pattern of south-ern progressivism described by historian Dewey Grantham, when, be-tween 1880 and World War I, social welfare was an urban phenomenon generally undertaken by private organizations. Churches and benevolent associations often filled the void left by local governments, which were reluctant to provide public welfare out of fear that it would thwart per-sonal initiative. According to Grantham, the one notable exception to an organized welfare program in the South prior to World War I was the care of Confederate veterans. Lost Cause sympathizers, especially south-ern women, were vehemently opposed to placing their ancestors in almshouses or on poor farms, the primary agencies of public welfare in the region. Thus, beginning in the 1880s and continuing through World War I, they turned to building soldiers' homes and widows' homes throughout the South. While many of these homes began as private charitable enterprises in the 1880s, by the early twentieth century most had become state property and were being maintained with state funds.[5]

The UDC's pledge to honor Confederate men and women, therefore, extended well beyond monument building. The Daughters believed that it was their duty to provide for aging and indigent veterans and widows, since neither was eligible to receive national pensions. They were equally committed to providing the poor children and grandchildren of Confed-erate veterans with educational assistance. Helping those less fortunate was also an integral part of a class tradition of noblesse oblige. What distinguished the UDC, however, was its Confederate progressivism, which was not simply for whites only, but rather for Confederates only.[6]

Southern women had long played an indispensable role in the region's early welfare movement, if not through their churches, then through organizational work.[7] In this regard, members of the UDC were no exception. Many Daughters engaged in progressive reforms unre-lated to the Lost Cause. UDC cofounder Caroline Meriwether Goodlett, for example, served on the board of managers of the Protestant Orphan Asylum and Mission Home, was vice president of the Humane Society in Nashville, lobbied her state's legislators to pass a bill raising the age of consent of girls from sixteen to eighteen years, proposed a bill to build a home for "feeble-minded children," and urged the state legislature to "abolish whipping women in the Penitentiary."[8] As an organization, however, the UDC's progressive impulse was directed toward Confederate men and women and their poor descendants.

During the first two decades of the UDC's existence, its members focused their benevolence on impoverished Confederate men and women. Later, as the generation of the 1860s dwindled in number, the Daughters turned their attention toward educating poor young men and women of Confederate descent. This eventually became an important mission of the organization, since it was linked to the greater objective of indoctrinating children with the basic tenets of the Lost Cause.[9]

Confederate veterans had long been the focus of the Lost Cause celebration by the time the UDC was organized in 1894. By the late nineteenth century, caring for "Johnny Reb" had become a pressing issue. Beginning in the mid-1880s, North Carolina and Florida became the first states to issue pensions to their veterans, and in 1882 Louisiana built the first state-supported soldiers' home.[10] Although defenders of the Lost Cause claimed that veterans were highly valued for their service to the Confederacy, using state funds to provide for common soldiers in their old age challenged the social tenet that charity begins and ends at home. Therefore, voluntary organizations like the UCV and the UDC stepped in to assist the region's needy heroes.[11]

Women in Confederate circles took an active interest in the construction of soldiers' homes around the South and were often instrumental in their founding. As early as 1892, Missouri women, who were the first group to call themselves "Daughters of the Confederacy," made possible the construction of their state's soldiers' home. When the Ex-Confederate Association of Missouri had exhausted itself trying to raise funds for the home, the Missouri Daughters stepped in to help. As one writer explained in his letter to the *Confederate Veteran*, "In two counties where the men could not raise a dollar, the local [groups of DOCs] raised over $1,000 each." The Missouri Daughters raised a total of $25,000 and "paid for the main building," ensuring that the indigent veterans in their state were cared for in their old age.[12]

It was evident within the first year of its founding that the general organization planned to use its influence to help establish soldiers' homes. UDC cofounder Caroline Goodlett, in a speech before the 1895 Atlanta convention, declared, "We want Legislatures to make appropriations or procure homes for our disabled homeless soldiers and to maintain them."[13] Daughters across the South heeded Goodlett's message and, in states where no home existed, raised funds to build one and lobbied legislators for state appropriations. In fact, in every state of the former Confederacy, UDC members used their political influence and fund-raising skills to support the construction of soldiers' homes.[14]

As the number of Confederate veterans dwindled rapidly toward the close of the nineteenth century, white southerners showed increasing concern for those who remained. Historian R. B. Rosenburg has noted that the soldiers' home movement that took place in the South between 1880 and 1920 was an effort to honor the living Confederates for their sacrifices on behalf of the region. Campaigns to build homes in southern states during these years were a direct outgrowth of the Lost Cause and thrived on the support of the South's leading Confederate organizations, the UCV and the UDC. Though Rosenburg downplays the role played by women's organizations, there is clear evidence their involvement was critical to the success of establishing the region's soldiers' homes.[15]

Despite the assistance of women's organizations, these homes were for soldiers only and did not admit Confederate women. Indeed, in numerous cases the wives of the very men being admitted to the soldiers' homes were denied entry. This inequality prompted UDC members to action, because they believed their female ancestors deserved benevolent assistance equal to that provided to the old veterans. "While I would not detract one iota from the courage required of these brave men," explained UDC historian-general Mildred Rutherford, "I must in justice pay tribute where it rightfully belongs—to the wives and mothers who sustained and cheered them during [days] of gloom and despondency." Rutherford's sentiments were shared by many in the UDC who recognized the sacrifices made by Confederate women.[16]

While provisions were being made across the South to place numerous soldiers into homes for veterans, Daughters in Richmond, Virginia, conceived a plan to build a home strictly for women. Their efforts began in 1897 and within three years, on October 15, 1900, the Home for Needy Confederate Women formally opened. The building was tangible proof of what the UDC considered a "sacred duty"—caring for Confederate women. And while the UDC was responsible for the home's existence, one of the home's managers, Mrs. Andrew Jackson Montague, reminded men that it should be an "honor [for them] to do their manly part in this work," by providing their financial support. She also considered the home a most appropriate monument to "the courageous women of the Confederacy."[17]

The Home for Needy Confederate Women in Richmond became the model for future homes for Confederate women, although it served as the only women's home for several years. Its officers and managers were all women, but an advisory board "composed of men of business experience" also served. However, as Montague was quick to explain, "these gentlemen do not desire or pretend in any sense to manage the Home, leaving that absolutely to the ladies," who were presumed to be fit for this work because it was an extension of their traditional role as caretakers.[18]

Many of the home's first residents, referred to as "inmates," were from Virginia. But since the home was the only such institution in the South for many years, women from other states were admitted. It was open to needy widows, sisters, or daughters of Confederate soldiers. Residents were required to be "free from mental derangement, contagious diseases, morphine or alcoholic habits, and epilepsy." A further condition of acceptance was that "all furniture, property or money belonging to an inmate" became property of the home. In exchange, the women received perpetual care until their death. Just as in the soldiers' homes, women were required to abide by rules of conduct that reflected the paternalistic attitudes of the managers. Inmates who exhibited "disrespectful conduct or presumptuous attitude to those in authority" were to be reprimanded or, if need be, dismissed from the home.[19]

The fact that the Richmond home was the lone institution of its kind in the South worried many Daughters, particularly Florence Barlow of Kentucky. Barlow was the associate editor and manager of the *Lost Cause*, a periodical published and edited by women in Louisville.[20] She wrote scathing editorials about the lack of facilities for needy Confederate women and questioned the manhood of the region's elite white men who failed to provide for the women. Her acute criticisms of male contemporaries highlighted the Daughters' frustrations with southern men for their waning interest in the Lost Cause. She believed they had essentially shirked their responsibility to care for Confederate women—women whom the Daughters, and surviving veterans, wanted to honor for their wartime sacrifices.[21]

Florence Barlow was incensed that women were being turned away from the Richmond home because of lack of space. She regarded this situation as a primary failure of southern men who, in many forums commemorating the Lost Cause, often gushed about their indebtedness to Confederate women. In the early years of the twentieth century, these men had even raised money to build a monument to the women of the South. Barlow's editorials chided men for being hypocrites. "These women of the Confederacy, for whom the men of the South have exhausted the vocabulary of the English dictionary and pirated on the French language to find words to express their praise and admiration . . . are told there is 'no room.'" She challenged southern men to explain why they had not provided for women they feigned to honor. "Stop your adulations until you have provided for these women," she admonished. "When you have given them something to eat and a place to sleep and protected them from the cold blast of winter, then they can listen in comfort . . . to your exalted expressions of admiration for them."[22]

Like many Daughters, Barlow protested against building monuments to Confederate women when so many of them still required living assistance. Pointing out that many of the surviving Confederate women still lived in poverty, Barlow wondered in 1903, "what difference does it make? . . . [I]n a few years they will all have passed away, but a great monument of stone will be erected recording them as the bravest, most courageous, self-sacrificing women on earth."[23]

Southern men seemed to have turned a deaf ear to Barlow's criticisms, since they were rarely involved in the campaign to build homes for women. Nevertheless, the Daughters responded to what they saw as a pressing need and, on a state-by-state basis, campaigned to build homes for Confederate women. The Home for Needy Confederate Women in Richmond reasonably accommodated only twenty-five to thirty women, though eventually that number doubled. Yet hundreds of women throughout the South wished to become occupants. While a few soldiers' homes—those in Mississippi and Missouri, for example—allowed veterans to bring their wives, numerous Confederate women who lived in poverty continued to rely on the Daughters' charity.

Fig. 5.1. The Mississippi UDC was instrumental in establishing Beauvoir
as the state's soldiers' home.

The general organization of the UDC eventually considered financing
a regional home for women, taking up the issue in 1910. Until then, state
divisions engaged in campaigns to build homes for Confederate women.
UDC members in Texas and North Carolina, for example, began campaigns to build Confederate women's homes in their states within five
years after the opening of the Richmond home. The campaigns in both
states were successful: the Texas home opened in 1908 and the North
Carolina home in 1915. The North Carolina home was built with state
funds, and both homes were eventually maintained by their state's government, a testament to the Daughters' influence among southern legislators.[24]

As campaigns to build homes for women continued across the South,
state divisions of the UDC acted to provide immediate relief for Confederate women in the interim. At the general conventions, delegates
discussed the need to pressure states to provide for their Confederate
women, and the organization looked to state divisions to carry out its
relief work. In Mississippi, for example, the state division of UDC made
the support of Beauvoir, the soldiers' home in Biloxi, their "chief and
united work." By 1905 they had raised enough money to build an annex
"for the men who have their wives with them." A few years later, they also
built a dormitory for the widows of soldiers and sailors.[25]

At their annual meetings, UDC members held earnest discussions on the best approach to providing relief for the needy women. At the 1907 annual convention, Sallie Faison of North Carolina spoke for many in the UDC when she described how "hard and cruel" it was to force aged veterans who entered soldiers' homes to leave their wives. She suggested that Daughters in each state send a petition to their respective legislatures, "begging" them to appropriate enough money for the soldiers' homes "as would enable the managers to take care of the wives of the old veterans."[26]

State appropriations, however, were not always forthcoming, and where there were none, UDC divisions began raising funds for separate homes. Such campaigns often generated popular support and forced the hand of state governments to assume care of their indigent Confederate women. Three years after the Texas Home for Confederate Women opened, the Texas Division presented the home as a "gift" to the state. In North Carolina, UDC members stood in plain view of their state senators as the senators voted on appropriations for a Confederate women's home. Indeed, local newspapers recorded that the Daughters' presence "without doubt, influenced a favorable vote on a proposition the appropriations committee had previously turned down."[27]

A regional home for needy Confederate women, sponsored solely by the UDC, was offered as yet another solution to the problem of providing for indigent wives and widows. At the general convention held in Little Rock, Arkansas, in 1910, Caroline Helen Plane of Atlanta, whose address was delivered to the convention by fellow Georgian Mildred Rutherford, outlined her proposal for a UDC home. "We have long neglected . . . the women of the Confederacy [who] made the Confederate soldier what he was," she told the Daughters. Noting what she thought to be a "callous attitude towards aged women amongst us," Plane asked the membership to commit itself to "build a home which shall be worthy of them [Confederate women] and an honor to us."[28]

The home Plane envisioned was one for women of elite status. She recognized that homes for old women, "without regard to social position or education," existed; however, such homes were "totally unfit for women of refinement." She suggested that the UDC model its home after the Louise Home in Washington, D.C. Philanthropist William Corcoran had built and endowed that home in 1869 for "gentlewomen who have been reduced by misfortune." When Rutherford finished reading

Fig. 5.2. Caroline Helen Plane of the Georgia UDC proposed building
a home for Confederate women and spearheaded the movement
to establish the memorial at Stone Mountain, Georgia.

Plane's address to the convention, she presented the UDC with a resolution that a Home for Aged Confederate Women "be the next work of the
[organization]."[29]

Reaction to Plane's proposal was swift and highly critical, pitting
UDC leaders against one another. The Daughters in attendance at Little
Rock were concerned "that it was the intention of [the home's] promoter
to draw lines of social distinction; that none other than ladies of refinement could be admitted." Such distinctions were taken into consider-
ation for admission into the UDC; however, as Confederate progressives,
the Daughters were intent on assisting less-fortunate white women. Cornelia Branch Stone, a past president-general from Texas, entered a plea
"in behalf of the poorer classes" and vowed not to lend her support to an
institution modeled after the Louise Home, where restrictions of class
were enforced. Indeed, Stone argued, "the wives and daughters of the

humblest soldiers were as much entitled to such homes as the wives and daughters of officers of the army."[30]

Rutherford tried to defend the plan by arguing that Plane's proposal had been misunderstood. Unmoved, Cornelia Stone retorted that the UDC should never "support a home that discriminates against any Confederate Soldier's family." Then, Janet Randolph, the highly respected president of the Richmond chapter of UDC, stepped in with a compromise. She recommended that the UDC form a relief committee whose responsibility would be to "investigate and relieve as far as possible, present pressing needs of Confederate women." The convention approved her idea and dropped the subject of a UDC home altogether; Randolph was then appointed committee chair, a post she held until her death.[31]

The relief committee became the UDC's watchdog for needy Confederate women; however, no organizational funds were budgeted for the work, and relief continued to be the province of state divisions. Still, Janet Randolph was pleased that her committee had generated good publicity for the Daughters, proving that they had not failed "to care for the living as well as for the graves of their dead." She pointed with pride to the work of UDC divisions in Maryland and Texas, where homes for Confederate women existed, and to Mississippi, where wives were allowed to join their husbands at the soldiers' home. She took special pride in her own state, where the first home for needy Confederate women was built and where the Virginia Daughters supported numerous Confederate women with monthly allotments.[32]

While state divisions of the UDC provided relief to needy Confederates, the general organization was reluctant to supply the relief committee with its own budget. Randolph's requests for funds were often ignored; however, she remained a staunch advocate of social welfare for women and kept the issue before conventions of the UDC. Moreover, she remained confident in the UDC's ability to accomplish great tasks. "We can afford to build our monuments, educate our children, and . . . help the Confederate women," she told Daughters at the 1913 general convention.[33]

Benevolence remained an important activity of the UDC throughout the organization's early years, although state divisions were responsible for most of the work. Thus, the Virginia Daughters pressed their state

Fig. 5.3. The Virginia Daughters, seen here at Mt. Vernon, succeeded in establishing the first home for needy Confederate women, in Richmond, Virginia.

legislature for widows' pensions and succeeded, and in North Carolina Rebecca Cameron stated with confidence that "the North Carolina Legislature usually gives the United Daughters of the Confederacy what they ask for."[34] Therefore, when the UDC was unable to raise sufficient funds to care for needy Confederates, members used their political influence to help accomplish that goal at the local and state levels of government.

Education for the poor of Confederate descent was also part of the UDC's benevolent mission. However, the Daughters' response to assisting poor whites in getting an education was mixed. While many Daughters supported industrial education for poor whites, particularly in the rural South, on the whole the UDC did not lend its full support. Individual members and chapters of the UDC often acted independently to promote and support a program of industrial mission schools, while the general organization balked at providing financial assistance for several years. This reluctance was primarily because of the Daughters' pledge to provide for the region's aging Confederates, as well as their resolute commitment to building monuments, which took financial precedence.

A clause in the UDC bylaws, consistent with the organization's objectives, stated that members were responsible for educating "the needy descendants of worthy Confederates," yet the organization itself did not establish a committee on education until 1908. Until then, state divisions and local chapters took up the cause of educating disadvantaged Confederate descendants. In fact, when President-General Cornelia Stone appointed members to the UDC's education committee, four states already had established committees: Mississippi, North Carolina, South Carolina, and Missouri. When the general organization's committee was finally established, the Daughters chose to provide financial assistance to young men and women seeking a college education, neglecting industrial education altogether.[35]

That the UDC chose to spend its money on college scholarships rather than industrial education suggests that the Daughters sought to preserve class distinctions. The uplift of poor whites was not as important as the larger goal of the organization—perpetuating the message of the Lost Cause. Indeed, the majority of money the UDC raised for education went to fund scholarships in southern colleges, particularly in the region's normal schools. Scholarships were also established outside the South at Columbia Teacher's College, Vassar, and the University of Chicago, to name a few. Moreover, assisting young men and women to become teachers served the organization's larger goal of transmitting Confederate culture to future generations.[36]

Within the first ten years of its founding, the UDC became one of the most socially and politically effective organizations in the region—in large part because of the size and influence of its membership. As a result, the organization became a target for pleas from southern reformers wishing to take advantage of the UDC network—a network of women who had close connections to the leading male politicians of the region. Chief among them was Rebecca Latimer Felton, a Daughter from Carrollton, Georgia, whose personal crusade was to educate rural farm women—not only to empower them personally, but in order to sustain "Anglo Saxon" supremacy. In many respects, her progressivism was Confederate, since she often made the point that many of these young farm women were the direct descendents of Confederate veterans. As she sought to enlist other southern women in this cause, she saw other UDC members as her most obvious allies.[37]

Rebecca Felton spoke to small groups of the UDC throughout Georgia, arguing that they should take action to relieve the plight of southern farm women. Then, in 1897, she had the opportunity to address the entire convention of the UDC. Felton traveled to Baltimore, Maryland, where the Daughters were holding their general convention and delivered a speech entitled "The Importance of the Education of Poor Girls of the South." Motivated to action by the poverty and ignorance visible in her own state and conditions she knew existed throughout the South, Felton presented her case to the UDC. The poor southern white girls of whom she spoke may not have been "cultured ladies" like the Daughters, but the fathers and grandfathers of those girls had also fought to defend the Confederacy. Therefore, southern men and women had a "duty" to help the descendants of those who died during the "unequal struggle of the sixties," by providing poor white girls with higher education.[38]

Felton's speech appealed to the Daughters' race, class, and gender interests. An avowed white supremacist, she implored the Daughters to assist poor white girls because they were "the coming mothers of the great majority of the Anglo-Saxon race in the South." She pointed with disdain at the money northern philanthropists had given to educate African Americans in the region. While Felton believed that "giving literary cultivation and the ballot to a race before it was fitted for either" was a "waste of money," she also feared that poor whites would not be able to compete "with the children of the former slaves" who received a technical or university education. The Daughters must help these young women, Felton pleaded, because "the destiny of the white population rests in their [white girls'] hands."[39]

By referring to UDC members as "cultured ladies," Felton distinguished between those she wished to assist and those whom she asked for assistance. She referred to the poor as "country people" and "orphans of this class of men" (i.e., poor veterans). The Daughters, on the other hand, were from a class of "honorable" men and women whom Felton suggested had come back to their homes after the Civil War "in peace, if not in plenty." Therefore, the UDC, as members of a privileged group, had a mission to help the poor orphans of "dead veteran soldiers."[40]

Finally, Felton appealed to the Daughters as women, who, according to traditional definitions of gender, were society's guardians. Indeed, she argued, these poor girls were the "wards" of the UDC. "Must [they] appeal to you [women of the South] for help in education and sympathy," Felton asked, "and fail to get the best work of your life in their behalf?" The Daughters, she concluded, should assume the "office of guardian and caretaker" for these white girls, because "the progress of [the] race" depended upon it.[41]

Initial reaction to Felton's speech was enthusiastic and resulted in prolonged applause from her UDC audience; nevertheless, assistance from the general organization was not immediately forthcoming. Providing benevolent assistance to surviving Confederate men and women remained the Daughters' top priority. They were also committed to a campaign of monument building across the South, believing that such public symbols were critical to preserving the memory of the region's fallen heroes. Still, in 1908, when Cornelia Stone appointed members to the UDC's new committee on education, providing needy white girls with a higher education had moved up on the Daughters' list of priorities.

As members of the region's elite, and as a politically influential women's organization, the Daughters believed they were in a position to play an important role in the uplift of the less fortunate of their race. Southern progressives touted industrial education as a curative for rural poverty; as Confederate progressives, UDC members supported similar measures for the poor descendants of veterans. They believed that industrial education helped alleviate illiteracy and provided poor whites with practical skills for living. Still, the UDC's education initiatives were focused on higher education. The Daughters worked to fund scholarships and build dormitories at normal schools to assist those descendants, primarily young women, struggling to earn a college degree. Training women to become teachers, moreover, provided some assurance that the narrative of the Lost Cause, with its lessons about race and class, would be spread to coming generations.[42]

Certainly individual UDC members were personally committed to the uplift of their race through education, and several actually taught in the public schools. Their task was a prodigious one, indeed. White illiteracy in the early-twentieth-century South was epidemic. Rural areas were especially dismal, as illiteracy was often accompanied by abject poverty. Students seldom attended school beyond the elementary level; their attendance was generally irregular during the three or four months schools were open. Southern social reformers addressed the problem through school reform and, later, anti-illiteracy campaigns. These campaigns were waged throughout the region, primarily by women who zealously sought to emancipate the South from ignorance.[43]

Among the South's educational reformers was Martha Gielow of Alabama. Little is known of Gielow personally except that in 1905 she helped to found the Southern Industrial Education Association (SIEA), whose purpose was to promote "industrial and practical education for white children throughout the South." She hoped to establish industrial "mission schools," especially for the most destitute white children living in the mountains, and to support such schools that were already operating in those areas. To gain help in this task, Gielow sent a circular to the presidents-general of the local, state, and general divisions of the UDC, requesting their assistance.[44]

Like Felton, Gielow was also a Daughter, and her appeal was as both a member and a reformer. She implored the UDC to join her in educating "neglected Southern white children" in order to prepare them "for the duties of citizenship." She asked the Daughters for personal and financial assistance in establishing schools where young girls would be taught cooking, sewing, and "every kind of housework," and both boys and girls would learn "the improved arts of agriculture." An industrial education for poor whites, she believed, provided them with the necessary tools to "extricate themselves from the limitations of their present environment."[45]

Gielow's appeal to the UDC followed Rebecca Felton's example. She solicited the Daughters' help by asking them to assist the less fortunate of their race, people who were "white, of the pure Anglo-Saxon race." She raised concerns about the money spent by northern philanthropists to educate African Americans in the South and then critically questioned the UDC about the way it spent the money it raised. "What good will monuments to our ancestors be," Gielow asked, "if our Southland is to become the land of educated blacks and uneducated whites?" She concluded by asking the Daughters to join her crusade so that it too did not become a "LOST CAUSE."[46]

The response to Gielow's circular was mixed at best. Forty-seven chapters of the UDC joined the SIEA by 1907, yet hundreds of other chapters did not. The problem, it seems, was the way Gielow had worded her appeal. She asked that state divisions of UDC become state associations of the SIEA for the purpose of establishing industrial schools. In other words, she asked that UDC divisions make pledges to the "mother association" (i.e., SIEA) and become auxiliaries.[47]

Fig. 5.4. President-General Lizzie George Henderson (1905–1907)
was also the daughter U.S. Senator James Z. George,
author of the Mississippi Plan.

UDC President-General Lizzie George Henderson of Mississippi issued her own response to Gielow. The UDC should not "educate any but
Confederate children," and definitely not "the children of the mountain
whites who fought against the South," Henderson wrote—highlight-
ing the classism of the UDC's membership. As head of the South's
leading women's voluntary organization, she also disavowed any group
that sought to make the UDC its auxiliary. Rebuffed, Gielow tried to
cover her tracks by explaining that the term "auxiliary" simply meant
"helper." The clarification was too little too late, and though Gielow continued to seek the UDC's assistance, her credibility had been severely
damaged.[48]

Martha Gielow's request may have offended the leader of the UDC,
but she was not alone in the belief that industrial education had the
potential to alleviate many of the South's social ills. Her allies included

Fig. 5.5. In an early will, Varina Davis, widow of the Confederate president, stated that she wanted the Davis family home in Biloxi, Mississippi, to become a school for industrial education.

Varina Davis, widow of the Confederate president; UDC cofounder Caroline Goodlett (whom Gielow consulted prior to the conflict with Henderson), and Elizabeth Lumpkin Glenn, a Daughter who had achieved enormous popularity as a speaker at veterans' reunions. In a 1901 speech to the UDC in Monteagle, Tennessee, Glenn spoke about providing industrial education to the thousands of girls and boys currently working long hours in the textile mills of the region. In an early will, Varina Davis considered leaving Beauvoir, the Davis family home in Biloxi, to the Protestant Episcopal Diocese of Mississippi "to be used as a Children's Industrial Home." Although Beauvoir became a Confederate soldiers' home instead, Varina's original will revealed her support for educating poor white children through a program of industrial education.[49]

If there was one person who could motivate the Daughters to act on behalf of needy white youth, it was the woman the UDC affectionately referred to as "Mother Goodlett." In fact, Caroline Goodlett's speech to the UDC at the general convention in 1908 appears to have motivated President-General Cornelia Branch Stone to create the UDC's Committee on Education. Goodlett, whose home state of Tennessee was also the home to many poor mountain whites, expressed her disappointment that the general organization had not moved forward in its campaign to educate needy descendants of Confederate veterans.[50]

Goodlett spoke to the convention, expressing disappointment in the organization and in herself. While thousands of dollars went into building monuments, she described how she "sat by . . . thinking that the monument fever would abate." She also believed that "the most thoughtful and best educated women" in the organization should have realized that the "grandest monument [they] could build in the South would be an educated motherhood." Goodlett challenged the Daughters to help poor whites, not by going into "the stone and mortar business . . . erecting monuments to [their] pet idols." Rather, the UDC should spend its money on a "nobler cause—in raising the standard of Southern women."[51]

President-General Stone responded to Goodlett's challenge by creating the UDC's Committee on Education, appointing South Carolinian Mary B. Poppenheim as chair. Poppenheim, an active member who never married, gave enormous energy to this post, which she held until 1917, when she was elected to the UDC's highest office. Between 1908 and 1917, she guided the Committee on Education to seek out and establish scholarships, primarily in the region's public universities, but also outside the South in more prestigious institutions such as her alma mater, Vassar.[52]

Prior to Poppenheim's appointment, state divisions of the UDC had actively supported the cause of educating disadvantaged young women in their respective states. Assistance took the form of scholarships and efforts to build women's dormitories in the region's normal schools. The Tennessee Division campaigned to build a women's dormitory at the Peabody Normal College in Nashville beginning in 1903. The following year, the Georgia Division began its fund-raising drive for a women's dormitory. The drive was a success, and the dormitory, which the division named the Winnie Davis Memorial Building, opened at the Georgia State Normal School (now the University of Georgia).[53]

The North Carolina UDC, one of the first state divisions to have a committee on education, supported scholarships at its State Normal and Industrial College, located in Greensboro. Ella Brodnax, a member of the Greensboro chapter, chaired the committee and handled all applications to "The Normal," where the North Carolina Division sponsored two scholarships. She had the unenviable task of having to decide who should get scholarships, as many women applied.[54]

Applications, such as the one from Mary Mauney of Newton in 1908, were accompanied by desperate pleas for an education. As Mauney explained, "unless I am successful in this [application] my school days are at an end." Sallie Faison, who served on the committee with Brodnax, made her own recommendations based on letters from applicants in similar circumstances to those of Mary Mauney. Faison wrote Brodnax about another young woman: "if she does not have the chance to improve herself now . . . it means she must go to the factory."[55] The young women, like Mary Mauney of North Carolina, who applied for UDC scholarships across the South were the disadvantaged Confederate descendants that the UDC's Committee on Education wished to assist.

While young men were the recipients of UDC scholarships in the early twentieth century, the organization had a greater interest by far in sponsoring the education of young white women. Indeed, the UDC's interest in educating women went a long way in addressing the organization's larger goal of transmitting the values of Confederate culture. The majority of young women on UDC scholarships were training to be teachers. By supporting this endeavor, the Daughters accomplished two important objectives: assisting needy descendants and training young women "to teach the children . . . of the South." In other words, providing young white women with the means to receive an education at an institution of higher learning in the South served the higher purpose of preserving the Confederate past. For as these women became teachers, the Daughters reasoned, thousands of the region's white youth were sure to learn reverence for the Confederate past, including the principle of states' rights and the value of white supremacy.[56]

The UDC's benevolent activity helped remind contemporary southerners that those who sacrificed their lives for the Confederacy, as well as their descendants, were valued in the New South. Homes for widows and soldiers were, undoubtedly, powerful public symbols on the south-

Fig. 5.6. Carr-Burdette College in Texas provided young women with what the
UDC thought all new teachers should have—a pro-southern education.

ern landscape. They represented a firm commitment to preserving the
integrity of the defeated. Educating women and men of Confederate
descent was another, even more effective, way of ensuring that the traditions and values of the Old South would be perpetuated for generations.

→ 6 ←

Combating "Wicked Falsehoods"

To perpetuate the truth of Southern history and to search out
and immortalize its facts and traditions is our dearest aim. . . . We ask
only for truth and justice . . . we condemn histories that are
false or misrepresent life in the South.

Rassie Hoskins White, president-general, 1913

Adelia Dunovant, a Texas Daughter recently elected president of her division, traveled to the UDC's general convention in 1902 to give an address about the importance of history to the work of the organization. The Daughters convened their meeting in Wilmington, North Carolina, where the violent crusade to end "negro rule" had succeeded just a few years earlier. Mayor Alfred Moore Waddell, a white supremacist who led the campaign, welcomed the Daughters to the city and complimented them on their efforts to restore the reputation of Confederate men. The outcome of the Wilmington Race Riot of 1898 may have helped restore Waddell's reputation, but it was important to the UDC that all veterans receive their due. The Confederate generation had been branded "rebels," which Dunovant regarded as a "very grave error," and she contended that an accurate account of the past was needed to change this misconception. "History should be made to serve its true purpose by bringing its lessons into the present and using them as a guide to the future," Dunovant asserted, and she believed that those best suited for the task were the women of the UDC. "What lies before us is not only loyalty to memories, but loyalty to principles; not only building of monuments, but the vindication of the men of the Confederacy," she reminded convention delegates.[1]

Fig. 6.1. Adelia Dunovant, former president of the Texas UDC,
wrote passionately about the importance of "unbiased" history
and about southern citizenship.

The United Daughters of the Confederacy and other proselytizers of
Lost Cause mythology agreed that history, especially that written by
northerners, was biased against the South. The organization considered
it a "very grave responsibility," as Dunovant's address attests, to preserve
and promote "true" history. It was the Daughters' chief tool of vindication and was used to influence future generations of southerners. UDC
members generally applied such modifiers as "correct," "authentic," and
"impartial" to describe a history that was favorable to the Confederacy.
Their commitment to historical "truth" was firmly established in the
UDC constitution, and much of the organization's activity focused on
meeting this objective.[2]

The Daughters believed that an "authentic" history of the "War between the States," their official term for the Civil War, would help them
achieve important objectives. What counted as "authentic," of course,
was generally history written with a pro-southern slant. History written

"correctly," they reasoned, vindicated Confederate men, recorded the sacrifices of Confederate women, and exonerated the South. "Biased" history, on the other hand, regarded secession as an act of rebellion and argued that the South fought the war to defend slavery.

The importance the Daughters placed on historical work cannot be overstated, because they acted on the assumption that duty required them to defend the honor of Confederate men and women. The primary means of doing so was to "instruct and instill into the descendants of the people of the South" a respect for the Confederate past and its principles (see chapter 7 following). As a result, the UDC's historical and educational objectives were closely linked. The myriad ways in which the Daughters sought to preserve the history of the Old South and the Civil War, therefore, are crucial to understanding the organization's purpose and the extent of its influence.[3]

The Daughters were not the first southerners to press for a pro-Confederate perspective on the Civil War. Beginning in 1876, the Southern Historical Society published articles written by former Confederate officers, which primarily assessed military tactics. The UCV, founded in 1889, created a Historical Committee that issued formal statements condemning biased history written and published by northerners. Then, in 1893, Sumner A. Cunningham began publication of the *Confederate Veteran* in Nashville, Tennessee. It quickly became the official organ of every Confederate organization. All groups expressed concern that histories biased against the South would have a long-term negative impact on the region and its people.[4]

Soon after its founding in 1894, the UDC became the Confederate organization most actively engaged in combating what one Texas Daughter called "wicked falsehoods." Many UDC leaders spoke about the importance of impartial history, but their organization's efforts to preserve history were also concrete and systematic. The Daughters collected artifacts for museums and supported their male counterparts in setting up state departments of archives and history. They gathered manuscripts and collected war reminiscences from veterans and Confederate women, some of the earliest examples in what has since become the field of oral history. The UDC encouraged the study of history by establishing essay contests for its membership, and many Daughters were active amateur historians. They wrote history for local newspapers, published articles in the *Confederate Veteran* and other magazines, and even wrote historical novels or textbooks for use in southern schools.[5]

The UDC established a history committee to assist its members in their crusade to vindicate southern men. "Our duty is clearly defined," declared the committee's chair, Mildred Rutherford, in 1899, "to strive to vindicate, by a truthful statement of facts we can prove, the heroism of our fallen comrades and surviving Veterans." Adelia Dunovant of Houston, Texas, echoed these sentiments when she chaired the history committee in 1901, noting that the Daughters' historical work was important to "the vindication of the men of the Confederacy." Mayor Alfred Moore Waddell welcomed the UDC general convention to Wilmington, North Carolina, in 1901 by asserting that southern women had achieved enormous success in "vindicating before the world the causes in which their Southern countrymen engaged."[6]

History, therefore, was highly regarded as a powerful tool of persuasion. While the Daughters were convinced that the South was misunderstood because of the influence of northern histories, they were equally convinced that "unbiased" histories could rectify any false impressions and bring about vindication. As they saw it, their mission was to reverse the trend of vilification to one of vindication. They rejected the contention that southerners had been traitors and rebels and instead promoted them as heroes and defenders of a just cause. "Not only will men of the South stand justified among her people," Chief Justice Francis Nichols of Louisiana reminded the UDC at its 1902 general convention, "but the women of the South will be honored."[7]

The UDC sought to correct what they believed were interpretive inaccuracies and in doing so offer an interpretation that suited their cause. Above all, the Daughters resented claims that the South fought the Civil War to defend slavery and that Confederate soldiers were traitors to the United States. UDC members, as well as their male contemporaries, wanted history to record that the South fought the war to defend states' rights, not slavery. Moreover, they insisted, Confederate soldiers were American patriots because they were the true defenders of the Constitution. The Daughters believed that correcting such errors was essential if Confederate men were to be vindicated.

Vindication was not limited to rehabilitating Confederate manhood. Many Lost Cause devotees, including the Daughters, believed that biased histories had both maligned the Confederacy and generated false impressions of southern life before the war. According to UDC members, nonsoutherners had been misled into believing that citizens of the Old South were impoverished and illiterate. Even worse, for them, books like Harriet Beecher Stowe's *Uncle Tom's Cabin* had successfully challenged whether the Old South elite were true Christians, given that they had owned slaves. Lost Cause organizations were particularly defensive about the latter subject, because they regarded planter benevolence as inherently Christian. Thus, a revised historical narrative was also important in telling the truth, as they understood it, about slavery in the South.

The UDC's devotion to impartial history was motivated, to a large degree, by class pride. The Daughters were descendants of the Old South elite and refused to remain idle while historians condemned their fathers. They were unwilling to accept the allegation that slavery was a cruel institution and pledged themselves to defend the region's people and its past. As one Daughter put it, the organization intended to continue its crusade until "all the world admits that the Confederate soldiers were loyal, brave, patriotic, gallant men, justified in their construction of constitutional right." Convincing "all the world" was a difficult task; still, the UDC was committed to perpetuating a benevolent image of their ancestors as kind masters of faithful servants.[8]

The Daughters' efforts to provide impartial history were first launched by the state divisions, which received some directives from the general organization. Writing correct history required documentation, so in addition to gathering artifacts, the Daughters also collected manuscripts. Preserving documents was important if the UDC was to defend its version of history. "Unless we rouse ourselves," Mildred Rutherford reported to the Richmond convention in 1899, "most valuable records will slip from our grasp and beyond the proving power of witnesses." Daughters heeded her advice and took action in their respective states.[9]

State divisions of the UDC supported a movement, initiated by the SCV, to establish departments of archives and history in southern states. In 1904, at the Confederate veterans' reunion, the SCV announced its intention to pressure state legislatures to support the creation of state archives. The following year, the UDC added its power and influence to the movement. At its 1905 general convention in San Francisco, the UDC pledged its assistance in the development of departments of archives and history, similar to those already operating in Mississippi, Alabama, and Tennessee. The Daughters encouraged the creation and maintenance of "separate departments of State" as the best means of preserving historical material.[10]

UDC members acquired archival materials to place in these new state agencies. The most often donated items were war reminiscences, essentially oral histories conducted by UDC members. They placed a high priority on collecting the stories of remaining Confederate veterans, whose numbers were rapidly dwindling. Nearly every southern state archive received soldiers' reminiscences, because the UDC believed that "unwritten history" offered the "most vivid" evidence of the truth.[11]

The Daughters' efforts to preserve history extended beyond collecting archival material. They also gathered material culture associated with the Confederacy and the antebellum South. The UDC exhibited Confederate "relics" in a variety of venues. Under UDC management, rooms were set aside for the display of artifacts in several of the South's state capitol buildings. Led by Caroline Helen Plane of Atlanta, the Daughters sponsored an exhibit of Confederate relics at the Cotton States and International Exposition in 1895. At the 1904 World's Fair in St. Louis, and at the 1907 Jamestown Exposition, the UDC had its own building—a replica of Jefferson Davis's home, Beauvoir—where cultural artifacts were displayed.[12]

In 1896 the Confederate Memorial Literary Society (CMLS) established the Confederate Museum in Richmond, Virginia, which served as a permanent and central repository for Confederate material culture. The museum was housed in the former White House of the Confederacy, which had been home to Jefferson Davis and his family during the Civil War. Each state of the former Confederacy was assigned a room in the house, where artifacts from that state were exhibited. The museum also sponsored a "Solid South" room to which all states were asked to submit a Confederate item of significance. The UDC and CMLS held members in common, and while the CMLS managed the museum, the UDC carried reports of its operation and encouraged the Daughters to lend their support to this enterprise.[13]

State divisions of the UDC also collected and displayed items in their own states in addition to making contributions to the Confederate Museum. Doing so was in keeping with their duty to the Confederate gen-

Fig. 6.2. The White House of the Confederacy became
the Confederate Museum in 1896.

eration. As one writer to the *Confederate Veteran* put it, southerners owed
it to the "memories of its Confederate dead" to preserve their state's "best
relics." The activity of state divisions of the UDC is evidence that the
Daughters agreed, as the material culture they gathered provided a three-
dimensional narrative of the war.[14]

UDC members intended to display the items they collected, and they
often set up exhibits in government-owned buildings. The Mississippi
Division reported in 1900 that the plans for the new capitol building
included "a large room designated as the 'Hall of History.'" The Hall of
History was to be under UDC control, "used as a repository for their
archives." In 1904 the Texas state legislature set aside a room in its capitol building in Austin for use by the UDC to "deposit, classify, and exhibit
relics of all wars in which Texas and her people had taken part." Members of the Alabama Division organized the First White House Association to preserve the Montgomery home briefly occupied by Jefferson
Davis and his family when he became the Confederacy's first and only
president. The home served as a repository for the "valuable and numerous relics" the Association received from Varina Davis.[15]

The Daughters took their role as history's guardians seriously, as evidenced by the fight to preserve the Old Capitol in the state of Mississippi. Division President Laura Martin Rose from West Point, who later served as historian-general for the general organization, reported in 1909 that the division was "using its influence in every way" to secure an appropriation from the legislature to ensure the building's preservation. The UDC valued the Old Capitol because it had served the state before and during the period of the Confederacy. It was doubly valued because the Daughters hoped to use it as a museum for Confederate relics. Members of the division lobbied the state for an appropriation in 1910, and although none was granted, they were undaunted in their mission to save the building.[16]

Two years later, in 1912, UDC member Eron Rowland organized a petition drive to restore the Old Capitol. Rowland, whose husband was director of the Mississippi State Archives and History, sought support from a variety of organizations across the state. While Laura Rose spoke with state representatives and senators, encouraging them to fund the preservation of this historic landmark, Rowland authored a petition to save the building. It was signed by members of the Colonial Dames, the Daughters of the American Revolution, the Daughters of 1812, the Mississippi Federation of Women's Clubs, the Mississippi Women's Christian Temperance Union, the Mississippi Woman Suffrage Association, the UCV, and the SCV.[17]

The state legislature declined an appropriation for a second time, despite Rowland's petition, but UDC members persisted. Although former state President-General Lucy Yerger had once claimed that the Daughters of Mississippi were not a "political body," the women wrote their legislators, asking them to approve the bill to save the Old Capitol. When it came up for a vote in 1914, the bill was defeated by just eleven votes. The Daughters attributed the outcome to the "ravages of the boll weevil," which had devastated the state's cotton crops, contributing to financial depression. Laura Martin Rose, chair of the committee to save the building, still urged the Daughters not to give up on their work. She asked that they continue to speak with legislators about preserving the building as a repository for Mississippi's history. The UDC's tenacity paid off after six years of lobbying, when, on April 8, 1916, the state approved a bill appropriating $125,000 to restore the Old Capitol.[18]

The success of the Daughters' efforts to preserve Confederate material culture, both artifacts and buildings, was aided by the fact that UDC members were dedicated students of history. Meetings of local chapters always included some discussion of southern or Civil War history. A historical program was a central element of the annual meetings held by state divisions and the general organization. Studying history was considered essential preparation for UDC membership. Florence Barlow, a Kentucky Daughter and editor of the *Lost Cause* magazine, urged her female readers to "enlighten and educate yourselves and those around you in, at least, literature pertaining to your own section." Tennie Pinkerton Dozier, historian of her chapter in Franklin, Tennessee, agreed. "Every Daughter of the Confederacy—in fact, every Southern woman— should know this history [of the South]," she said.[19]

Historical knowledge was important to the Daughters for a variety of reasons, not the least of which is that it made them better role models for children and other adults. Appalled by the "ignorance of the adults in Texas" regarding the real history of the Civil War, Cornelia Stone recommended that every southern woman read the works of Jefferson Davis, Alexander Stephens, and Mary L. Williamson, the author of several books for children, including *The Life of Robert E. Lee*. Stone reasoned that since a child's education began "at the mother's knee," the responsibility for learning the true history of the South's participation in the Civil War devolved upon women.[20]

State divisions and local chapters of the UDC established history committees and appointed historians to carry out the directives from the general organization, as well as to develop a course of study specific to their respective states. Adelia Dunovant, chair of the UDC's history committee in 1901, suggested that individual chapters should study and discuss history at their meetings, as well as sing "southern" songs. Dunovant believed, as did most Daughters, that studying history helped the UDC fulfill its obligation to defend the Confederate generation. History was useful, she wrote, because it contributed to the "vindication of the men of the South" and offered "proof that [southern men] were patriots."[21]

The UDC's Committee on History guided the organization's efforts to perpetuate pro-southern history for more than a decade. It urged each state division and every chapter to elect a historian. Committee chair Mary Poppenheim of South Carolina reported that after ten years of the

UDC's perseverance, "the truth is gradually being revealed through Southern historians." The organization's historical work had become so critical in its effort to transmit Confederate culture that in 1908 the UDC established the office of historian-general to guide its members. The women who filled this position wielded considerable power, as they established the course of study for the membership and were key spokeswomen for the organization.

Virginia Morgan Robinson, a member of the Richmond chapter, became the UDC's first historian-general. The daughter of a Confederate colonel, Robinson had helped care for wounded soldiers as a young girl during the Civil War. She was an active club woman and founding member of the Confederate Memorial Literary Society, the group responsible for creating the Confederate Museum in Richmond, now the Museum of the Confederacy. A savvy and experienced administrator, she was an appropriate choice for the new post within the general organization because it came with enormous responsibility.[22]

Robinson had to report to the convention on the work of the divisions, develop a program of study, and suggest the course the UDC should take in preserving and promoting impartial history. Her first report was delivered to the 1909 UDC convention, and in it she asked that Daughters continue to collect "papers, books and documents of every kind, relating to Southern History." Robinson also suggested that the UDC establish "Exchange Libraries" for preserving and collecting books and manuscripts. Finally, she implored members to write essays using primary sources for "accuracy and truth."[23]

Robinson's efforts were admirable, since by her own admission she "knew absolutely nothing about the whys and wherefores of this additional general office." As she explained in a letter to Mary Stribling, a UDC historian in West Virginia, she felt overwhelmed by the work before her. "I came home from Atlanta, where I was elected," Robinson wrote, "almost appalled at the work that the Office represented." She was admittedly unclear about the *"exact duties"* of the office, but remained faithful to the cause. "As long as I am [historian-general] I am willing to do what I can," she wrote.[24]

Given the responsibilities of the office, Robinson felt that the woman elected historian-general should serve at least three to five years "without being subjected to the annual upheaval." Such time was needed, she explained, in order to fully develop a historical plan. Robinson also thought the office was something only a few people would be willing to do. The work was "nothing but plodding and digging," she complained, and few had the stamina to "do it thoroughly."[25]

Mildred Lewis Rutherford of Georgia, who succeeded Robinson in 1910, proved to be one of the few. Rutherford, the daughter of respected educators in Athens, was the president of the all-girls Lucy Cobb Institute and of the Athens Ladies' Memorial Association. She was a zealous advocate of pro-Confederate literature of every kind. She immersed herself in the "plodding and digging" and was so thorough in her promotion of history that her successors pale by comparison. Rutherford established a course of study for UDC members, as well as for children. She traveled the country, giving lectures as part of her campaign to promote true history, and wrote prolifically about southern history and literature. Her reports to the general conventions of the UDC were extremely detailed, as she noted every small victory in the battle for vindication.[26]

Lost Cause supporters regarded Rutherford's speeches to the general conventions as crucial to the study of southern history. Thousands of copies of her essays and speeches were published, and she personally mailed the majority of them. Numerous individuals, schools, and libraries owned copies of Rutherford's writings. During her five-year tenure as historian-general, her commitment to correct anti-southern bias in history can aptly be described as a vindication crusade.[27]

In her first report to the UDC general organization, in 1911, Rutherford asked the Daughters to engage in all types of historical work. She encouraged them to write history, collect reminiscences and photographs, publish pamphlets and books, write essays, and sponsor essay contests.[28] Rutherford led the way by publishing her own pamphlets, and many Daughters followed suit. Their essays, published in the *Confederate Veteran* and other Lost Cause publications, provide revealing evidence of what UDC members considered impartial history.

While southern men wrote about military battles and tactics, the Daughters wrote about life on the home front and examined the character of Confederate men, especially their heroes Robert E. Lee and Jefferson Davis. More often, however, the Daughters wrote essays about southern life and culture. They added to the Lost Cause narrative with their stories of plantations and of the relationships between master and slave. They also wrote about Reconstruction and its effects on the South, about southern women's role during the Civil War, and about what they saw as the region's rescue from "negro rule" by the Ku Klux Klan (KKK). Vindication was always the goal, whether it was to resurrect the reputation of Confederate veterans or southern culture.[29]

Local meetings of UDC chapters provided forums for sharing essays, many of which were published in the *Confederate Veteran*. The historian-general of the UDC created a yearlong program with suggestions for topics of study for each monthly meeting. June, for example, was dedicated to the study of Jefferson Davis, since he was born on the third day of that month. At the monthly meeting of the Robert E. Lee Chapter in Houston, for example, members read their essays on "the spirit of Jefferson Davis."[30]

The Daughters' essays about the prewar South often emphasized and idealized plantation culture and the good relationship between master and slave. Slaves were faithful, the Daughters believed, because of the benevolence of masters. According to an essay by a UDC member from Tennessee, there had never been "a peasantry so happy . . . as the negro slaves of America." Mildred Rutherford concurred when she wrote that slaves "were the happiest set of people on the face of the globe." She assumed that the reason for slave contentedness was the paternalism of whites who looked upon slaves as "their people." Rutherford encouraged the Daughters to preserve their own historical record of slavery by writing sketches of the "old mammy" and the "many faithful slaves."[31]

Although young members of the UDC had never actually lived on an antebellum plantation, they idealized the South based on the memories of their parents and grandparents who had owned plantations and slaves. A Daughter from Nashville, Tennessee, read to her chapter an essay that described the prewar South as a haven for "plantation folk living with their servants on large estates." Mildred Rutherford's essay "The South of Yesterday" described a similar setting where "contented slaves" served their master. Their memories of the Old South were fixated on the elite and their faithful servants; significantly, poor white southerners were never among the cast of characters.[32]

Nostalgia and sentimentality colored the Daughters' essays, particularly when the master-slave relationship was the subject matter. Like other members of their class, these women believed that race relations were at their peak prior to the Civil War. The Old South, moreover, represented a region and time whose values had lessons for the current generation. Cornelia Branch Stone's "Vivid Reminiscences of the Old Plantation," submitted to the 1912 essay competition sponsored by the Texas Division, is a prime example. Stone, one-time president-general of the organization, romanticized her parents' plantation. What she described was a paternalistic, even maternalistic, setting. According to Stone, both her mother and father were responsible for the happiness of her family as well as their "other family," whom she referred to as the "darkies in the quarters." Stone wrote about the "sweet melody of the banjo" and of the "pickaninnies" who danced in front of their cabins. In sum, her descriptions of the Old South offer flattering portrayals of the master class and idealize the subordinate position of slaves.[33]

Although Stone's reminiscence of plantation life presented this idyllic portrait of slavery and described the relationship between master and slave as one of mutual fondness, she maintained that she did not wish to see slavery reestablished. While she insisted that race relations were better in the Old South, like many Daughters, she argued that slavery had been more difficult on the masters than the slaves. Stone's principal memory of the South's peculiar institution was its impact on her mother. "Aside from the wrongness of servitude," Stone believed that the majority of labor required to operate a plantation devolved on her mother. "She was the greatest slave on the plantation," Stone wrote.[34]

In addition to describing the master as benevolent, the Daughters' essays also sought to justify slavery by claiming the institution had a "civilizing" influence on slaves. Mildred Rutherford, the longtime UDC historian, believed the UDC had a responsibility to future generations of southerners to see to it that they understood that slavery was not an evil institution. She feared, as late as 1915, that children growing up in the South were already being misinformed about slavery, and she blamed parents for not teaching their children the truth. If southern children were surveyed, she believed, one was likely to find large numbers of "abolitionists, intense and fanatical, and in full sympathy with the Northern side." She addressed this perceived problem in her widely published essay "The Wrongs of History Righted."[35]

Mildred Rutherford's personal crusade was to correct what she believed were false impressions of southern slavery as harsh and cruel.

"Slavery was no disgrace to the owner or the owned," Rutherford argued. She defended the institution for its "civilizing power," over Africans brought to the southern colonies. In racist language, she described how former slaves were "savage to the last degree" and contended that contemporary blacks should "give thanks daily" that they were not now living in the land of their ancestors in Africa. In her view as a spokeswoman for the UDC, former slave owners had done the world a service by providing their African slaves with the gift of Christianity. Indeed, she argued, the Old South planters should be recognized for having participated in "the greatest missionary and educational endeavors that the world has ever known." She concluded her essay by proclaiming that any history to the contrary was mistaken. "These wrongs must be righted" for the defense and vindication of former slaveholders, she asserted.[36]

Rutherford's justification of slavery was also a justification of white supremacy and racism in her own time. Her views, moreover, represented the views of the UDC, which is significant, given how influential the organization was in the early twentieth century. As the Daughters wrote to vindicate the Confederate generation, they made obvious their own views on race, views they wished to instill in future generations. White supremacy was considered an important measure of social control; black deference (i.e., "faithfulness") to white authority in the Old South, moreover, was regarded as an instructive example for good race relations in the New South.[37]

UDC members clearly resented any change that tampered with the racial status quo. Their essays about Reconstruction sought to prove that chaos ensued when white authority was jeopardized. The Freedman's Bureau, in particular, raised the ire of a UDC member from Mississippi, Mrs. M. V. Kennedy. As she explained in *Our Heritage*, the official organ of the state division, the bureau constituted the "most infamous outrage visited upon the South after the war." Its only service to the region, she charged, was to "demoralize" former slaves and make it impossible "to manage them sufficiently, to reap any profit from their labor." Not only was the federal government's money spent on "worthless negroes," she argued, but the bureau's agents also created racial strife between southern whites and freedmen.[38]

Kennedy's compatriot in the Mississippi Division, Mrs. W. Z. Higgins of Aberdeen, also loathed the Freedman's Bureau. She, too, blamed the agency for causing conflict between southern whites and blacks. She asserted that race relations were under control until bureau agents arrived and taught freedmen "to distrust and hate their former owners." Worse yet, southern whites were forced to endure a government composed of carpetbaggers, scalawags, and freedmen "who could neither read or write." Mildred Rutherford of Georgia further argued that "negro suffrage was a crime against the white people of the South."[39]

The Daughters clearly resented any threat to white supremacy, and, as much as they criticized Reconstruction, they hailed the South's Redeemers. Higgins, for example, cited the father of former President-General Lizzie George Henderson for his part in redeeming the state of Mississippi from "negro rule." She praised James Z. George, author of the Mississippi Plan, for his role in "placing white supremacy on an enduring and constitutional basis."[40]

Members of the KKK were also included among the Redeemers, and the UDC officially recognized the Klan for helping to restore southern home rule and white supremacy. Founded in 1866 in Pulaski, Tennessee, the organization counted among its members former Confederate officers, including Nathan Bedford Forrest, the first Grand Wizard. During Reconstruction, the Klan engaged in a campaign of violence and terror against Republican leaders, black and white, as well as the general population of freedmen. Its purpose was to thwart social and political change by any means necessary, and the Daughters regarded Klansmen as heroes.[41]

UDC member Laura Martin Rose of West Point, Mississippi, rose to prominence as an authority on the Ku Klux Klan. Though a member of the Mississippi division, Rose was born in Pulaski, Tennessee, where the Klan was founded. She claimed to personally know many of the group's founding members and drew from her interviews with them to write essays and speeches that praised Klansmen as saviors of the white South. Using documentation she claimed to have received from original Klansmen, Rose published widely on the subject between 1912 and 1916, even authoring a primer on the KKK for use by schoolchildren.[42]

Rose wrote a special essay on the subject of the Klan for the *Confederate Veteran* in early 1916, not long after the premiere of D. W. Griffith's film *The Birth of a Nation*. She responded favorably to Griffith's interpretation of Thomas Dixon's book *The Clansmen*, which she thought was

Fig. 6.3. Laura Martin Rose of West Point, Mississippi,
achieved notoriety for her writings on the Ku Klux Klan.

"more powerful than all else in bringing about a realization of 'things
as they were' during Reconstruction." Rose believed that Griffith had
accomplished "untold good" in his portrayal of the "tragic era," and she
elaborated on why the KKK was important to the resurrection of the
South.[43]

Rose spoke for her contemporaries in Confederate organizations when
she referred to Reconstruction as "the dark cloud that enveloped the
Southland." She regarded Klan activities as necessary to restore law and
order to the region and to restore Anglo-Saxon supremacy to the South.
Her portrayal of Klansmen as chivalrous knights was part of her personal effort to vindicate the organization "before our boys and girls of
today." These men, she maintained, had been "maligned, misjudged,
and misunderstood" by northern historians. She insisted that such "false"
impressions should be rectified, because the white South owed these
men a debt of gratitude. She sought to repay her portion of the debt by
producing an "unbiased" history of the organization.[44]

Rose found her niche as a crusader for a "true" history of the Klan.
The white South's collective memory of Reconstruction saw it as a time

THE KU KLUX KLAN
Or Invisible Empire

"K. K. K. Banner"

Just Out —Most Fascinating Book of the Day. Profusely illustrated. Letters from charter members of the Klan, biographical sketch of its great leader, Gen. Nathan Bedford Forrest. Indorsed by leading educators, historians, the U.D.C. and S.C.V., who will co-operate in placing the book in schools and libraries. Interesting from start to finish. Price, 75 cents; postage, 10 cents. Order from author, **Mrs. S. E. F. Rose, West Point Mississippi**

Fig. 6.4. Advertisement for Rose's primer for children, adopted by the State of Mississippi as a supplementary text for public schools.

when white southerners had been "trampled underfoot by ignorant and vicious negroes." This memory gave credence to Rose's claim that the KKK was founded to restore the previous order. She described with pride how devoted southern women made the costumes worn by Klansmen and delighted in telling how KKK members, wearing their ghostlike apparel, terrified the freedmen. Rose also took delight in telling the story of the Klansmen who, during one of their hooded raids, offered to shake hands with some freedmen, only to leave "a skeleton hand with the negroes as a pleasing souvenir of their visits."[45]

Laura Martin Rose achieved popularity within Lost Cause circles, and in 1916 she was elected to succeed Mildred Lewis Rutherford as historian-general. She influenced UDC members and countless children by developing a program of study in which the history of the KKK was prominently featured. In 1913 the UDC gave Rose's primer, *The Ku Klux Klan or Invisible Empire,* its official endorsement and asked that division presidents promote its use in schools. The book was adopted as a supplementary text in Mississippi, and abstracts of it appeared in the *Confederate Veteran*. Undoubtedly, her writings helped to perpetuate the white South's public memory of the Klan of Reconstruction as a noble organization.[46]

While the UDC's primary mission was to vindicate men through impartial history, the organization was committed to preserving a past in which their Confederate mothers also figured prominently. The UDC constitution specifically stated that one of the organization's objectives was to record "the part taken by Southern women" during the Civil War. Confederate women were respected for their sacrifices, to be sure, but they were also honored for their work as nurses, for sewing uniforms and flags, for maintaining plantations, and for their work in munitions factories.[47]

The South Carolina Daughters initiated one of the most comprehensive efforts to document the activities of Confederate women. They began their project in 1896, when Mrs. Thomas Taylor, a member of the Wade Hampton chapter, sought to collect "photographs and records of women who had been active in Confederate work." What began as one woman's idea soon became the project of the entire South Carolina Division.[48]

During its annual meeting in 1897, the division established a committee whose objective was "to collect statistics of woman's work in the war." Taylor envisioned a book that recorded all of the contributions made by South Carolina women during the "War for Southern Independence." She wanted the book to describe more than women's domestic activity, because their work was not limited to "making banners." She wanted it to be made known that women were a "potent factor" during the war. They furnished food and clothing for men in battle; they nursed the wounded and dying in hospitals; and they had gone to work in munitions factories. In sum, they had answered their country's call to duty, and their efforts should be recognized.[49]

The South Carolina Division was successful in acquiring a substantial amount of historical material for its book about women's work during the war. Several essays were contributed on the work of relief associations or women's work in Confederate hospitals. Articles entitled "Burning of Columbia," "Personal Experiences with Sherman's Army at Liberty Hill," "In the Track of the Raiders," and "Incidents of the Anderson Raid" provide women's firsthand accounts of their encounter with the military aspects of the war. There are also individual stories with titles like "Mrs. Lottie L. Green's Experience," "Some Heroic Women," and "Tales of a Grandmother."[50]

The committee that oversaw the project was equally successful in its petition to the state legislature to support the publication. In fact, the legislature appropriated $500 to purchase 300 copies of *South Carolina Women in the Confederacy* upon its publication in 1903, which UDC members subsequently distributed to schools and libraries throughout the state.[51]

South Carolina's effort spurred other states to sponsor books on Confederate women's work. North Carolina and Georgia, for example, followed suit. Florence Barlow, publisher of the *Lost Cause,* promoted this trend in her magazine editorials. "We want to know, and we have a right to know the part our mothers played in that wonderful conflict," she claimed. Barlow solicited articles that described women's wartime activities. In fact, her illustrated monthly journal was dedicated, in part, to the South's "faithful and loyal women." UDC historians further encouraged members to write about the women of the Confederacy by sponsoring essay contests on that very subject.[52]

Just prior to World War I, the UDC committed to publish an official history of Confederate women's work. Assisted by regional historian Matthew Page Andrews, who compiled and edited the volume, women collected and wrote sketches about Confederate women's organizations and the heroic deeds of individual women. The result of this effort was *The Women of the South in War Times,* first published in 1920. Similar in scope to the book on South Carolina women, it was well received by the public and went through six printings by 1927. Its success prompted the UDC to proudly announce that through its official history "many erroneous ideas of Northern people . . . have been recast after reading this book."[53]

Northerners, more than anyone else, were the ones the UDC believed were in dire need of the "truth." Although the years leading up to and including the Spanish-American War had given birth to warm feelings of sectional reconciliation, those feelings often turned cold when the subject of history and the Civil War were discussed. Even though professional historians, several of whom were trained by William Dunning at Columbia University, legitimized the Lost Cause narrative through their own scholarship, Confederate organizations remained convinced that a northern bias still permeated historical writing. In an effort to erode this perceived bias, the Daughters sought to influence those living above the Mason-Dixon Line to learn and write impartial history.[54]

The UDC, which considered itself a national organization, sought to extend its influence to the North. Chapters were firmly established in the metropolitan cities of Boston, New York, Philadelphia, and Chicago, and the Daughters believed that a good way to promote the unbiased study of southern history was to establish scholarships and essay contests in northern universities where teachers were being trained. Their intent in awarding these academic prizes was to generate "unbiased history" outside of the South. Thus, students at the University of Chicago, the University of Pennsylvania, and Columbia Teachers' College received UDC scholarships and prize money by writing essays on southern history.[55]

The Daughters fully expected the winning essay to reflect favorably on the South; they also assumed that the judges they chose were going to protect the UDC's interests. The winning essay of 1907, written by a student at Columbia University, challenged both assumptions. Christine Boyson, a native of Minnesota, wrote an essay on Robert E. Lee that, upon its publication, drew a hostile reaction from the Lost Cause community. The essay, judged by an independent committee appointed by the UDC, was criticized for its inclusion of flagrant "untruths" about the South and its famed general and brought great embarrassment to the Daughters. For two years the essay was vilified in the *Confederate Veteran*, and eventually the UDC withdrew its scholarship at Columbia along with the essay prize.

The Boyson controversy illustrates how the UDC naively thought it could correct the perceived bias of northern historians by simply encouraging the study of the Civil War from a southern viewpoint. Leonora Rogers Schuyler, a UDC member from New York, recommended sponsoring the Columbia essay prize in 1905. The sum of $100 was to be awarded to a student from the Teachers' College on a topic "relating to the South's part in the War Between the States." The UDC appointed an internal prize committee that included Schuyler and former President-General Lizzie George Henderson of Mississippi. The committee, in

Fig. 6.5. Leonora Schuyler, a Daughter from New York, served
on the UDC committee that awarded an essay prize to students
at Columbia Teachers' College.

turn, chose the judges for the contest. In 1906, the first year the prize
was awarded, the judges were respected academicians: Edwin Alderman, president of the University of Virginia; D. L. Burgess, dean of Political Science at Columbia; and Woodrow Wilson, president of Princeton College.[56]

The UDC was actively involved in commemorating the centennial of
Robert E. Lee's birth in 1907 and had decided that the Confederate general should be the topic for that year's essay contest. Edwin Alderman
served again as a judge and was accompanied by C. Alphonse Smith,
president of the University of North Carolina, and John H. Finley, president of the College of the City of New York. They awarded the prize to
Christine Boyson for her essay "Robert E. Lee: A Present Estimate."[57]

When the text of Boyson's essay reached the southern press in late

1908, it was viciously attacked by Confederate organizations. Specifically, they condemned Boyson's blasphemous statement that Lee was a "traitor." They were also upset by Boyson's conclusion that by the time of the Civil War the South was "intellectually dead" and, furthermore, most of its people were "densely ignorant." For the next several months, the essay was ripped apart by readers of the *Confederate Veteran,* who engaged in an even larger debate on the importance of "true" history.[58]

Significantly, UDC members were the essay's most vocal critics. Virginia Morgan Robinson, the historian-general, issued her own circular, in which she attacked the essay as a "contortion of Southern History" that defeated the purpose for which the prize was given.[59] Boyson's "dense ignorance of conditions and institutions of the South" offended the Cape Fear chapter of Wilmington, North Carolina. The Charleston, South Carolina, chapter of the UDC wished to be "among the first in pouring oil on the troubled waters," and the Florida Division expressed its concern that the UDC's "stamp of approval" on the essay was certain to cause "untold harm, not only in the South, but in the North as well." Many chapters shared the sentiments of one Daughter when she expressed how unfortunate it was that the statement "Lee was a traitor" was to be remembered as having been "endorsed by *our* leading educators."[60]

Chapters in New Orleans and Baltimore were particularly offended by Boyson's comments about the ignorance of the southern people. The New Orleans chapter attributed the South's high illiteracy rate to the emancipation of 4 million slaves. "These were the illiterates forced upon us," the chapter noted, "and to this day they are a burden patiently borne by the Southern people." Daughters in Baltimore agreed with the women of New Orleans. They believed that "the negro population in the South was certainly ignorant," but refused to concede that illiteracy was a problem among white southerners—certainly not among the planter elite.[61]

Interestingly, the blame for the essay debacle was never placed on the young woman who wrote it, Christine Boyson. She was excused for being a "Northern schoolgirl" whose false impressions of the South no doubt "evolved from her Northern education and environment." Cornelia Stone, the president-general, suggested that the textbooks Boyson had used probably provided her with "misleading" information about the South and its people.[62]

Initially, the UDC blamed the essay fiasco on the judges. The Daughters had chosen reputable scholars, two of whom were southern and understood the UDC's position regarding "true" history. The Richmond chapter condemned Alderman, Smith, and Finley for having "shown themselves grossly neglectful of the [UDC]." Women from Charleston, South Carolina, including a former and future president-general, criticized the judges for their "failure to appreciate the true purpose of the UDC."[63]

Edwin Alderman defended the judges' decision by arguing that the prize was awarded for an essay, "not a eulogy." Indeed, he argued, the essay prize was established at the "most cosmopolitan" university in the country, where men and women from "every section and every nation" were allowed to compete. Therefore, Alderman believed, critics should have allowed for "differences in historical viewpoints." Were papers to be disqualified because they failed to "conform entirely to the Southern viewpoint?" he asked.[64]

Ultimately, the UDC members on the committee who selected the judges were held accountable. Many in the organization believed that its own committee did not read the essay before awarding the prize. "The Daughters in Convention in Atlanta evidently endorsed something they knew nothing about," said one member. The Richmond chapter publicly asked why a committee of Daughters allowed the essay to "pass without comment."[65]

South Carolinian Mary Poppenheim, longtime chair of the UDC Committee on Education, was furious. She wrote her friend Janet Randolph of Virginia that she held the UDC committee solely accountable for this embarrassment. "*They were our official* agents and representatives and should have selected the essays that were acceptable to *us first.*" Poppenheim claimed that she never approved of the prize to begin with, and she blamed the Daughters for allowing Leonora Schuyler to have "free reins" with the UDC's "*name, influence, and treasury.*" "This will be a lesson to the UDC not to run away and let every charming woman start a plan *outside* of our territory," she lectured, "and so bring us into unpleasant situations."[66]

Committee members Leonora Schuyler and Lizzie George Henderson, along with President-General Cornelia Stone, admitted that mistakes had been made. Still, they defended the ultimate goal of the prize, and Stone promised that in the future the award would be made with "every safeguard" to prevent the same mistake from ever happening again. The award continued with a new set of judges—men in whom the UDC placed even greater confidence. They included Dunbar Rowland, historian and director of the Mississippi Archives and History, whose wife was a UDC member, and Ulrich B. Phillips, a Georgia native and history professor at the University of Michigan. Ironically, Phillips had received his own training at Columbia.[67]

Although the essay contest remained in place, Adelia Dunovant of Texas spearheaded the movement to withdraw the UDC scholarship from the Columbia Teachers' College. At the 1909 general convention, held in Houston, she "sprang the negro question," which, she claimed, disrupted the meeting. In effect, Dunovant questioned the UDC's common sense for supporting a scholarship at a college that accepted "negroes . . . on a perfect equality" with white students. Dunovant, moreover, was thoroughly upset at what she described as the "humiliating spectacle of the Daughters of the Confederacy sitting at the feet of a Northern schoolgirl." Her campaign to remove the scholarship succeeded, and four new awards were established—at Vassar (Poppenheim's alma mater), the University of North Carolina, Alabama Polytechnic Institute (now Auburn), and the University of Alabama.[68]

The Daughters' attempt to promote impartial history outside the South was optimistic, at best. The UDC expressed hope that promoting history in northern colleges would ultimately contribute to the Confederacy's vindication. The fact that the Columbia essay contest failed to accomplish its objective is instructive. The UDC learned that training northern students to adopt a southern viewpoint about the past was not only difficult, but also unrealistic. The Daughters also learned that southern intellectuals did not always agree with the UDC's particular historical perspective, as was the case with Edwin Alderman.

The failure of the Columbia essay contest was a minor setback in a much larger and more successful regional campaign by the UDC to promote "true" history. Prior to World War I, the Daughters were highly successful in documenting their generation's memory of the Civil War. Like male Confederate organizations, the UDC believed that history from a southern perspective served as a corrective to existing histories they perceived to be biased.

History came in a variety of forms, and the Daughters' efforts to promote a truthful account of the Civil War were wide ranging. They preserved material culture, donated manuscripts and reminiscences to state archives, and helped establish museums. The Museum of the Confederacy, the Alabama State Department of Archives and History, and the North Carolina Museum of History were all founded with collections of Confederate relics gathered by the Daughters. In addition, they exhibited Confederate relics in government buildings and at regional expositions. UDC members also competed in essay contests and published essays in their local newspapers and Lost Cause periodicals. To assist its members in actively pursuing and perpetuating true history, the organization appointed historians at the local, state, and national level.

The UDC's efforts to vindicate Confederate men, honor Confederate women, and defend southern culture through an impartial history of the Civil War were exhaustive. And while its efforts to preserve unbiased history were less successful outside the South, within the region the UDC's influence was unequaled. To be sure, the organization had a membership whose commitment to correct historical inaccuracies was extremely personal—the men they wished to vindicate, and the women they honored, were their parents and grandparents. The Daughters' emotional ties to the past, moreover, provided the motivation required to preserve the "truth," not only for the sake of their Confederate ancestors but also for future generations.

Confederate Motherhood

Daughters of the Confederacy, this day we are gathered together,
in the sight of God . . . to do homage unto the memory of our gallant
Confederate soldiers, and to perpetuate the fame of their noble
deeds unto the third and fourth generation.

From the UDC Ritual, by Mrs. J. D. Beale, 1904

We are the adamantine chain transmitting their [Confederate dead]
cherished memories to the ages yet unborn, not one link of which is to
be lost, and let me ask, who more worthy the trust, more willing the duty!
For, are not women the mothers and molders of men,
from the cradle to the coffin?

Virginia Clay Clopton, address to Daughters of the Confederacy, ca. 1900

On a spring day in 1902, Laura Talbot Galt, a thirteen-year-old from Louisville, Kentucky, was sent home from school for insubordinate behavior. She had refused to obey an instruction from her teacher to sing "Marching through Georgia," a song that celebrated William T. Sherman's destructive march through the state in the spring of 1865. Galt perceived the song as an affront to her Confederate heritage and not only refused to sing the song but put her fingers in her ears while her classmates sang.[1]

"Little" Laura Galt became a regional heroine and was praised for following the admonishment of her grandmother, a member of the UDC, to protest the song. Galt put her fingers in her ears, she told the *Confederate Veteran*, because she refused to listen to a song that glorified "such a tyrant and coward as Sherman." Her action brought her accolades from around the South. She was honored by the UCV and made an honorary

Fig. 7.1 "Little" Laura Galt of Louisville, Kentucky.

member of the UDC chapter in Kittrell, Kentucky, for rebelling against a song that glorified "crimes against Southern womanhood." Members maintained that singing it in the presence of a southern woman was "worse than dancing on the grave of her mother." They further argued that the song damaged the current relationship between northerners and southerners by perpetuating "sectional strife and hatred." Their contempt for the song, however, was tempered by Laura Galt's response, because it was vivid proof that pro-Confederate education worked.[2]

Southern women had long involved the region's white youth in the rituals and ceremonies of the Lost Cause. Ladies Memorial Associations (LMAs), the first groups to commemorate Memorial Day in the South, led children in paying homage to their Confederate ancestors. They instructed southern girls and boys to maintain the graves of the region's fallen heroes and to place flags and flowers on those graves during annual ceremonies. When the UDC was formed, a new generation of southern women became leaders of the Lost Cause, and the effort to involve children in the Confederate tradition expanded in scope.

Fig. 7.2. The UDC involved children
in the Confederate celebration at an early age.

Although involving children in the care of Confederate graves remained an important ritual linking generations, educating them to revere and uphold Confederate ideals assumed even greater importance.
As the UDC ritual makes clear, southern women were committed to instilling the region's white youth with a respect for the Confederate past
and its heroes. Members believed that if white children were properly
instructed, they would become "living monuments" to the Confederacy.
Unlike marble statues, these children served as future defenders of the
"sacred principles" for which their Confederate ancestors had died—
namely, states' rights and the preservation of white supremacy.[3]

Convinced that education served this higher purpose, and that women
were especially suited for the task, the UDC committed itself at once to a
program of indoctrination. The Daughters joined male Confederate or-

Fig. 7.3. Children were critical to the preservation of Confederate culture.

ganizations in a campaign to eradicate "unsuitable" textbooks from southern classrooms, and they established their own textbook and education committees for that purpose. Yet the Daughters saw the removal of these textbooks as only one tactic in the campaign to shape children's understanding of the Confederate past. These women took their message directly to the schools.

UDC members placed Confederate flags and portraits of Confederate heroes in southern classrooms and worked with teachers to plan history lessons. They planned Confederate commemorative activities for students, often at the invitation of principals and school superintendents, and they sponsored essay contests to encourage public school children to learn about the Confederacy and its heroes. Descendants of Confederate veterans between the ages of six and sixteen were also recruited to join the Children of the Confederacy, where they were immersed in the study of Confederate culture as instructed by a UDC member. In fact, the UDC hoped to sustain its own membership, and possibly that of the SCV, by forming children's chapters.

Through their active involvement with the region's white children, the Daughters believed they could help shape the New South guided by the principles of the Old. It was a campaign of indoctrination with serious consequences for the region. There was nothing innocuous about imparting the Lost Cause narrative to a younger generation, as that narrative was replete with racial stereotypes, emphasized the inferiority of blacks, and exaggerated the benevolence of slave ownership. Moreover, the Lost Cause narrative provided more than lessons on the past; it served as a political and social road map for the future.

The UDC's efforts to instill in white children a reverence for the principles of southern citizenship, particularly the region's commitment to states' rights, resembled a precedent set by women a century before. In the years following the American Revolution, public perceptions of women's role in society underwent a significant change. In the new republic, women's traditional role as mother was enlarged to include the training of good citizens. As mothers, women assumed a public role as society's moral guardians, charged with the crucial responsibility of training children to become patriotic, virtuous citizens. The philosophy that women were responsible for instructing and instilling in children a proper respect for the principles that guided the new nation was known as "republican motherhood." Accordingly, women were not only mothers to their children, but as society's moral guardians, they were also mothers to the nation's citizens.[4]

Similarly, members of the UDC were engaged in Confederate motherhood.[5] Though their ancestors' attempts to form a separate nation had failed, the Daughters were determined to keep alive the values of the Old South and the Confederacy and hold off the intrusion of northern values. UDC members served as public guardians of the Confederacy's sacred principles and sought to impart the same to southern white children. Both men and women of the Lost Cause assigned critical importance to this role. "We must teach our children to uphold the lofty standards of southern womanhood," Virginia Clay Clopton of Alabama told an audience of Daughters, "and prove themselves worthy to shape the moral and social destiny of the fairest region." Adelia Dunovant, chair of the UDC's Historical Committee in 1901, made a similar appeal to the general organization: "Mothers of the Southland, the preservation of constitutional liberty depends . . . upon your instilling its principles into the minds and souls of your children." The Daughters agreed with Dunovant and Clopton that the responsibility for the way the Confederacy and its heroes were remembered devolved upon the UDC.[6]

The Daughters' commitment to the Confederate motherhood ideal made the UDC's role in the Lost Cause celebration more significant than the part played by their male counterparts, the UCV and SCV. Men may have felt a responsibility to teach children the "truth" of history, but their activity rarely extended to social guardianship of the region's white youth. Historian Charles Wilson correctly asserts that the Daughters, leaving nothing to chance, were "even more aggressive and single-minded than Southern men" in shaping the minds of the children of the region.[7]

The primary difference between republican motherhood and Confederate motherhood was that the UDC was motivated in part by fear—fear that textbooks with a northern bias had already accomplished irreparable damage, fear that their ancestors might not be vindicated, and fear that future generations of white southerners may never know the sacrifices made by their Confederate ancestors. "Of what profit is it to proclaim that our fathers were conservators of constitutional liberty," Adelia Dunovant asked, "if their children and their grandchildren and their great-grandchildren are not?"[8]

The Daughters' fears were eventually allayed by the success of their activity among southern children. To assure this achievement, UDC members devoted enormous energy to the cause of educating Confederate descendants. Since the UDC had become such a large and influential organization in the late nineteenth and early twentieth centuries, Confederate motherhood, while a social concept, also had political overtones. This was especially true when the Daughters used their influence to accomplish organizational objectives related to education.[9] "Teach a child well and let him feel that he owes a debt to the men who fought by his father's side, to the women who suffered as his mother suffered, and he will pay that debt," Elizabeth Lumpkin Glenn assured a group of UDC members.[10]

In fact, of the many activities in which Lost Cause advocates engaged to defend the honor of Confederate men, they are best known for their campaign for pro-southern or pro-Confederate school textbooks.[11] The UCV, UDC, and the SCV each formed history committees to monitor textbooks used in the region's white public schools, to remove those that were unacceptable, and to endorse those that Confederate organizations thought to be "fair." These activities began in the mid-1890s, shortly after the formation of the UDC and, after 1900, were usually spearheaded by the Daughters. UCV membership was dwindling rapidly, and the SCV, according to historian Gaines Foster, "never became an important group." Indeed, SCV members were often criticized for being "too busy" to honor their ancestors. In the pro-Confederate textbook campaign, as in other Lost Cause activities, women assumed a leadership role.[12]

From its founding in 1894, the UDC took an active interest in providing southern youth with "impartial" history. In 1897, when the UDC established its committee on history, the organization passed a resolution to "take immediate steps" to produce and publish suitable histories of the United States so that the "Southern cause and Southern people were truly vindicated."[13] State divisions took the lead in monitoring the textbooks used in white public schools. In some cases, UDC chapters were large enough to form their own textbook committees. For example, the J. Z. George Chapter of Greenwood, Mississippi, had its committee "interview the Textbook Commission to eliminate from the schools . . . all books not dealing fairly with the . . . War Between the States." This committee also conferred with the state's superintendent of education in an effort to make women eligible to serve on the Mississippi Textbook Commission.[14]

Not surprisingly, Lost Cause advocates showed a decided preference for school textbooks written by southerners. Susan Pendleton Lee's *A School History of the United States* (1895) was a favorite among Confederate organizations. Lee was the daughter of a Confederate general and a native of Lexington, Virginia. In her school history the South played a more prominent role than did the North in the nation's development. Moreover, Lee's interpretation of slavery and the Civil War was consistent with the ideology of the Lost Cause. Katie Daffan's report on school textbooks to the Texas Daughters reiterated what other state divisions had found in Lee's history—that it touched "a responsive chord in the hearts of the Southern people."[15]

Books by Thomas Nelson Page, Joel Chandler Harris, and Mary L. Williamson were also popular choices. Page's stories of the Old South were extremely popular in the North and South but were considered especially useful by Confederate organizations seeking to preserve idyllic images of plantation life. Likewise, Harris's Uncle Remus stories were regarded as entertaining and authentic. Williamson's readers, *The Life of Robert E. Lee* and *The Life of Stonewall Jackson,* were esteemed for their "accuracy."[16] Mildred Rutherford personally distributed her own publications to schools to familiarize students with the "impartial" facts. Significantly, white public schools were not the only ones to receive Rutherford's writings. *The Wrongs of History Righted* (1914) was mailed to black schools as well.[17]

J. N. Bennett, principal of the Colored Training and Industrial School in Faison, North Carolina, thanked Rutherford for mailing him a copy of her essay. Bennett wrote that he was "pleased" that Rutherford was "interested in the success of [his] race." He also spoke highly of the UDC, recognizing the Daughters for "scattering [the] same shower of love among the product of the master and the slave." Bennett claimed that he planned to distribute the address for use by his students. "I am praying for the friendship of our Southern white women," he concluded, "for our students are your cooks, nurses, housekeepers, etc. and when we get your friendship, suggestions, encouragement and help, it will be the means of a closer tie between servants and masters." Bennett's response may have been tongue-in-cheek, though it certainly could have been about self-preservation. For in the Jim Crow South, there were repercussions for not being deferential to white women.[18]

The fact that Rutherford sent her pro-Confederate writings to a black school suggests that she saw clearly the benefit of having black pupils understand the past as the Daughters understood it. If indeed black students accepted the UDC's version of what constituted appropriate race relations in the Old South, then perhaps those students would realize the necessity of maintaining the status quo in the Jim Crow South. In other words, blacks could be persuaded of the benefits of white supremacy. "True" history, therefore, served both an educational and political purpose.

Nothing seemed to raise the ire of the Daughters more than the adoption, by a southern school or college, of a "biased" textbook. Such was the case with Henry W. Elson's *History of the United States of America* (1904), adopted by Roanoke College of Salem, Virginia. Confederate organizations were unanimous in their condemnation of Elson's *History*, particularly at an institution of higher learning in the South. Cordelia Odenheimer, a Daughter from Maryland, denounced the book, claiming that certain statements made her "blood boil." Not only did Elson refer to the Civil War as "The Slaveholders' War," but Odenheimer fumed that "the relations of our people in regard to the slaves are falsified in a language unfit for print."[19]

The use of Elson's *History* was a perfect example of what the Daughters wanted southern educational institutions to avoid. This episode prompted the UDC to renew its commitment to monitoring textbooks. At the general convention of 1911, held in Richmond, the UDC passed two resolutions against "biased" histories in general—a response to the Elson *History*. The resolutions were very similar, stating that the UDC was committed to using its influence to "combat and condemn, with all [its] strength and might, individually and collectively, this Elson's *History*, or any other history defamatory or unfair to the South." This renewed commitment by the UDC eventually had its desired impact; in 1914 the chair of its Committee on Education could proclaim that "twenty years of UDC work along historical lines has borne rich fruits for the harvests of truth."[20]

As UDC membership grew, the Daughters' influence was widely recognized in the campaign for pro-southern textbooks. For example, when Virginia UDC members entered the debate in 1911 over Roanoke College's adoption of Elson's textbook, a writer to the *Veteran* described the Daughters as "a force to be reckoned with." Indeed, he maintained, "they make public sentiment in this country, and in the last analysis are the final and conclusive power."[21]

The UDC, like other Confederate organizations, wanted children to believe that although the Confederacy suffered military defeat, the cause was still just. Furthermore, Lost Cause supporters did not want children to regard their ancestors as traitors or rebels. As textbooks with a pro-Confederate slant made their way into southern classrooms, children learned instead that the region's veterans were heroes and defenders of states' rights. These "unbiased" texts were also useful for preserving a version of the southern past in which elite culture was held in high esteem. Indeed, historian Fred Bailey argues that by glorifying the patrician culture of the Old South, southern textbooks were instrumental in preserving traditional class and race relations for the New South.[22]

Historians of the Lost Cause have, for the most part, limited their discussions of pro-Confederate education to the textbook campaign. Only recently have they begun to investigate the impact of women, whose ideas for pro-southern education extended well beyond the promotion of suitable textbooks. The UDC, in particular, was inventive in its approach to inculcating children with a reverence for the Old South and the Confederacy. Indeed, the textbook campaign was enhanced because the Daughters made it their mission to have direct contact with children both in and out of the South's white public schools.

In her autobiography, *The Making of a Southerner* (1946), Katherine DuPre Lumpkin recalls the clarion call of Confederate organizations to educate southern children. At veterans' reunions and within her own home, pro-Confederate education was considered important to the preservation of conservative values. The changes brought about by the movement to monitor what children learned about regional culture and the southern past, Lumpkin recalled, "had come to pass in the schoolrooms of [her] childhood." She attended school in South Carolina, but her experience as a student in the early twentieth century was the experience of thousands of children who attended white public schools in the region. Their contact with the Lost Cause, in fact, was no accident.[23]

The Daughters maintained a constant presence in the South's white public schools between 1894 and 1919. Members made school visits, organized ceremonial activities to honor the birthdays of Robert E. Lee (January 19) and Jefferson Davis (June 3), and placed portraits of Lee and Davis in the classrooms. The UDC sponsored essay contests for both students and teachers, and through the Daughters' influence, public schools were renamed for Confederate heroes. In effect, the UDC modified the southern classroom so as to immerse students—literally—in Confederate culture.

School visits by members of the UDC became increasingly common as Daughters sought to discern whether southern schools were toeing the Lost Cause line. President Katie Currie told the 1899 general convention of her visits to schools, where she saw for herself "the earnestness with which the young teachers were telling the story aright." However, this cooperation was not always the case, and UDC members often complained of having teachers who did not tell the story of the Civil War "correctly." "A large proportion of these teachers are from the North," wrote a disgruntled Daughter. "Just so long as the South continues to employ teachers from the North," she continued, "it will be necessary for the parents [and UDC] to keep a vigilance over what their children are being taught." Her complaint spoke to the larger problem of educating, within the region's own institutions of higher education, a sufficient number of southern teachers to instruct children to revere the southern past.[24]

Daughters' visits to the schools, therefore, served to balance the presence of northern teachers as well as assist teachers trained in the South. In 1902 Ava James, a Daughter from Alabama, claimed that she and her chapter were "especially interested" in what children learned about the Civil War. "*Our* public schools use Southern histories," she explained, "but we as a chapter are trying to impress the teachers to put the causes of war in very simple language, and drill [students] in reverence for names of heroes."[25]

Lucy Closs Parker, a UDC member from North Carolina, was even more emphatic than James was. Writing in 1907, Parker remarked that it was "high time" that the UDC "correct false impressions" made on "the Youth of our Southland." She was furious that northern histories depicted Confederate soldiers as "rebels," and even more angry that Abraham Lincoln was lionized. "Any school in [North Carolina] that should declare Abe Lincoln a greater man than [George] Washington," she contended, "is a disgrace to their teachers and to the Board of Education of the State."[26]

Annie Allison, another member in the North Carolina Division, received a personal invitation to speak on Confederate history to a third-grade class. Allison felt that the children understood "states' rights pretty well." During her visit, she asked the class to explain the cause of the "War Between the States." One boy raised his hand and answered, "The Old Northern Yankees kept meddling with our business and we kept telling them to let us alone and they wouldn't do it, so we pitched in and fought them." Pleased with his answer, Allison remarked, "Pretty good for a nine year old Southern boy, isn't it?"[27]

The UDC sponsored essay contests in the public schools to encourage students to respond favorably to the Confederate cause, as well as to provoke further interest in the study of the South and the Civil War. Students wrote essays, usually on a subject chosen by the state division, and competed for cash prizes. Pupils were required to refer to a UDC bibliography in choosing their sources, a list that usually included the essays of the historian-general Mildred Rutherford.

The Henrietta Morgan Duke Chapter of Georgetown, Kentucky, sponsored essays for both students and teachers in 1904. White public school children were offered a medal for the best essay on Jefferson Davis. Teachers in the same county were asked to write an essay by answering such questions as "What is the Doctrine of States' Rights?" "What is Rebellion? Is it ever Justifiable?" and "What is Secession?" The winning essays were awarded a copy of Jefferson Davis's *The Rise and Fall of the Confederate States of America*, Thomas Dixon's *The Leopard's Spots*, and a set of Confederate prints.[28]

Students often wrote essays about Confederate military heroes, particularly when the UDC sponsored contests in conjunction with the birthdays of Lee and Davis. Essays about the Old South, plantation life, and slavery were also sponsored. In 1914, for example, a New Orleans UDC chapter sponsored a contest for the best essay on "The Institution of American Slavery." The winner, Louis Levile of the Rugby Academy, described slavery as a benevolent institution, but his discussion of race relations was not limited to the prewar South.[29] Levile compared the "slavery question" of the Old South to the "Negro question" of his own time. The institution of Jim Crow laws, he wrote, had placed "so many restrictions . . . on the Southern negro" that he concurred with the contemporary conclusions of white men in declaring that "the negro himself was better off as a slave, provided he had a kind master." He concluded that "the negro will stay socially distinct, an alien element, unabsorbed and unabsorbable." Levile's essay revealed how well versed he was with the Lost Cause narrative.[30]

The promotion of essay contests was just one example of how teachers and superintendents in the region's public schools assisted the Daughters in the task of inculcating children with conservative values. In many cases teachers were UDC members. Virginia Redditt Price reported in *Our Heritage* that "many . . . Mississippi Daughters are teachers." Katie Smith, who attended public school in Ellisville, Mississippi, recalled that her teacher was a member of the UDC who held lessons on the "War Between the States." Smith recalled that while they were studying the war, her teacher asked "every student to tell something about his [Confederate] ancestor." Although Smith's experience was fairly common, the Daughters still complained of northern-trained teachers, particularly in border states like Kentucky and even West Virginia. Thus, they continued to pursue an agenda to promote the study of Confederate culture with the full support of principals and superintendents.[31]

The most visible evidence of the Daughters' influence in the white public schools was the thousands of portraits of Robert E. Lee that adorned southern classrooms. Lee was the Confederate hero par excellence. His portrait often hung next to that of George Washington in hopes that white southern children would equate Lee's significance to that of the nation's founding fathers. Jefferson Davis's portrait was also placed in schools, though less systematically. These portraits served as daily reminders of what the Daughters often called the Confederacy's "glorious heritage." In fact, the portraits of Lee and Davis took on added significance when the UDC, with the approval of school superintendents, held commemorative celebrations on the birthdays of these southern heroes.[32]

The Daughters also insisted that students learn about Lee's life. They wanted students to know of his military genius and to emulate his patriotism. "The placing of General Robert E. Lee's portrait in the public schools, and having children instructed as to his life and character," reported a Kentucky chapter, "was the most important accomplishment of the year." The Texas UDC urged its chapters to request that school superintendents "instruct teachers" to commemorate the birthdays of Davis and Lee so that "pupils may become familiar with the names and characters of these great men."[33]

Frances Thornton Smith, of Mississippi, remembered how her class commemorated Robert E. Lee's birthday in her hometown of Hattiesburg in the 1920s. "We'd have programs on him, and have his picture up all around," she recalled. To commemorate the day, students "might have to write [an essay]." Smith, whose mother was a UDC member, explained that Lee's portrait was not the only one in her school. "We had all the southern generals we studied about."[34]

Portraits of Lee and Davis were hung in the white public schools of the South in great numbers in 1907 and 1908, since those years marked the centennials of the births of Robert E. Lee and Jefferson Davis, respectively. To commemorate Lee's birthday, the Johnston-Pettigrew Chapter of Raleigh, North Carolina, purchased enough "Confederate pictures to supply every schoolhouse in Wake [County]." Edith Royster, the chapter's representative, mailed a circular to the teachers, informing them that the Daughters were "very anxious to see a picture of General Lee in every Schoolhouse." She insisted that the schools "get one of these pictures promptly" to show their appreciation for the UDC's "gift." She also urged teachers to celebrate Lee's birthday "with appropriate exercises and formally hang [his] picture."[35]

Robert E. Lee's portrait was also placed in Yankee classrooms. UDC chapters were active throughout the country, and though the majority of them celebrated Lee's birthday at their local meetings, some northern chapters risked pointed criticism for publicly paying homage to the Confederate general. An Ohio UDC chapter, for example, managed to "place pictures of General Lee in every public school in Dayton," as the UDC chapter in Helena, Montana, did likewise. The Montana chapter received harsh criticism from the Grand Army of the Republic (GAR), which tried to have the picture of Lee removed. However, the GAR faced an uphill battle because three southerners served on the local school board. Ironically, the editor of the *Helena Independent* suggested that the GAR (and not the UDC) "was still living in the dark days of '61–'65."[36]

UDC chapters around the country greeted the centennial of Jefferson Davis's birth with similar enthusiasm. Daughters, with the help of teachers and principals, involved students in the study and celebration of his life. A chapter in Kentucky was particularly inventive. Members suggested that Davis's birthday be commemorated by assembling all the boys in their county who were named "Jefferson Davis." Once gathered, the boys could enter the formal ceremony "to the music of a states' rights march," composed by a Daughter.[37]

The Mississippi UDC spearheaded the regional celebration, since the state claimed Davis as its most illustrious citizen. The Winnie Davis Chapter of Meridian passed resolutions, adopted by the state division, formally requesting that the superintendent of public education "introduce the supplementary study of the life of Jefferson Davis" in the schools. Indeed, hundreds of Davis portraits were placed in schools

Fig. 7.4. Portraits of Jefferson Davis were placed in southern classrooms, and several schools were renamed in his honor.

throughout the South, and thousands of white children studied his life. The UDC approved a portrait of Davis that depicted him "as he looked when he assumed the administration of Government of the Confederate States." The Daughters did not want children to gaze upon an image of their hero "when worn with defeat, disappointment, imprisonment, and sorrow."[38]

The effort to place portraits in schools continued even after both centennials were commemorated. President-General Cornelia Stone, speaking to the general convention in late 1908, maintained the importance of placing "authentic portraits" of Lee and Davis in the public schools—a duty Daughters should continue to fulfill "until every school in the South is supplied." As president-general, Stone also encouraged "an earnest and widespread study" of Davis by public and private schools, as well as among the general public. She believed that a thorough study of Davis's life was an effective way to stimulate southern youth to emulate his "nobility of character and patriotic citizenship."[39]

Portraits were not the only items of Confederate material culture that the Daughters used to inspire and instruct southern children. The UDC chapter in Greenwood, Mississippi, proudly announced to the general convention of 1910 that through its efforts "the Ordinance of Secession of Mississippi is engrossed and hung upon the walls of our public school building" and suggested that other chapters do the same.[40]

Hanging a copy of a state's ordinance of secession in a public school was unusual, but displaying Confederate flags was not. Southern children were frequently exposed to the flags of the Confederacy, both in and out of their classrooms, and certainly came to understand their significance to the white South. Every Confederate Memorial Day, white public schools closed so students could participate in local ceremonies, including placing miniature Confederate flags on the graves of southern soldiers in local Confederate cemeteries. At the 1911 general convention, a choir of 200 children from a Richmond public school "arranged picturesquely upon the stage to form the 'Stars and Bars.'" These "living" Confederate flags were also a common feature at monument unveilings.[41]

Confederate flags were undoubtedly an important symbol of Confederate culture. Virginia Redditt Price, historian of the Mississippi Division, argued in 1914 that providing schools with a Confederate battle flag was very "patriotic." She dismissed criticism that such actions kept alive "the feeling of strife and bitterness." Indeed, chapters in her division were encouraged to give schools a Confederate flag to accompany the portrait of Lee or Davis, since it was nothing more than a "piece of bunting."[42]

However, Price herself was not convinced that the Confederate flag was mere bunting, because she went on to defend its placement in the classroom. She argued that the flag's visibility was intended to have "no baleful effect upon the minds of growing generations." Furthermore, it served as a symbol of southern heroism and patriotism. "No youth, wherever reared," Price continued, "can but have his citizenship and statesmanship broadened and elevated by contact with that which recalls Davis, Lee and Jackson." She concluded that if the Confederate flag were placed out of sight, "the nation was robbed of half of its heroes and a full quarter of its glory."[43]

Placing cultural symbols of the Confederacy in public schools was important to UDC members because they believed in the power of such icons to influence southern and, in some cases, northern school chil-

Fig. 7.5. Children of the Confederacy chapters, like this one
in Pittsburg, Tennessee, were important to preserving Confederate
culture and sustaining the parent organization.

dren. Putting a face with a name such as Robert E. Lee, whose life ex-
ample children were taught to emulate, was an effective way for the
Daughters to achieve their goal of instilling respect and reverence for the
Confederate past.

Equally important to the indoctrination of children was the activity
that took place away from school. Indeed, UDC members' contact with
the region's white youth was far-reaching. Confederate motherhood, as
practiced by the Daughters, included organizing children to participate
in the Confederate celebration in their communities. Local chapters of
the UDC were the first to establish children's groups known as Children
of the Confederacy (CofC). The general organization supported this action, but organizing children's chapters continued to be the domain of
local groups of UDC and state divisions for many years. The formation
of children's chapters within the states became such a successful venture

that in 1917 the general organization made the CofC its official auxiliary and appointed a director who held the official post of third vice-president general.[44]

The first chapter of the CofC was chartered in Alexandria, Virginia, in 1896. The parent organization, the Mary Custis Lee Chapter, organized the children to take part in commemorative activities within their community. The larger goal of the Lee chapter was to "unite the children . . . of the South in some work to aid and honor ex-Confederates." This first chapter was not small and included "over a hundred little girls and boys." One of their first acts was to participate in Memorial Day ceremonies, one of the white South's most sacred rituals.[45]

Organizing children's chapters was a significant UDC activity between 1894 and 1919. The success of the first CofC prompted great enthusiasm among the Daughters, and local chapters throughout the UDC began forming their own auxiliaries. The general organization was reluctant to assign official status to the children's chapters early on, because the UDC's primary focus early in the organization's history was caring for aging veterans or their widows. Thus, state divisions were primarily responsible for the success of the CofC in the late nineteenth and early twentieth centuries.[46]

The movement to organize children's chapters expanded particularly after 1910, as the obligation to care for a thinning population of Confederate men and women became less burdensome. Indeed, as death took its toll on these aging Confederates, transmitting the conservative values of their generation became a more relevant pursuit. Benevolence for the generation of the 1860s remained a priority; however, the organization began to place critical importance on the descendants of Confederate veterans. Indeed, many Daughters believed that the future membership of the UDC depended on the organization of children's chapters whose members, they believed, eventually would sustain the adult organization. "Let each chapter establish an auxiliary of children," Cornelia Stone told the 1905 general convention, "for the older chapter to always draw on." Two years later she reiterated her plea, saying that "on this training of the children will depend the perpetuity of our organization."[47]

The activity of children in the auxiliaries, moreover, was important to the perpetuation of conservative class values, as well as a pro-southern version of history. Often, they were the children and grandchildren of

UDC members. Organizing these children into chapters of the CofC was considered an important step in preparing them "to creditably fill the place of men and women who have in the past given the [South] both name and fame."[48]

Boys as well as girls were eligible to join the CofC. Membership sometimes began as early as the day a child was born, since UDC members were quick to enroll their children and grandchildren. However, most active CofC members were between the ages of six and eighteen. At their monthly meetings children studied history and the Confederate catechism (a book of call and response to questions about the "facts" of the southern past), wrote essays, and sang favorite Confederate songs, such as "Dixie" and "The Bonnie Blue Flag." Children also raised money for local and regional Confederate monuments and made visits to veterans' and widows' homes. Children had long been a regular feature at monument unveilings and Memorial Day commemorations, and the CofC continued this activity.

Key to the success of children's chapters was the chapter leader. They were Daughters who were very enthusiastic about the responsibility of instilling children with a reverence for Confederate men and women, as well as the sacred principles of states' rights. Former members of the CofC remember their chapter leaders as inspirational women. Minnie Bell Barnes, who grew up in Chatham County, North Carolina, attributed her interest in Confederate history to her CofC leader. "Miss Carrie Jackson . . . was just a live wire," Barnes recalled. Jackson always started the meeting with an enthusiastic rendition of "Dixie," and, according to Barnes, she made Confederate history "so interesting."[49]

Leaders of children's chapters used the meetings to teach southern youth about the Old South, slavery, the "War Between the States," and Reconstruction. Like the UDC, children began their meetings with prayer and an opening ritual in which they pledged themselves to honor veterans and study and teach the "truths" of history—most important, that the war was "not a REBELLION," nor was it to "sustain slavery." During actual meetings, some chapters required children to respond to their name "with an incident relating to the war." This practice was common with the Julia Jackson Chapter in Charlotte, North Carolina, where children were asked to give information about a Confederate leader, or perhaps "the part played by the women or little children." A CofC leader in another North Carolina town also required children to respond to their names by stating something significant about the Confederacy.[50]

Chapter leaders were assisted in this endeavor by a monthly program developed by the historian-general, as well as a Confederate catechism. Mildred Lewis Rutherford, a tireless UDC member, developed and published comprehensive monthly programs for the CofC during her five-year tenure as historian-general.[51] Her program for the year 1915, for example, covered a variety of Confederate subjects. In January children studied Robert E. Lee and Stonewall Jackson, whose birthdays were being commemorated that month. For February, the subject was "secession and the result." March featured the study of "our leaders" and singing "Dixie." Memorial Day was studied and commemorated in April, while in May Jefferson Davis and Abraham Lincoln were to be compared by asking the question, "Which violated the Constitution?"[52]

Women's history was also part of Rutherford's program of study for children, which was consistent with the organization's message that Confederate women, as well as veterans, deserved recognition for their wartime sacrifices. In July members of the CofC were asked to learn about their grandmothers. Using Thomas Nelson Page's *The Old South,* they were challenged to write an essay describing "the life of 'Ole Mis' on the old plantation." The subject for August was "Young women of the Old South," when children were asked to answer such questions as "Who was called 'the best bred lady in the land?'"[53]

Rutherford also wanted children to learn about the South's heroines, the topic of study for September. The North Carolina women who participated in the Edenton Tea Party, by refusing to drink British tea during the American Revolution, were worthy southern heroines. So was "cross-eyed" Nancy Hart of Georgia, who, according to legend, held a group of British officers at gunpoint until they could be taken prisoner— she succeeded because they could not tell where she was looking. Helen Keller, born in Alabama, was also recognized as a southern heroine. From August until the end of the year, children studied Confederate heroes, "Christmas in the [Old] South," and even the UDC.[54]

In order to answer the questions posed, children were provided the necessary bibliography. Rutherford compiled the list of books, which included *The South in the Building of the Nation,* the *Library of Southern Literature,* Mary Williamson's *Life of Robert E. Lee* and *Life of Stonewall*

Fig. 7.6. Decca Lamar West of the Texas UDC wrote
a Confederate catechism for children.

Jackson, the *Confederate Veteran,* Page's *The Old South,* Laura Rose's *Ku
Klux Klan,* and Rutherford's own *The South in History and Literature.* The
UDC made most of these books readily available to children, if not in
their schools, then in their public libraries.[55]

Cornelia Branch Stone, who eventually became president-general of
the entire organization, prepared the *UDC Catechism for Children* in
1904. Leaders asked questions from Stone's catechism, and children responded as they had been taught in their meetings. "What causes led to
the War Between the States, from 1861 to 1865?" asked the Daughter in
charge. "The disregard, on the part of the States of the North, for the
rights of the Southern or slaveholding States," the children were admonished to respond. "What were these rights?" "The right to regulate their
own affairs and to hold slaves as property." "How were the slaves treated?"

"With great kindness and care in nearly all cases, a cruel master being rare."[56]

Children's learned responses to the questions from the catechism were a key ingredient in their indoctrination. Moreover, the catechism, combined with information children learned at school and at home, provided lessons that remained with them through adulthood. Interviews with former members of the CofC reveal that states' rights, plantation myths, and heroic tales of Confederate ancestors form vivid facets of their historical memory.[57]

Many women who are current members of the UDC were also active in the Children of the Confederacy. Moreover, they were often educated in the South's public schools, and their early education was decidedly pro-southern. For example, Helen Foster, a former member of the CofC in South Carolina, learned about the Civil War both at school and in the children's chapters. She was born in 1911; in 1990, when asked what she believed caused the Civil War, she replied, "I still think they were fightin' for states' rights." Her ancestors owned slaves prior to the war, and she grew up on a 3,000-acre farm worked by sharecroppers. That experience led her to believe that she had grown up "like it was before the [Civil] War." "I'm sure the people [white slave owners] didn't mistreat their slaves," she remarked. "I'm not saying slavery was right . . . but I'm saying a lot of them [slaves] were treated well."[58]

Mildred Youngblood Grant was born in Fayetteville, North Carolina, in 1900. She shared many of Helen Foster's perceptions of the Civil War and slavery. Like Foster, Mildred Grant was a member of the CofC and went on to become a UDC member. In her interview she stated that the War Between the States—"we don't like to call it Civil War"—was not fought over slavery. Moreover, Grant commented, "The slaves were not treated like sometimes it's written that they were because in the South they were treated well, and they didn't even want to leave their master's home."[59]

The UDC's objective to teach white southern children the lessons of "unbiased" history and to instill in them a reverence for the Confederacy, its heroes, and its "sacred principles" kept the Daughters extremely busy in the years between 1894 and 1919. As practitioners of Confederate motherhood, the Daughters actively assisted Confederate men in the campaign to provide children in the white public schools with pro-southern textbooks. The women of the Lost Cause, however, had a broader vision for training future generations of the South's citizens. Daughters maintained direct and constant contact with pupils, as well as teachers, in the region's public schools. They also organized children for further indoctrination and with the object of sustaining the parent organization.

The UDC left no stone unturned to ensure that the next generation was motivated to honor and uphold the values of the Confederate generation, as they had. Not all children, of course, were influenced to perpetuate the cultural myths and racist assumptions found in the Lost Cause narrative. Yet oral history evidence suggests that the UDC had succeeded in keeping that narrative present in the minds of several generations of southerners. By promoting Confederate culture during the era of Jim Crow, the Daughters were able to influence the development of the New South based on their reverence for the Old.

✦ 8 ✦

Vindication and Reconciliation

Some think of the [UDC] as several thousand militant and contentious women keeping alive sectional feeling. We are not organized to stir up sectional bitterness, and there is too much important work to be done to waste time on that. If we are at times apparently contentious, we are only insisting upon truth and justice for the Southern Confederacy, for the South, for our noble men, for truth.

Rassie Hoskins White, president-general, UDC General Convention, 1913

If the war through which the world has just been passing should have accomplished no other thing, it has surely knit closer than ever before the great ties of union in our land.

Charles Sears Taylor to President-General Mary Poppenheim, May 1919

"I am pained to see and realize that so many of our people have accepted and are preaching the Creed that there is no North or South, but one nation," Anna Raines complained in a letter to Caroline Goodlett in the spring of 1894. As the two women hammered out an agenda for their new organization, Raines vehemently expressed her opposition to sectional reconciliation. "NO true Southerner can ever embrace this new religion," she wrote, "and those WHO DO should be ostracized by the 'Daughters of the Confederacy.' They are like vipers warmed on the hearth of a good farmer, and as soon as life is restored, it turns and stings the good man's children." Raines's views about sectional reconciliation arose in the context of creating a new southern women's organization. The UDC intended to stand firm against the "new religion" of sectional reconciliation, because in 1894 bitter feelings for the North remained, as Raines's comments attest. Over the next twenty-five years, however, those feelings softened as the Daughters succeeded in redefining the image of Confederate men as defenders of Constitutional principle. Even northerners grew to admire the patriotism of southern men, and the Daughters interpreted this as proof of Confederate vindication.[1]

Sectional reconciliation was a common theme of the national dialogue when the UDC formed in 1894. Expressions of goodwill were exchanged between the North and the South in the late nineteenth century, as the regions courted one another in what historian Nina Silber describes as the "romance of reunion." By the 1890s the Democratic Party controlled state and local government throughout the South, and the region officially sanctioned white supremacy without northern resistance. The North, in fact, lost interest in "reconstructing" the South and had effectively given white southerners carte blanche to solve their "Negro problem." With self-government intact and white supremacy secured, white southerners were more at ease with the idea of reconciliation, though not entirely. After the Spanish-American War, reunification appeared to be within reach. Nearly one million southern white men joined northern white men on behalf of Cuba's "self-determination" to defeat a common enemy, and there was a general feeling among southerners to "rejoice in a reunited republic."[2]

The South's participation in the Spanish-American War brought former Confederates a step closer to vindication, yet bitter sectional feelings still remained. White southerners, especially women active in the Lost Cause, wanted more than praise for the performance of southern men in 1898. The honor of the Confederate generation was still in question, and as historian Charles Wilson has argued, the Spanish-American War was simply "one stop on the road to reconciliation." To be sure, members of the region's elite, including the UDC, were still coming to terms with defeat at the turn of the century. They did not feel as though they were citizens of a reunited country, especially while northern histories continued to refer to Confederate men as traitors and rebels. As long as such sentiments had life, white southerners believed that their American citizenship was still in question and that the South was still being treated as the nation's red-headed stepchild.[3]

The Daughters were active participants in the debate over reconciliation for nearly twenty years after the Spanish-American War. They remained steadfast in their belief that reconciliation was possible only when the Confederate generation was exonerated. Monument building, caring for the men and women of the 1860s, campaigning for impartial history, and transmitting Confederate ideals to southern children were all part of the UDC's crusade for vindication. For these women, vindication was the quickest path to reconciliation.

By the time war broke out in Europe in 1914, the UDC had made great strides to fulfill its mission to absolve Confederate men of failure. The Daughters' success, however, was visible primarily in the South. Yet when the United States entered the First World War, the UDC recognized a golden opportunity to prove southerners were, and always had been, American patriots. And by war's end in 1918, the Daughters expressed confidence that through their own wartime commitment, their organization brought honor to, and helped exonerate, the Confederate generation. For the first time in the organization's twenty-five-year existence, UDC members noticed how their efforts to vindicate their ancestors were now recognized outside of the South. The nation seemed to agree with what the Daughters had worked so hard to prove: southerners were loyal and patriotic Americans.

The road to reunion was a long one, perhaps made longer by the UDC's insistence on vindication. No sooner had the Spanish-American War ended than the debate over sectional reconciliation resumed. It continued for several reasons. Some northerners remained highly critical of the South, and their comments, which circulated in Lost Cause periodicals, generated lively replies from members of the UCV and the UDC. In addition, basic philosophical differences remained about the rights of states within a politically reunited nation. Finally, the issue of whether or not official histories of the United States revealed the "truth" about the Civil War was unresolved. In all aspects of the debate, members of the UDC were vocal participants.

What rankled Confederate organizations—other than the reality of Confederate defeat—was that, at times, northern critics seemed to deliberately offend southern people. For example, in 1900, when the commander of the GAR, General Albert D. Shaw, spoke at the Chicago reunion of Union veterans, he condemned the "school histories of the South" and suggested that they perpetuated sectional differences. This was especially galling to Confederate organizations because Shaw represented an organization whose members were the South's former foes.

His comments were particularly offensive given that Confederate veterans had agreed to participate in reunions of the "blue and gray."[4] The Campbell-Graves Camp of UCV in Danville, Virginia, passed resolutions condemning Shaw's statements. According to Danville's veterans, the South was simply "striving for the truth" with their histories, and they denied that they were "perpetuating the prejudices of 1861." The camp also pledged to "continue to teach southern children the *truth*."[5]

The UDC received its share of criticism for keeping reunification at bay. After the organization proposed to erect a monument to Captain Henry Wirz in 1908, a "bitter attack" on the Georgia Daughters ensued. Wirz had been in charge of the Andersonville prison during the Civil War, and northerners despised him for the atrocities that occurred there. As far as they were concerned, the UDC might as well erect a monument to the devil. A writer defended the Daughters in the *Southern Historical Society Papers*, and asked, "Why is it that the people of the North . . . will continually try to poison the minds of people at home and abroad against us?"[6]

The Daughters were also reproved for their efforts to influence children with their Lost Cause philosophy. In 1912 P. J. Noyes of Lancaster, New Hampshire, wrote a letter to the *Confederate Veteran* describing the UDC's efforts as "sinister" and an attempt to "debauch [southern] youth." When a "vicious partisan comment" appeared in a New York newspaper, referring to the UDC as a society of "rabid and disloyal fire eaters," Sumner Cunningham used his Nashville periodical to admonish the paper for printing "libel."[7] Another critic denounced the Daughters because they glorified that which "cost the blood of a nation to suppress." He suggested that the work of the UDC was, in fact, treason. As long as the Daughters were allowed to speak freely with such disregard for the Union, he argued, then "why not allow Emma Goldman . . . the 'Daughter of Anarchy'" the same right to free speech?[8]

The UDC was undaunted by such criticism, yet it hindered reconciliation as far as its members were concerned. The Daughters, in fact, held that certain conditions must be met before the South would pursue a relationship with the North. The terms of reconciliation required that northerners refrain from using the terms "rebel" and "traitor" to condemn Confederate men and recognize that the South fought to defend the Constitution, not slavery—thus making patriots out of the defeated.[9]

Adelia Dunovant, a leader of the UDC's Texas Division, was a vocal critic of reconciliation. Her speeches, and her articles in Lost Cause periodicals at the turn of the century, are noteworthy because she expressed a general sentiment within the organization that resisted reconciliation. Dunovant, by her own admission, was one of the "unreconstructed." In 1902 she still referred to the North as "the enemy." A staunch defender of states' rights, Dunovant was highly regarded for her ability to speak "vigorously and intelligently" about the Constitution.[10]

Interestingly, Dunovant opposed the use of the term *nation* and argued that the United States was "not a nation" and had "never been a nation." Instead, she described the country as a "federative system of free, sovereign, and independent states." Like other Daughters who defended the Confederacy, Dunovant wrote about defending the legacy of their Revolutionary forefathers who "jealously . . . guarded against even the suggestion of centralization." The Constitution, she argued, "still sustained" the rights of states in her own time.[11]

Adelia Dunovant insisted that the Daughters recognize the significance of upholding states' rights. If the UDC failed to do so, she said, it risked "throwing down the South's great bulwark of defense." Perhaps more seriously, the Daughters risked "destroying the very basis" upon which the UDC stood if they did not defend the principle of states' rights. Finally, she argued, the UDC must avoid the term *nation* because it inhibited the organization's purpose, which was to vindicate Confederate men and uphold state sovereignty.[12]

Adelia Dunovant's stance against nationalism, while extreme, was not inconsistent with the UDC's goal to command the respect of the North without compromising its conservative political philosophy. Vindication and sectional reconciliation, moreover, were not necessarily at odds with one another. The Daughters did not believe that achieving respect as patriotic Americans meant disavowing southern citizenship. On the contrary, the UDC assumed that a dual allegiance—to the South and to the United States—was possible. Even reconciliation was possible if former Confederates were welcomed back into the American fold as patriotic citizens.

Although some northern journalists criticized the UDC for stoking the fire of sectional discord, southern leaders praised the organization for trying to find common ground. Francis Nichols, former chief justice of Louisiana, defended the Daughters during the meeting of their general convention in New Orleans. The organization, he argued, did not "desire the bygone bitterness to be perpetuated," nor did members wish to instill "into their children's hearts" hostile feelings toward the federal government. On the contrary, the Daughters felt obligated by duty "to reestablish friendly relations and cordial feelings toward their fellow citizens of all sections." Members adopted this stance, Nichols argued, on the condition that they were not "to be traduced as traitors . . . and wrongly denounced."[13]

Nichols's assessment offers a clear definition of what the Daughters hoped to achieve with regard to sectional reconciliation. They wanted to encourage cordial feelings with the northern people, without disregard for Confederate men and women. Vindication remained their primary goal; sectional reconciliation was welcome, but only on terms they determined and accepted.

The Daughters believed that northerners had to do their part if sectional reconciliation had any chance of succeeding. Aside from a few vociferous critics, most northern whites had made great strides toward renewing their relationship with southern whites. Southerners' participation in the war with Spain contributed to their improved image in the North, and according to historian Nina Silber, the war also "seemed to confirm the natural unity of southern and northern white people." Confederate manhood, in fact, had achieved a new modicum of respect in the North. Yet despite these winds of change, members of the UDC continued to guard the South's sectional identity.[14]

One event that marked the Daughters' own "road to reconciliation" was their general convention of 1912, held in Washington, D.C. UDC members chose to showcase their organization in the nation's capital to bring publicity to the Confederate monument in Arlington, but their meeting also tested whether cordial feelings between the sections actually existed. The UDC claimed that this was the first time that the organization had held a meeting "outside" of the South, by which they really meant "in the North," since they had met in San Francisco in 1905. The Washington convention did represent a change in the Daughters' attitude toward the North, and it provided northerners with the opportunity to prove their sincerity by making the leading organization of southern women feel welcome. The local press even predicted that the UDC's convention would "permanently mark the union between the North and the South."[15]

Three UDC chapters were based in the District of Columbia and thus formed their own division. The division had issued the invitation to hold the UDC general convention in Washington in 1912 and promoted the meeting as an opportunity to show the nation that the UDC was a patriotic and national society of women. The convention was further regarded as a symbolic effort toward sectional reconciliation.

Florence Butler, wife of North Carolina Senator Marion Butler, was in charge of the local arrangements for the convention. As president of the District of Columbia Division, she was responsible for inviting President William Howard Taft to address the Daughters and, at the urging of President-General Rassie White, persuading President and Mrs. Taft to honor the UDC with a White House reception. "I know the delegates expect a reception at the White House, and if there were not one it would kind of hurt us especially as other organizations are accorded this courtesy," White explained to Butler. Both women agreed that the White House reception "should be especially arranged for" because they believed it would have a positive effect on the public's opinion of the UDC.[16]

When the Daughters gathered for their Washington convention, they held some of their largest sessions in Memorial Continental Hall, the national headquarters of the DAR. DAR President-General Mrs. Matthew Scott offered the UDC use of the building as an expression of her organization's goodwill. Several DAR chapters sent greetings of welcome to the UDC president-general, who reported that she had even received flowers from a DAR chapter located in "far-away Abolitionist New England."[17]

Nearly 2,000 delegates attended the convention and were pleased at their reception. Virginia Clay Clopton, a suffragist and UDC leader from Alabama, stated that the Daughters were "doubly grateful" for the invitation to Washington because it gave the UDC an opportunity to prove to nonsoutherners "that our object is not to keep alive the fire of sectionalism." President-General White concurred, saying that "good fellowship and glory in a common heritage of American valor has been strengthened" as a result of the meeting in Washington.[18]

One of the most important moments of the meeting occurred when

President Taft addressed convention delegates. The UDC had already expressed some confidence in Taft for appointing white southerners to "high positions of trust." The Daughters were also pleased that he had not made any "offensive appointments in the South"—a reference to his "Southern strategy" not to appoint blacks to office. His speech to the UDC convention was well received, and even as he took special care to address the theme of sectional reconciliation, he was careful to acknowledge southern patriotism.[19]

President Taft began his address by noting the "patriotic sacrifice" of the southern people. He expressed faith that the bitterness caused by the Civil War had dissipated enough that northerners were able to join southerners in expressing "just pride" in southern men and women. Taft acknowledged that the "story" of the war was a common heritage that both regions shared and apologized for northerners who had contributed to sectional antagonisms, suggesting that they were being "unreasonable" for their inability to accept regional differences.[20]

The president maintained that he had done everything in his power to reduce sectional animosity and to "make the divisions of this country geographical only." Still, he felt more needed to be done and was confident that the incoming president would succeed in reunifying the sections. Taft believed that with Woodrow Wilson, of whom he spoke, the country would have an administration "in which Southern opinion will naturally have greater influence." In other words, under a president sympathetic to the South, there existed a real opportunity to heal "the wounds of sectionalism."[21]

On the whole, the UDC convention was shrouded in an atmosphere of cordiality. Delegates attended teas and receptions held in their honor, including an opening reception in the ballroom of the new Willard Hotel. There was a limit to congeniality, however, because this was, after all, a meeting of a southern woman's organization founded to vindicate the Confederacy. Some chapters of the DAR were upset that the UDC was invited to use DAR headquarters and cited the display of Confederate flags in the hall as a "desecration." An article published in the *National Tribune* during the week of the UDC convention was even more derogatory.[22]

Isabel Worrell Ball, correspondent for the *National Tribune*, assailed the UDC and its convention. She was furious that delegates were invited to the White House, where, she wrote, they "insolently flaunted in that stately edifice the flag representing sectional strife and bitterness." She was appalled that Washington agreed to host women she described as the "howlers of the UDC . . . from whose white throats came the rebel yell." Ball claimed that the Daughters were "a menace to the South" and that they did not know "the war is over." She concluded her assault by criticizing the organization for sowing "seeds of treason where the lilies of peace are trying to take root."[23]

In the week following Ball's attack, a male friend of Florence Butler's tried to make sense of the criticism. He suggested that the "numerous" inaccuracies printed by newspapers during the week of the Daughters' meeting were the product of "irresponsible" correspondents. He furiously referred to Ball as "an absolute vixen." He was so angry with Ball, he told Butler, that he could "in no sense give you an idea of my estimate of her, because what I say will not be inscribed on asbestos."[24]

The Daughters left Washington, D.C., believing their convention was a success. They had felt welcome; delegates had been feted throughout the city over the course of their stay; and the president of the United States had addressed their meeting and hosted a White House reception in their honor. The ceremony to lay the cornerstone of the Confederate monument in Arlington National Cemetery, a primary reason for holding the meeting in the District of Columbia, was also a success. William Jennings Bryan, the nationally recognized Democrat and former presidential candidate, was keynote speaker for the ceremony. He praised the women of the UDC for building the monument, which he asserted was vivid "evidence of a reunited nation."[25]

Significantly, the UDC's gradual movement toward sectional reconciliation was enhanced by its association with other patriotic organizations on behalf of peace, or to be precise, the settlement of political disputes by peaceful negotiation. The Daughters considered themselves natural allies with women's organizations in the national peace movement.[26] As southerners they believed that they knew better than most Americans did about the horror and devastation caused by war. Thus, when invited to have representatives at meetings of peace advocates, the UDC was quick to respond.

When the National Peace Congress (NPC) held its 1907 convention in New York City, members of the UDC's New York Division were present.

The day's speakers included nationally known peace advocates like millionaire Andrew Carnegie, president of the National Arbitration and Peace Congress, and Jane Addams of Hull House in Chicago. The president-general of the UDC at the time, Lizzie George Henderson, was invited, but because she was unable to attend, her telegram of greeting was read before the meeting instead. Henderson declared that the UDC was pleased to be associated with the NPC, and she remarked that "we of all people in the world know of the necessity of doing all we can to promote universal peace." Henderson backed her statement by appointing a representative from each state division of the UDC to serve as delegates to future NPC conventions.[27]

The Daughters remained associated with the peace movement for several years and, just prior to the First World War, expanded their involvement in the movement. In 1911, while meeting in Richmond, the UDC passed its first peace resolutions. Elvira Moffitt, a North Carolina Daughter, proposed the resolutions, which were accepted after a motion by Georgian Mildred Lewis Rutherford. Moffitt's resolutions appealed to the UDC to support a national policy to settle international disputes "by other means than war and bloodshed."[28]

Moffitt asked the Daughters to become involved in the movement by promoting peace through education. She also asked the Daughters to encourage teachers to observe May 18 as "Peace Day." Just as the UDC sought to instill in children a reverence for Confederate heroes and principles, Moffitt encouraged UDC members to teach children "that the glories of peace are greater than the glories of war." As part of this effort with children, Moffitt also suggested that Daughters "introduce a Peace Flag in the schools." Such symbols, she argued, had the power to "impress upon the minds of the children the sentiment of peace."[29]

The UDC passed Moffitt's resolutions, but within a few short years they faced, along with the rest of the nation, the reality of a world war. The organization's official position on war was reflected in new resolutions, which stated in even stronger terms than its declarations for peace the UDC's distaste for war. "We deplore the spirit of militarism that holds war to be inevitable in the course of civilization," one resolution stated. Another revealed the organization's confidence that it could influence public opinion, as the Daughters pledged themselves to try to sway public sentiment on "questions of arbitration, international disarmament or limitation of armaments."[30]

Fig. 8.1. President-General Daisy McLaurin Stevens (1913–1915)
created the UDC's Peace Committee at the outbreak of World War I.

President-General Daisy Stevens officially committed the organization to peace work when she established the UDC's Peace Committee in
1914. As the leader of the organization, she had received numerous invi-
tations to participate in various meetings of peace groups, and she argued for the necessity of a peace committee to work with similar committees in other national organizations.[31]

The South had economic reasons to support a peace movement, as
they relied on European markets for the sale of cotton. Most southerners, however, supported the Allied cause and the Wilson administration.
Their enthusiasm for war was fostered by their own feelings of national
unity and the sense that their patriotism was the purest form of American patriotism. Few southern congressmen opposed the war, nor did
southern merchants, even though their business was most negatively
affected. Instead, the merchants appealed to women within the region
to buy their products. In her address regarding the creation of a peace
committee, UDC President-General Daisy Stevens of Mississippi sec-
onded their appeal. Repeating the slogan of the region's businessmen,
she asked the Daughters to "Wear a Cotton Dress." Still, she maintained

that it was important for the UDC to be involved in the peace movement, which it was until 1917.[32]

Stevens appointed a fellow Mississippian, Eron Rowland, to chair the newly formed peace committee.[33] Rowland was a zealous advocate for peace, and during her first year as committee chair, the UDC set and met most of its peace goals. The Daughters cooperated with the American Association for International Conciliation by establishing an essay contest in the South's public high schools on the subject of international conciliation. Not surprisingly, any student who wrote an essay for the UDC was required to be a descendant of a Confederate veteran. Rowland noted individual efforts to promote peace also. The president of the District of Columbia Division of the UDC, Maud Howell Smith, participated in a peace rally in the nation's capital, where she played the role of Woman in the "Peace tableaux" presented on the grounds surrounding the Washington Monument.[34]

State UDC divisions were also active in the movement for peace and in 1916 found themselves in the unaccustomed position of being at odds with other white southerners in the region. Most southerners supported the war and showed little tolerance for antiwar sentiment. Still, Rowland reported to the general convention on the necessity to continue the movement for peace in spite of the "white heat [of] military spirit" that existed throughout the world. She expressed great pride in the Daughters from Arkansas and Louisiana, who were particularly active peace advocates, despite support for military preparedness in their respective states.[35]

Judith Hyams Douglas, chair of the peace committee for the Louisiana Division, reported the difficulty she had as a peace advocate. Douglas felt her accomplishments were not as successful as she had hoped because of "unreceptive minds." In her hometown of New Orleans, there was a "preparedness parade" that, according to Douglas, made a powerful impression on local citizens. The parade's leader was so strident, she reported, that he threatened to "tar-and-feather and burn alive any Peace advocate who would express unpatriotic Utopian views in his presence."[36]

Douglas continued her work of "planting the seed of Righteousness." As she put it, her plan was one of "subsoil plowing—distributing literature, furnishing the same for lectures, debates at school, etc." She requested that churches, schools, and women's clubs address the subject of peace in their educational programs. And, as secretary of the Public Playgrounds Commission, she received permission to encourage children who used the city's playgrounds to participate "in one splendid rally for Peace." Though discouraged by the apathy of the press, whom she believed had misrepresented her efforts, Douglas stood firm in her commitment to peace.[37]

Members of the peace committee of the Arkansas Division worked as peace advocates as a means of proving their worthiness as an organization. "The women of the Confederacy are those on whom the leaders [especially Woodrow Wilson] may depend in time of stress and storm," committee chair Mrs. W. E. Massey proclaimed. She instituted a campaign for peace that was unique in the South, as it was geared toward promoting "Americanization." Massey thought peace was best served by efforts to "Americanize" immigrants to the United States. "The great foreign population is going to make chalky the backbone of this great republic of American ideals," she argued, especially if such ideals were "not instilled into the newcomer." Thus, she recommended to the general convention in 1916 that Daughters attempt the following: "help Americanize one immigrant; get one immigrant to become a citizen; teach one foreign-born mother English; put one immigrant family on your calling list." Doing these things, Massey asserted, proved that UDC members were "worthy" of their ancestors "who preserved the Union in 1776, and who fought again to preserve those principles in 1861."[38]

"Peace without victory" never materialized, even though the UDC campaigned for peace through 1918. Although the Daughters supported peace efforts, they also believed it was their duty to support any military action taken by the United States. The UDC regarded itself as a national patriotic organization even before the war and had formally pledged its support to President Wilson. Once the administration moved to adopt an official declaration of war, the UDC reiterated its support.

Immediately after Wilson severed diplomatic relations with Germany in February 1917, President-General Cordelia Odenheimer offered the services of the UDC to the president. Odenheimer, a resident of Baltimore, attended a meeting of the Red Cross in Washington, whose purpose was to mobilize "the womanhood of the United States" to provide wartime assistance. Speaking to the Daughters through her column in

Fig. 8.2. President-General Cordelia Powell Odenheimer (1915–1917) offered the services of the UDC to President Woodrow Wilson as the United States prepared to enter World War I.

the *Confederate Veteran,* Odenheimer urged members to pledge their loyalty to President Wilson and prepare themselves "to render service in any emergency that may occur."[39]

Ironically, the war they had hoped to avoid offered the Daughters a unique opportunity to bring attention to the South's particular brand of patriotism. They spoke of their support of the Wilson administration as a "patriot's duty," as something that made them worthy of their forebears. They described their role in the war relief effort as similar to the patriotism shown by their fathers and mothers. Addie Daniels, whose husband Josephus was Wilson's secretary of the navy, appealed to this sense of duty and opportunity. The Daughters, she claimed, had a chance to "emulate their mothers in the spirit of self-sacrifice for the benefit of their country." A member of the New Orleans chapter concurred, noting that the UDC's war relief work was like that of their mothers during "the dark days of the Confederacy."[40]

The impact of the war on the UDC also meant a shift in focus for members, from fund-raising for monuments to a comprehensive commitment to war relief. President-General Odenheimer encouraged the Daughters to complete their obligations to monuments like the one in Arlington as swiftly as possible, in order to devote their time, energy, and resources to meet the demands of war. Odenheimer, who represented the UDC at countless meetings related to war relief, outlined the Daughters' plan of action.[41]

The UDC, like women's organizations across the nation, became actively involved in food conservation efforts. "Southern women face an opportunity for enormous usefulness," wrote Mrs. J. Norment Powell, the organization's registrar-general, and she suggested that they serve their country by helping to conserve the nation's food supply. "There should not be wasted one bean, one tomato, or one particle of food," Powell instructed, and she encouraged all Daughters to "instruct the children in this industry."[42]

Mrs. Walter Preston, president of her UDC chapter in BelAir, Maryland, headed a "Department of Thrift and Conservation" in her county. She organized five thrift clubs of "colored women" in her town and gave lectures on "food conservation." Some Daughters lectured in "negro churches" on conservation and trained both white and black women in canning food. UDC members were also asked to support Prohibition as a "war measure." President-General Odenheimer noted that other women's organizations favored this plan of action not only to help conserve the food supply, of grain and other items used to make alcohol, but also to protect "against the blighting influence of the saloon and commercialized vice."[43]

Throughout the war, the Daughters also invested in liberty bonds and were active in the Red Cross. An article about the UDC's war relief activity that appeared in the British magazine *Town and Country* explained that the Daughters worked, like "other women of the world," to form committees for national defense and the sale of liberty bonds. Moreover, members had formed Red Cross units "in every Southern town."[44]

The Daughters were proud of their war relief work and were especially proud of a project that gave publicity to the UDC in Europe, specifically in France. At the UDC general convention in November 1917, the Daughters learned that an American military hospital in Neuilly, near

Paris, took in soldiers wounded at the front. The hospital needed funds to cover the costs of caring for those soldiers, and the Daughters were in a position to provide important assistance if they agreed to maintain a bed in that hospital at a cost of $600 per year.[45]

What especially piqued the Daughters' interest in the project was that the UDC would be allowed to attach a brass plate to the bed in memory of a Confederate veteran, with the UDC listed as the donor. South Carolinian Mary Poppenheim, who succeeded Cordelia Odenheimer as president-general in 1917, recommended that a War Relief Committee be created to carry out the plan to maintain beds at the Neuilly hospital. It was the committee's responsibility to encourage state divisions to sponsor additional hospital beds.[46]

A few months after the convention, in February 1918, the first "endowed bed" was placed in American Military Hospital Number One in Neuilly. It was a moment of great pride for the Daughters, as the brass plate on the bed read, "The United Daughters of the Confederacy—A Tribute of Honor and Devotion to Jefferson Davis." The endowment of the first bed was greeted with much enthusiasm, and President-General Poppenheim encouraged each state division to maintain at least ten beds in the hospital.[47]

The Daughters accepted their president's challenge, and within two months the UDC had endowed enough beds to fill an entire ward of the hospital. Poppenheim encouraged the UDC to continue its efforts "until peace comes back to earth." Invoking the legacy of the Confederate generation, she proclaimed, "It is part of our inheritance that we shall stand faithful to [war relief] unto the end."[48]

The expansion of UDC efforts to endow hospital beds continued, and in June 1918 Mary Poppenheim enthusiastically announced that the Daughters had provided for "a third UDC hospital ward in France!" By July the UDC was well on its way to endowing a fourth ward at the hospital, and some Daughters labored to endow a ward to honor Confederate women who nursed "soldiers at home or in hospitals during the War Between the States." By September a fifth ward was under way. The UDC was now supporting forty-two hospital beds, at a cost of $25,000 per annum.[49]

The UDC's war relief efforts were impressive. President-General Mary Poppenheim reflected on her organization's achievement by suggesting that "the touchstone of war brought out all the latent power" of the organization. Mrs. J. A. Rountree of Alabama, chair of the UDC's War Relief Committee, reported that in the last year of the war alone, the UDC had endowed seventy hospital beds at the American military hospital in Neuilly, France; made 3.5 million hospital garments; wrapped 4.5 million surgical dressings; knitted 100,000 garments; donated $82,000 to the Red Cross; subscribed $9 million in liberty bonds; and supported 830 French and Belgian orphans "at a cost of $20,000."[50]

When the UDC held its first postwar convention in 1919, the Daughters felt strongly that their efforts on the home front had honored their Confederate ancestors. President-General Mary Poppenheim congratulated UDC members for proving that theirs was truly a "National Patriotic Society." She asked the UDC to continue to be an influential organization, "walking in the earnest footsteps of the women who first saw the vision of our Association." The Daughters had successfully "shouldered the duty of immediate war needs," Poppenheim remarked; now they had to return to "making plans to prepare the boys and girls of today for their [life's] work."[51]

As it turned out, war, rather than peace, contributed to the mood of sectional reconciliation within the UDC. Significantly, at the postwar convention President-General Mary Poppenheim did not address the Daughters about the need to return to the work of vindication. She spoke instead of the "work to be done . . . for our reunited country." As far as UDC members were concerned, southern patriotism was no longer in question. The only question, in fact, was what the organization intended to pursue next. "We are equipped to be of vast service wherever we put our strength," stated Poppenheim.[52]

After World War I the Daughters did not return to monument building with the same sense of purpose as they had before the war. In fact, the task of monument building as set out by the founders was nearly complete. By the 1920s there were increasingly fewer Confederate men and women who needed the UDC's assistance. The Daughters' success, as much as the passage of time, led the UDC to a change in emphasis. Textbooks in the South's public schools now emphasized "true" history, and the Daughters' work with children continued outside of the classroom; in 1917 the Children of the Confederacy became the organization's official auxiliary. The UDC had also earned respect as a national patriotic organization, as evidenced by their partnerships with other voluntary associations during the war. The Daughters interpreted their success and expressions of respect as vindication. White southerners were praised for their patriotism without having to relinquish their belief that the Confederate cause was a just cause. Because patriotism was integral to the doctrine of states' rights, southern whites regarded northern admiration of the South's patriotism as evidence of vindication.

Vindication for the Confederate generation, of course, had been the primary goal of the UDC from its founding in 1894. Every monument placed in a courthouse square, every veteran or widow cared for, every history book removed from a library or school for being biased against the South, and every chapter of the Children of the Confederacy formed was done to vindicate Confederate men and women. World War I, moreover, gave the UDC its best opportunity to vindicate the Confederate generation, and they capitalized on it. "In this crisis in our country's national life," Poppenheim wrote during the war, "we must give our best and a best worthy of our Confederate lineage." When the war ended, the Daughters, at least in their own minds, were confident they had accomplished this task "without sacrificing a single principle."[53] For the first time in the twenty-five years since the UDC had formed, the Daughters genuinely believed that vindication for the Confederate generation had been achieved, as the feelings of reunion blossomed between the North and the South.[54]

National reconciliation had been achieved effectively on the South's terms, and certainly on the Daughters' terms. The North had accepted the Lost Cause narrative as fact, which was an essential element of reunion. That narrative, perpetuated most vigorously by the UDC, was, at its core, about preserving white supremacy. Reconciliation had allowed white southerners to return to the American fold as patriots, not traitors, one of the desired results of the Daughters' work. For African Americans, however, the results of this reunion would add decades onto their journey for freedom.[55]

Epilogue

Your unselfish efforts to preserve and maintain the priceless records
of our Southern heritage and to keep that heritage fresh in the minds
of our citizens have done much to keep us from being engulfed
in the chaos and slavery that the Communists and their sympathizers
seek for us in this country.

William D. McCain to the Mississippi Daughters, 1952[1]

In the winter of 2000, June Murray Wells, president-general of the United
Daughters of the Confederacy, found herself embroiled in the bitter debate over the Confederate battle flag that flew over the South Carolina
state capitol. She was invited to participate in a discussion at the governor's mansion in Columbia in January, along with members of the
state senate, the National Association for the Advancement of Colored
People (NAACP), the Sons of Confederate Veterans (SCV), and Governor Jim Hodges. The meeting allowed representatives of the different
groups to state how they each felt about the flag issue and the NAACP's
boycott of tourism in the state. The compromise that was eventually
reached within the state legislature did result in the flag's removal from
the capitol, but not the capitol's grounds. The Confederate flag now
waves on a 30-foot flagpole, lit at night, on the grounds leading directly to
the capitol's front doors.[2]

Throughout the controversy, June Murray Wells felt as though the
press had maligned her. In a public statement, she complained that the
media had taken her comments about the flag issue out of context. The
worst offenders, she claimed, "have been from my city and state, neither
of which wants to hear the pro-Confederate side of the story." Several

decades earlier, Wells would have been lauded for her efforts to defend the flag. The region that had once embraced the Daughters now regarded them as out of step with the times.[3]

The organization founded by Caroline Meriwether Goodlett and Anna Davenport Raines in 1894 met with great success in its early years, bolstered by a culture that celebrated the Confederacy and white supremacy, while at the same time stripping African Americans of their civil rights and making them second-class citizens. The UDC thrived, in part, because it actively supported the racial status quo. Though the UDC was not a political organization, the Daughters' activities were a natural complement to Jim Crow politics. Southern women, moreover, were rewarded by state and local governments for their commitment to conservative values with appropriations that reached the modern equivalent of millions of dollars for monuments, homes for soldiers and widows, and museums, while African Americans in the region were barely afforded enough money to maintain their schools.

The legacy of the United Daughters of the Confederacy in the creation of the New South is, in many ways, tarnished by the organization's insistence on perpetuating the values of the Confederate generation. Members certainly intended to honor their Confederate ancestors, and if the hundreds of monuments scattered across the South are an indication, they succeeded. They also took care of aging men and women who had sacrificed for the Confederate cause. It was their promotion of pro-Confederate history and education, however, that ultimately defines the organization's historical reputation.

By the 1920s most southern states had adopted pro-Confederate textbooks. Public schools created curricula that included the study of the Confederacy. Students were released from classes to attend Confederate Memorial Day ceremonies, and their classrooms often included a portrait of Robert E. Lee next to that of George Washington. As late as the 1970s, neither textbooks nor curricula veered far from Lost Cause interpretations, especially in the Deep South. In his study of civil rights in Mississippi, historian John Dittmer argues that as recently as the 1990s, most whites in the state still believed in the Lost Cause myths of Reconstruction, which he attributed to "an interpretation drilled into the minds of generations of schoolchildren."[4]

White supremacists during the period of massive resistance to desegregation revived many of the tactics once used by the UDC. Just as the Daughters had fought to ensure that white students were not unduly influenced by "biased" texts, segregationists screened the curricula of the South's public schools, as well as the content of books in school libraries. Following the example set by the early UDC, white supremacists sought to eliminate material that denigrated southerners or "the southern way of life." In 1956 the Mississippi House of Representatives even passed a bill requiring the State Library Commission to purchase books that promoted white supremacy.[5]

Although the intentions of the UDC and white supremacists were to preserve and instill their values among the region's white youth, the sad reality is that those textbooks eventually made their way into the hands of black students, since they received the cast-off books of the white schools. Thus, young African Americans were also exposed to a Lost Cause narrative, which included assertions about the inferiority of their race.

By the end of the First World War, members of the UDC had already begun to express their concern about the waning interest in the Lost Cause. Sally Archer Anderson, president of the Confederate Memorial Literary Society and a UDC member, told the Daughters at their 1919 convention that "young people are not eager to join in Confederate work. Many of them think it is time we should forget, and live for this era overflowing with new activities."[6] Anderson's concerns were valid, as the UDC had accomplished many of its objectives, while the appeal of memorializing the Confederacy seemed to be lost on young children, who were now four generations removed from the Civil War. Yet she did not have to worry whether children were learning about Robert E. Lee, or whether they understood states' rights and white supremacy. Those lessons were being taught in the schools, which were often named for Confederate generals, and were being supplemented by southern communities, where Memorial Day rituals were observed and where political leaders draped themselves in the rhetoric and symbols of the Confederacy, as they institutionalized white supremacy.

The generation of children raised on the Lost Cause and Confederate culture in the early decades of the twentieth century is also the generation that was actively engaged in massive resistance to desegregation at mid-century. Certainly not all southern children who were taught to revere their Confederate heritage by defending states' rights and white supremacy did so. Many rejected the Lost Cause narrative that the UDC and school officials insisted was necessary to the preservation of those values. And yet from this generation came James O. Eastland, Strom Thurmond, Bull Connor, Byron de la Beckwith, and others. In fact, Beckwith's aunt, Lucy Yerger, was president of the Mississippi UDC and made some of the most virulently racist speeches to come out of the organization.[7]

The UDC's effort to plant seeds of reverence for states' rights and white supremacy among southern youth bore fruit during the fight to preserve Jim Crow, as a new generation of men and women employed the rhetoric once associated with the Lost Cause. The Citizens' Councils, organized throughout the South in the 1950s and 1960s, employed that rhetoric and used tactics very similar to those of the UDC to defend their cause—the preservation of "states' rights and racial integrity."[8] Just as members of Lost Cause organizations like the UDC used the language of states' rights to justify slavery and de jure segregation, the Citizens' Councils used it to react to the advancement of black civil rights in their own time. In its heyday the UDC was the primary nonpolitical organization promoting preservation of the racial status quo; during the period of massive resistance, the councils operated with the same goal.

While the Daughters sought to protect southern youth from historical bias, council members expressed concern that pupils of their day should be protected from ideas of egalitarianism. Like the UDC before them, the councils sought to purge from school libraries and classrooms those books they considered "unfair" to the South. In Mississippi, a woman directed this effort, and one of the groups she called on to fight a war against "brainwashing" was the United Daughters of the Confederacy—still very much respected for their work with white children, as the epigraph of this epilogue attests.[9]

Council members regarded their efforts as protecting constitutionalism, just as Confederate organizations argued that southerners had fought the Civil War to defend constitutional principle. The Lost Cause argument, which had been pressed most vigorously by the UDC in the early twentieth century, was resurrected at mid-century by white supremacists for their own purpose—to defend against desegregation.[10]

In the early years of the organization, the Daughters were able to engage in the rhetoric of states' rights and white supremacy without serious criticism from outside the region. The nation generally agreed with the concept of white supremacy and the basic tenets of social Darwinism. By the 1950s and 1960s, however, much had changed, and the same ideology did not resonate as well outside of the South.

Although the Lost Cause had never been simply about preserving Confederate heritage, the Daughters' collection of artifacts and oral histories, their restoration of historic buildings, and their collection of veterans' reminiscences were all genuine efforts to safeguard the heritage of their white forebears. The definition of Confederate heritage changed radically in the 1950s, as segregationists draped themselves in symbols of the Confederacy, such as the Confederate battle flag, in their war to preserve white supremacy. Since then, most Americans associate Confederate symbols with the searing images of hate that made their way via television into the nation's living rooms. Thus, today's Confederate organizations have only segregationists, and not groups like the NAACP, to blame for having to adopt their defensive mantra "heritage, not hate."

Today, the Daughters have a reputation as a group of old women whose honor must occasionally be defended by the likes of the retired U.S. senator from North Carolina, Jesse Helms. It is true that the organization's membership is not as youthful as it once was. As of 2001, there were approximately 20,000 members in the entire organization, not all of whom were active. Most meetings continue to be held in private homes and essentially serve as book clubs for pro-Confederate history. The Daughters still commemorate Confederate Memorial Day, though they rarely get involved in controversy—the Confederate flag in South Carolina being an exception. On the other hand, the organization has modernized and now supports a website to promote membership.[11]

Despite the UDC's decline during the twentieth century, the organization's early history remains important to understanding how the New South was created in the image of the Old. The Daughters' efforts to preserve and perpetuate Confederate culture are also useful in understanding why, in addition to its politics, the region has struggled to disengage itself from its culture of segregation—a culture that was created, in part, by the activities of southern women in the early twentieth century.

Notes

Chapter 1. Journey into the Lost Cause

1. For the purposes of this work, the definition of Confederate culture is derived in part from Williams, *Keywords*, 91, and Geertz, *The Interpretation of Cultures*, 193–233.

2. *A History of the Origin of Memorial Day*; Poppenheim, *History of the UDC*. For a broader discussion of hereditary organizations, see Davies, *Patriotism on Parade*.

3. Studies of the New South that briefly explore the Lost Cause include Woodward, *Origins of the New South*, 155. The Lost Cause does not rate a place in the index of Ayers, *Promise of the New South*; Paul Gaston explores the problems that arise for New South businessmen who were hampered by the Lost Cause defense of agrarian traditions in *New South Creed*. In *Ghosts of the Confederacy*, Gaines M. Foster discusses what he sees as the "waning power of the Confederate tradition" by 1913 and suggests that "the transfer of responsibility for the Confederate tradition to women suggests that the tradition had become less central to society" (179). More recent scholarship recognizes the long-term, often negative impact of the Lost Cause on society, including Hale, *Making Whiteness*, and Blight, *Race and Reunion*. See also Brundage, ed., *Where These Memories Grow*, particularly Catherine Bishir's essay, "Landmarks of Power," 139–68.

4. Historians who have given a cursory examination of women in the Confederate tradition include Foster, *Ghosts of the Confederacy*; Wilson, *Baptized in Blood*; and Osterweis, *Myth of the Lost Cause*. More recent scholarship reveals a more significant portrait of women's involvement in the Lost Cause and its implications for the New South. These works include Wheeler, *New Women of the New South*, 3–37; Whites, *Civil War as a Crisis in Gender*; Faust, *Mothers of Invention*; Hale, *Making Whiteness*, 43–44; Hall, "'You Must Remember This'"; Johnson,

"'Drill into us . . . the Rebel tradition'"; and Montgomery, *The Politics of Education in the New South*.

5. The Lost Cause is described as a "myth" by Osterweis, *Myth of the Lost Cause;* as a "cult" by Woodward, *Origins of the New South*, 55; as a "civil religion" by Wilson, *Baptized in Blood*, 8; and as a "tradition" or "celebration" by Foster, *Ghosts of the Confederacy*, 7–8. For other discussions of the Lost Cause phenomenon, see Connelly and Bellows, *God and General Longstreet;* Rosenburg, *Living Monuments;* and, more recently, Gallagher, *Myth of the Lost Cause and Civil War History*.

6. For a discussion of the work of Ladies' Memorial Associations, see Whites, *Civil War as a Crisis in Gender*, 160–98.

7. On changes in the celebration over time, see Foster, *Ghosts of the Confederacy*, 88–103.

8. On white northern attitudes toward southern whites, see Silber, *Romance of Reunion*, 143.

9. Historian Fred A. Bailey has written several articles examining pro-southern textbook campaigns, all of which basically assume that the movement was supported by both male and female Confederate organizations. As for the effectiveness of the SCV, Foster argues that it "never became an important group" (*Ghosts of the Confederacy*, 197). On New Men, see Doyle, *New Men, New Cities, New South*, and Gilmore, *Gender and Jim Crow*, 64.

10. Letter from UDC cofounder Anna Raines to Eliza Parsley, A. M. Raines to Mrs. Parsley, February 10, 1896, Parsley Papers, SHC. Biographies of UDC leaders appear in state organizational histories, and biographical information was also gleaned from state histories of the GFWC, whose leaders in the South were also active UDC members. See also Collier, *Biographies of Representative Women of the South*.

11. In chapter 3, class is described in more detail. On the Washington convention, see "United Daughters of the Confederacy Gather Here for Big Convention," *Washington Post*, November 10, 1912; "Hosts to the UDC: Mr. and Mrs. Taft Will Receive Delegates Nov. 14," ibid., November 4, 1912.

12. Reaction of African-American women's organizations to the UDC's proposed "mammy" monument can be found in Joan Marie Johnson, "'By Our People, for Our People': African American Clubwomen, the Frederick Douglass Home, and the Black Mammy Monument" (unpublished paper, 1999, in my possession). For a broader discussion of African-American responses to the Lost Cause, see Blight, *Frederick Douglass' Civil War*. Blight discusses further the impact of the Lost Cause on race relations and reconciliation in *Race and Reunion*, 255–99.

Chapter 2. The Sacred Trust

1. Kyle, "Incidents of Hospital Life," 40.

2. Ibid., 44–45.

3. "History of Confederate Memorial Work," *Confederate Veteran* (February 1898), 76 (hereafter *CV*).

4. Foster, *Ghosts of the Confederacy*, 38–45.

5. Whites, *The Civil War as a Crisis in Gender*, 160–98.

6. For a discussion of the changes in women's roles, see ibid. and Faust, "Altars of Sacrifice," 177–99. Florence Barlow, a member of the UDC in Louisville, Kentucky, served as the managing editor of *Lost Cause*, a magazine primarily for UDC members (hereafter *LC*). Her comments on men come from her editorial "Daughters of the Confederacy: Their Mission," *LC* (December 1900), 72.

7. Mrs. A. M'D. Wilson, "Memorial Day," *CV* (April 1919), 156.

8. Mrs. M. L. Shipp, "Women of North Carolina," *CV* (May 1898), 227; "Why the Ladies' Aid Societies, Ladies' Memorial Associations, Daughters of the Confederacy?" *CV* (March 1916), 110; and Foster, *Ghosts of the Confederacy*, 45.

9. On the shift in emphasis, see Foster, ibid., 87–101.

10. Ibid., 80; J. W. Sandell, "'New South' and the 'Lost Cause,'" *CV* (December 1912), 573; Sarah Brewer, "Recollections of Jefferson Davis," *CV* (April 1894), 6; Gaston, *The New South Creed*, 6–13.

11. Gaston, ibid. On the Lost Cause narrative, see Hale, *Making Whiteness*, 51–67; see also Hall, "'You Must Remember This.'"

12. Foster, *Ghosts of the Confederacy*, 98–101. Foster explains the movement to erect a monument to Robert E. Lee by placing Early at the center of activity. Events make it clear, however, that Janet Randolph influenced many decisions regarding the monument.

13. Regarding the founding of the Southern Historical Society, see *Southern Historical Society Papers* 39 (1914), 13. On the formation of the UCV and the return of Jefferson Davis to Confederate social circles, see Foster, *Ghosts of the Confederacy*, 96–98.

14. Poppenheim, *History of the UDC*, 2.

15. Jim Crow disfranchisement is discussed in Woodward, *The Strange Career of Jim Crow*; McMillen, *Dark Journey*; and Chafe, *Remembering Jim Crow*.

16. See Gilmore, *Gender and Jim Crow*.

17. Poppenheim, *History of the UDC*, 2.

18. Ibid.

19. Ibid., 3.

20. Mrs. W. J. Behan, "Confederated Southern Memorial Association," *CV* (July 1904), 33.

21. Mrs. L. H. Raines, "United Daughters of the Confederacy: Origin, History, and Growth of the Organization," *CV* (October 1898), 451–53. See also Poppenheim, *History of the UDC*, 4–9.

22. Information about Caroline Goodlett is drawn from "The President of the National Daughters of the Confederacy," *CV* (October 1894), 307; see also "UDC Origins," *CV* (October 1898), 451–53; Poppenheim, *History of the UDC*, 6–9; and "National Daughters of the Confederacy," *CV* (October 1894), 306.

23. "UDC Origins," ibid.; Poppenheim, ibid., 8.

24. Caroline Goodlett to Mrs. L. H. Raines, April 24, 1894, and Mrs. L. H. Raines to Mrs. M. C. Goodlett, April 29, 1894, as transcribed in the Mildred Lewis Rutherford Scrapbooks, vol. 2, 70–74, MOC.

25. Information on the gathering of women in Nashville in September 1894 is sketchy; however, the *Confederate Veteran* and the official history of the UDC by Poppenheim make clear that both Raines and Goodlett were involved in the organization of the UDC. See Poppenheim, *History of the UDC*, 9–10; "UDC Origins," *CV* (October 1898), 451–53; Report of the Committee of History, *Minutes of the Fifteenth Annual Convention (UDC)*, 232.

26. Poppenheim, *History of the UDC*, 9–12; *Minutes of the First Annual Convention of the Daughters of the Confederacy*, 1–3. Goodlett's comments appear in the Rutherford Scrapbooks, vol. 2, 81–82, MOC. Currie's wedding is described in *CV* (April 1911), 179–80.

27. The NDOC, later UDC, drew its memberships from the LMAs and the DOCs. The first generation of UDC, the focus of this study, represented older, experienced women, as well as younger women who were gaining experience in the new organization.

28. *Minutes of the First Annual Convention*, 1–3.

29. Ibid.

30. Historians Wilson, *Baptized in Blood*, Foster, *Ghosts of the Confederacy*, and Rosenburg, *Living Monuments*, all regard men as the leaders of the Confederate tradition.

31. *Minutes of the First Annual Convention*, 1–3; "Suggestions from the North Carolina Division to the National," n.d.; E. H. Parsley to Mrs. L. H. Raines, October 1 and 29, 1894, both in Parsley Papers, SHC.

32. *Minutes of the First Annual Convention*, 1–3.

33. E. H. Parsley to Mrs. L. H. Raines, October 1 and 29, 1894; A. M. Raines to E. H. Parsley, November 1, 1894, all in Parsley Papers, SHC.

34. C. M. Goodlett to E. H. Parsley, May 8, 1895, Parsley Papers, SHC.

35. A. M. Raines to Mrs. Parsley, February 10, 1896, Parsley Papers, SHC. Seventeen years later, eligibility was still an issue. President Virginia McSherry rendered a decision during her tenure in 1911 that a chapter did not have to accept a member "on the ethic principle that no voluntary association is compelled to receive as a member one who is morally or otherwise objectionable" (Report of the President-General, *Minutes of the Eighteenth Annual Convention*, 98–99). McSherry's successor, Rassie White of Tennessee, also recommended that "as the organization grows in strength, popularity and prominence, membership in it becomes more desirable, and therefore should be hedged about and protected by more stringent rules" (Report of the President-General, *Minutes of the Nineteenth Annual Convention*, 95).

36. "Suggestions from North Carolina Division to the National," n.d., Parsley Papers, SHC.

37. *Minutes of the First Annual Convention*, 1–3; *Minutes of the Second Annual Convention*, 10–11. For the purposes of this book, the "politics of the Lost Cause" suggests the use of political influence and contacts to achieve the goal of perpetuating Confederate culture. As it relates to the UDC, many of its projects (monuments, pensions, and widows' homes) received government funding as a direct result of the organization's political lobbying.

38. *Minutes of the First Annual Convention*, 1–3; *Minutes of the Second Annual Convention*, 10–11.

39. A. M. Raines to Mrs. N. V. Randolph, August 1, 1895, Parsley Papers, SHC. Raines continued to fulfill her duties as first vice president, though she obviously resented that Goodlett and the Nashville chapter were credited with the founding of the organization.

40. C.D.M. Goodlett to Mrs. Edwin G. Weed, 190[?], UDC Collection, MOC.

41. Caroline Goodlett to Anna Raines, December 31, 1900, Rutherford Scrapbooks, vol. 2, 112–17, MOC.

42. Ibid.

43. C.D.M. Goodlett to Mrs. Edwin G. Weed, 190[?], UDC Collection, MOC.

44. On the national women's club movement, see Karen J. Blair, *The Clubwoman as Feminist*. Southern white clubwomen's activities are described in Scott, *The Southern Lady;* Wedell, *Elite Women and the Reform Impulse in Memphis;* Turner, *Women, Culture, and Community;* and Sims, *The Power of Femininity in the New South.*

Chapter 3. The Rise of the UDC

1. "United Daughters of the South," *CV* (December 1895), 374–77; "Daughters of the Confederacy," *CV* (January 1897), 34; and "United Daughters Reunion,"

CV (October 1897), 498–503. Actual figures on the total UDC membership are unavailable for the first few years, but the published minutes of the annual conventions intermittently provide estimates of total membership. I have estimated 35,000 members by 1904 based on a report in 1902 that claimed 25,000, of which close to 5,000 were from Texas; "Daughters of the Confederacy," *CV* (January 1902), 9. At the 1913 general convention, President-General Rassie White claimed in her report that the UDC had a "membership of over 90,000" (*Minutes of the Twentieth Annual Convention,* 13). The figure of 100,000 is taken from the *Minutes of the Twenty-Fifth Annual Convention,* 324. The Tennessee UDC, for example, grew by 1,000 members from 1906 to 1907; see "The Tennessee Division, UDC," *CV* (June 1907), 301.

2. Membership numbers from the General Federation of Women's Clubs Membership Records (Directories), 1890–1910, GFWC Archives.

3. This total is derived from WCTU membership records for the states of Alabama, Arkansas, Georgia, Louisiana, Mississippi, North Carolina, South Carolina, Tennessee, Texas, and Virginia, as published in the *Women's Christian Temperance Union Convention Minutes for 1900,* facing p. 112.

4. The organization's annual meetings are known as "general conventions" and will be referred to as such throughout this book.

5. Historical Report, *Minutes of the Tenth Annual Convention,* 119.

6. "Convention Alabama Division UDC," *CV* (April 1898), 155; President-General's Report, *Minutes of the Seventh Annual Convention,* 98–99; Mildred Rutherford, "Confederate Monuments and Cemeteries," *CV* (January 1903), 17.

7. Kate Mason Rowland to Mrs. R. Halm and Kate Mason Rowland to Colonel Oswald Tilghman, in Kate Mason Rowland Letterbook, 1896–97, UDC Collection, MOC.

8. A. M. Raines to Mrs. Parsley, February 10, 1896, Parsley Papers, SHC.

9. Quotation from McSherry, President-General's Report, *Minutes of the Eighteenth Annual Convention,* 98–99; quotation from White, President-General's Report, *Minutes of the Nineteenth Annual Convention,* 95.

10. Virginia Redditt Price, "Why I Am a UDC," *Our Heritage* (September 1913), 2; Caroline Goodlett to Mrs. L. H. Raines, April 24, 1894 (TS), Rutherford Scrapbook, Vol. 2, MOC. Historian Anastatia Sims found that in North Carolina, the UDC was the most popular of the women's voluntary organizations, often affecting membership rolls in other organizations (*The Power of Femininity in the New South*).

11. Address of Mrs. Alexander White, *Minutes of the Twentieth Annual Convention,* 12–13.

12. Ibid., 13.

13. Raines quoted from "Daughters of the Confederacy," *CV* (January 1897), 34. Woman suffrage provoked a hostile reaction from white southerners because it threatened "Southern civilization," where traditional "southern ladies" played an important role in maintaining the status quo. Historian Marjorie Spruill Wheeler argues that southern suffragists were held "hostage" by the limited thinking imposed upon them by the Lost Cause; see Wheeler, *New Women of the New South*, 33–37. Henderson quoted from "United Daughters of the Confederacy," *CV* (October 1907), 440.

14. Hallie Alexander Rounsaville of Georgia, who served as state president and then president-general from 1901 to 1903, was a charter member of the national DAR.

15. "The President of the NDOC," *CV* (October 1894), 307; "The Daughter of the Confederacy," *CV* (February 1901), 36; "Founder of the UDC," *CV* (November 1914), 496; Mrs. C. M. Goodlett to Mrs. Edwin G. Weed, ca. 1900, UDC Collection, MOC. Additional information on Goodlett can be found on the Internet at http://www.hqudc.org/Founder.htm.

16. *CV* (July 1909), 310; *CV* (December 1909), 590; Mrs. James Britton Gantt, "Mrs. Cornelia Branch Stone," *CV* (May 1911), 210. Stone's predecessor, Lizzie George Henderson, was president of the Women's Missionary Union as well as the Greenwood Woman's Club.

17. William Howard Taft hosted a White House reception for the entire UDC delegation when the organization held its annual convention in Washington, D.C., in 1912.

18. On Virginia Clay Clopton, see her memoir, *A Belle of the Fifties;* on Rebecca Felton, see Whites, "Rebecca Latimer Felton and the Problem of 'Protection' in the New South"; Gantt's quote is from "Mrs. Cornelia Branch Stone," *CV* (May 1911), 210. See also McArthur, *Creating the New Woman*, 3–5.

19. Most UDC members revered the first KKK, and the organization was often included in their articles on the Lost Cause. Laura Martin Rose of West Point, Mississippi, wrote a primer for children on the KKK. The Daughters generally distanced themselves from the second Klan of the early twentieth century, primarily because of what they considered class differences between the leaders of the first and second Klans.

20. Hale, *Making Whiteness*, 43–75; Hall, "'You Must Remember This.'" On emulating antebellum women, see McArthur, *Creating the New Woman*, 3.

21. Information on presidents-general has been gathered from the following sources: "Elizabeth George Henderson," Subject File, MDAH; "Mrs. Lizzie George Henderson," *CV* (December 1905); on Virginia Faulkner McSherry, see *CV* (April 1916), 152; "Daisy McLaurin Stevens," Subject File, MDAH; "New President Gen-

eral UDC," *Our Heritage* (November 1913), 4. Additional information on UDC presidents can be found in Collier, *Representative Women of the South*, and LaCavera, "Ex-Presidents General," *UDC Magazine* (special issue, September 1994).

22. Thomas Connelly and Barbara L. Bellows mistakenly identify the early UDC as "gray-haired" (*God and General Longstreet*, 2).

23. Bailey, "Mildred Lewis Rutherford and the Patrician Cult of the Old South," *Georgia Historical Quarterly* 77 (1994), 509–35; Collier, *Representative Women of the South*, 147–48; Genealogy and Biography, Mildred Lewis Rutherford Collection, UGA. Rutherford was also crowned "Patron Saint of the UDC." Additional biographical information appears in LaCavera, "Mildred Lewis Rutherford," *UDC Magazine* (February 1992), 14.

24. Hale, *Making Whiteness*, 61–62; Rutherford's addresses and speeches are collected in Mildred L. Rutherford Collection, UGA.

25. Circular, n.d., "Observations and Comment," by James Callaway, in Rutherford Scrapbooks, UGA. Callaway writes that Rutherford "gave an address before a committee of the House of Representatives."

26. Rutherford, "Address to the Georgia House of Representatives," handwritten, Rutherford Scrapbooks, UGA.

27. "Address Delivered by Miss Mildred Lewis Rutherford, Historian General, United Daughters of the Confederacy," New Willard Hotel, Washington, D.C. (Athens, Ga.: McGregor, 1912), 19.

28. Wheeler, *New Women of the New South*, 3–37.

29. "Miss Lumpkin to Georgia Veterans," *CV* (February 1904), 69–70; historian Jacquelyn Dowd Hall analyzes Elizabeth Lumpkin's role in the Lost Cause celebration in her article "'You Must Remember This,'" 452–57.

30. "Miss Lumpkin to Georgia Veterans," ibid.

31. "Address by Miss Elizabeth Lumpkin," *CV* (July 1905), 298–99.

32. Ibid., 299.

33. *Minutes of the Fifteenth Annual Convention*, 11; "The Women of the Confederacy," *LC* (October 1902), 37. This article describes the women as "fearless, yet shrinking; bold, yet timid, unyielding, yet gentle."

34. "United Daughters Reunion," *CV* (October 1897), 502.

35. Florence Barlow, "Daughters of the Confederacy: Their Mission," *LC* (December 1900), 72.

36. References to men and women who grew up in the Old South and went on to defend the Confederacy are central to Lost Cause ideology. On the development of "faithful slave" fiction, see Litwack, *Been in the Storm So Long*, chap. 1.

37. Men who were eligible to join the SCV were less likely to join it as women of the same generation were to join the UDC. And, as Gaines Foster has noted,

the SCV membership "never became an important group" (*Ghosts of the Confederacy*, 197). The UDC and the UCV were the organizations that essentially sustained the Lost Cause tradition. For discussions of the ideal woman of the antebellum South, see Scott, *The Southern Lady;* Fox-Genovese, *Within the Plantation Household;* Clinton, *The Plantation Mistress;* Rable, *Civil Wars;* Wheeler, *New Women of the New South,* 5–7; and Faust, *Mothers of Invention.*

38. For the purpose of this study, "New Men" refers to those men who were sons of Confederate veterans but who may or may not have been members of the SCV. They were men of the same generation as those women who joined the UDC. The UDC often referred to these men as descendants of Confederate veterans who had turned their backs on their heritage in their quest to make money. I refer to them as "New" because the UDC often remarked on the differences between these men and the generation of their fathers, men of the Old South. Other definitions of "New Men" can be found in the study of rank-and-file memberships in the 1890s North Carolina state legislature by Billings, *Planters in the Making of a "New South,"* and Woodward, *Origins of the New South.* Glenda Gilmore refers to these men as "New White Men" in *Gender and Jim Crow,* 64–66. Donald H. Doyle argues that "New Men" in the South's urban centers were not "new" in the sense that they were younger than members of the old planter class, but "new" in that they were self-made men who had earned their wealth since the war through business, and not agrarian, investments (*New Men, New Cities, New South,* 87–96).

39. On nationalism, Anglo-Saxonism, and empire, see Wilson, *Baptized in Blood,* 163; Gilmore, *Gender and Jim Crow,* 62–63; and Silber, *The Romance of Reunion,* 174–78. On "manliness," see Bederman, *"Manliness" and Civilization,* 6–7. Historian David Blight also argues that African Americans became "sacrificial offerings on the altar of reunion" (*Race and Reunion,* 139).

40. Gilmore, *Gender and Jim Crow,* 64–67.

41. "A Model Appeal: What a Daughter Says," *CV* (September 1911), 416; Judge J. M. Dickinson, "Women and Men of the South," *CV* (November 1909), 537; "What May Be Expected of Our Young Men," *CV* (February 1912), 56.

42. "What May Be Expected of Our Young Men," ibid.

43. Mrs. Thomas Taylor, "South Carolina Daughters," *CV* (January 1897), 14.

44. Herbert Mitchell, "A Plea to the Sons of Veterans," *CV* (October 1909), 484–85; a similar opinion was expressed in "General Evans to Sons and Grandsons," *CV* (January 1910), 3.

45. Doyle, *New Men, New Cities, New South,* 87–96.

46. For further discussion of Confederate men's failure as seen by New White Men, see Gilmore, *Gender and Jim Crow,* 65–67.

47. Henderson, "United Daughters of the Confederacy," *CV* (June 1906), 245–46; see also Mrs. Alexander White, "Greeting and Counsel with the Daughters," *CV* (March 1913), 250.

48. "Miss Lumpkin to Georgia Veterans," *CV* (February 1904), 69–70; Lost Cause periodicals often showered women of the UDC with compliments for emulating the women of the Confederate generation.

Chapter 4. The Monument Builders

1. White, Report of the President-General, *Minutes of the Nineteenth Annual Convention*, 95. For an analysis of monument building in the United States, see Savage, *Standing Soldiers, Kneeling Slaves*. H. E. Gulley makes the point that blacks did not participate in the celebration ("Women and the Lost Cause," 125–41). The fact is that they did participate, though perhaps unwillingly, as they provided the workforce that put the monuments into place.

2. Katie Behan, president of the CSMA, which formed in 1900, remarked that there had been "renewed interest in local memorial work" since the founding of the UDC. See "Women Who Meet with Veterans," *CV* (March 1903), 103.

3. Figures on monument building are from Winberry, "'Lest We Forget,'" 110; estimates of UDC membership appear in the official minutes of general conventions and in *CV*.

4. Cabell, "The Jefferson Davis Monument," *CV* (June 1899), 253.

5. Ibid.

6. "The Jefferson Davis Memorial," *CV* (May 1900), 209; "The Jefferson Davis Monument," *CV* (June 1900), 255.

7. "The Jefferson Davis Monument," ibid.; "The Confederate Memorial Association," *CV* (February 1913), 72. Behan describes in the article how the CSMA provided "material aid" in building the Davis monument.

8. *Minutes of the Fourteenth Annual Convention*, 5, 14. The general organization was approached to raise money for the Stone Mountain, Georgia, memorial, but refused because of commitments to Shiloh and Arlington. The Stone Mountain memorial became primarily a project of the Georgia Division UDC.

9. Greeting from the New President-General, ibid., 5; Report of the ACMA, *Minutes of the Fifteenth Annual Convention*, 275–78; Foster, *Ghosts of the Confederacy*, 153–54. On the history of the Arlington monument, see Cox, "The Confederate Monument at Arlington: A Token of Reconciliation," 199–218.

10. *Minutes of the Fourteenth Annual Convention*, 5, 24.

11. *Minutes of the Thirteenth Annual Convention*, 59; *Minutes of the Fourteenth Annual Convention*, 310.

12. Report of the Chairman of the Executive Committee, *Minutes of the Sixteenth Annual Convention,* 276–80.

13. Mrs. J. W. Irwin, "Our Neglect of Shiloh National Park," *CV* (November 1904), 537–38; "State Monument at Shiloh," *CV* (February 1907), 62.

14. White, "The Shiloh Monument to Confederates," *CV* (April 1908), 169; White, "History of the Shiloh Monument Undertaking," *CV* (May 1910), 198–99; "Initial Work for the Shiloh Monument," *CV* (November 1912), 500; Report of the SMC, *Minutes of the Fourteenth Annual Convention,* 236–39.

15. McSherry, "Construction of Arlington Monument," *CV* (April 1911), 147; "Design for Shiloh Monument Accepted," *CV* (December 1914), 542; ACMA Report, *Minutes of the Twentieth Annual Convention,* 339–44. For information on Moses Ezekiel and the creation of the Arlington Monument, see Gutmann and Chyet, eds., *Moses Jacob Ezekiel,* 438–41.

16. "Dedication of the Monument at Shiloh," *CV* (June 1917), 250.

17. The original contract for the work on the Arlington monument was $35,000, but the UDC pledged $50,000 and eventually raised over $60,000. See Report of the Chairman of the Executive Committee, ACMA, *Minutes of the Eighteenth Annual Convention,* 296–97. According to EH.net, a website administered by economists, the $70,000 spent on the Jefferson Davis monument is equivalent to $1.3 million in 2002. These calculations are based on the Commodity Price Index (CPI).

18. Untitled, *CV* (April 1900), 173; "Confederate Monument at San Antonio," *CV* (June 1900), 261; "Entertainment by Nashville Daughters," *CV* (November 1900), 503.

19. "The Confederate Monument at Raleigh," *CV* (May 1898), 229; Report of the Mississippi Division, *Minutes of the Thirteenth Annual Convention,* 263. In another example, the Hattiesburg, Mississippi, chapter of the UDC petitioned its board of supervisors for $10,000 for a monument fund. State division President Daisy McLaurin Stevens noted that it was "an unprecedented amount given by a board for this purpose, but so strictly Confederate a county bearing the name of [Nathan Bedford] Forrest," it was almost expected (untitled speech, ca. 1908, Daisy McLaurin Stevens Papers, MDAH). See also "An Act Relating to the Erection of a Monument to the Memory of Confederate Soldiers in Henderson, North Carolina," *Public Laws of North Carolina,* Session 1909, 839.

20. Mrs. W. J. Behan to Major-General J. B. Gordon, December 25, 1902, LHAC-UDC Papers, Tulane; "Jefferson Davis Monument," *CV* (November 1901), 489.

21. "Shiloh Post Cards: Attention UDC," *CV* (August 1911), 363; Report of the SMC, *Minutes of the Fifteenth Annual Convention,* 258–60; *Minutes of the Eigh-*

teenth Annual Convention, 277–81; and Minutes of the Nineteenth Annual Convention, 92.

22. "Confederate Christmas Seals," CV (November 1910), 500; Minutes of the Seventeenth Annual Convention, 88.

23. "Sharing Their Profits," CV (June 1912), 298.

24. "A Stirring Appeal," LC (February 1903), 103; "The Davis Memorial," CV (April 1903), 39; "The Davis Monument," CV (May 1903), 56.

25. "The Jefferson Davis Monument," CV (March 1902), 133; "Last Appeal for Monument Fund," LC (June 1902), 164.

26. ACMA Report, Minutes of the Twentieth Annual Convention, 339–44.

27. "Our Sacred Cause at Dallas, Texas: Dedication of the Grand Monument," CV (June 1898), 299–301.

28. Ibid. See also Henderson, "United Daughters of the Confederacy," CV (August 1907), 348–50; "Confederate Monument at Henderson" CV (April 1911), 170; "The Jefferson Davis Monument on the Jefferson Davis Parkway, New Orleans," CV (May 1911), 197–203; "The Monument at Arlington," CV (July 1914), 292–96.

29. "Our Sacred Cause at Dallas, Texas: Dedication of the Grand Monument," CV (June 1898), 299–301.

30. Ockendon, "Monument at Montgomery," CV (July 1899), 292; "Confederate Monument at Huntsville," CV (December 1905), 539; "Unveiling of Monument at Mt. Pleasant," CV (June 1908), 270–71.

31. "The Jefferson Davis Monument . . . New Orleans," CV (May 1911), 197–203; "Confederate Monument at Huntsville," CV (December 1905), 539.

32. This summary of monument building and its cultural significance is informed by Winberry, "'Lest We Forget,'" 107–121; Gulley, "Women and the Lost Cause," 125–41; Davis, "Empty Eyes, Marble Hand," 2–21; Radford, "Identity and Tradition in the Post–Civil War South," 91–103; Kubassek, "'Ask Us Not to Forget,'" 155–70; Bishir, "Landmarks of Power: Building a Southern Past," 5–45; Bodnar, Remaking America; Foster, Ghosts of the Confederacy, 127–44. The use of official or political landscape derives from Jackson, Discovering the Vernacular Landscape, who defines it as a landscape that "fosters order, security, and continuity of society and remind[s] people of rights, obligations, and history" (6). For a discussion of the ways in which landscapes are used to make political statements, see Schama, Landscape and Memory, 12.

33. Explanations for the increase in monument building are outlined in Winberry, "'Lest We Forget,'" 107–21; Foster, Ghosts of the Confederacy, 13. Gulley does recognize the impact of the UDC on monument building, but as a rule, historians have not. Winberry states (110) that approximately 93 percent of the monuments

erected in town squares can be dated after 1895, the majority of them built between 1903 and 1912—a period of significant growth for the UDC, as membership expanded from approximately 30,000 to nearly 80,000.

34. White, "History of Shiloh Monument Undertaking," *CV* (May 1910), 198–
99; "The Shiloh Monument," *CV* (April 1911), 149; Report of the SMC, *Minutes of
the Fourteenth Annual Convention*, 236–39.

35. ACMA Report, *Minutes of the Twentieth Annual Convention*, 339–44; Report
of the SMC, *Minutes of the Sixteenth Annual Convention*, 267–68.

36. "Daughters at Franklin: Address Made for Them at Monument Dedication," *CV* (April 1900), 172; "Georgia Daughters' Annual Convention," *CV* (January 1910), 9.

37. "Arrive for Unveiling," *Washington Post*, June 4, 1914; "Child to Bare Memorial," ibid., June 3, 1914.

38. Report of the President-General, *Minutes of the Twentieth Annual Convention*, 102–3; "The Monument at Arlington," *CV* (July 1914), 292–96; "Gray and
Blue Join," *Washington Post*, June 5, 1914.

39. Address of Daisy Stevens, "The Arlington Monument," *CV* (August 1914),
346–47; "The Monument at Arlington," *CV* (June 1914), 292–96; "Gray and Blue
Join," ibid.

40. "The Monument at Arlington," ibid.; "Turn Your Faces to the Future . . . ,"
Washington Post, June 5, 1914.

41. *History of the Arlington Confederate Monument*, 77. See also Cox, "The Confederate Monument at Arlington."

Chapter 5. Confederate Progressives

1. Caroline Goodlett to Mrs. L. H. Raines, April 24, 1894, Rutherford Scrapbook, vol. 2, MOC.

2. President-General's Address, *Minutes of the Twentieth Annual Convention*, 13.

3. Poppenheim, *History of the UDC*, 2–10.

4. Rebecca Montgomery describes the impact of the Lost Cause on Progressive
reform in Georgia in *The Politics of Education in the New South* (forthcoming).

5. On the emergence of social welfare in the region, see Grantham, *Southern
Progressivism*, 217–22. Soldiers' homes for Confederate veterans are the subject of
Rosenburg, *Living Monuments*.

6. The term *Confederate progressivism* is used here to distinguish the benevolent activity within the Lost Cause celebration from the larger progressive movement. Southern progressivism is analyzed briefly by Woodward, *Origins of the
New South*, 369–95, where he coins the term "for whites only," and more fully by
Grantham, *Southern Progressivism*, and Link, *The Paradox of Southern Progressiv-

ism. For a discussion of southern women and progressivism, see Scott, *The Southern Lady*, and Wheeler, *New Women of the New South*, 10–12.

7. Historian LeeAnn Whites has argued that LMAs, the primary Confederate organizations for women prior to the UDC, were part of early southern progressivism. Whites's essay "Stand by Your Man" can be found in Pope, *Women in the American South*.

8. Biographical material on Caroline Meriwether Lewis Goodlett emerges from "The President of the National Daughters of the Confederacy," *CV* (October 1894), 307; "UDC Origins," *CV* (October 1898), 451–53; "National Daughters of the Confederacy," *CV* (October 1894), 306; Poppenheim, *History of the UDC*, 2–9; and J. Turner, *The Courageous Caroline*.

9. Poppenheim, ibid., 95–127.

10. Rosenburg, *Living Monuments*, 3–12.

11. "What the South Is Doing for Her Veterans," *CV* (June 1915), 255; Rosenburg, ibid., 30.

12. W. P. Barlow, "History of the Missouri Confederate Home," *CV* (October 1893), 302. In *Living Monuments*, Rosenburg gives women little credit for the soldiers' home movement and suggests they were nothing more than a nuisance; see esp. 141–42.

13. *Minutes of the Second Annual Convention*, 10–11.

14. Rosenburg, *Living Monuments*, 141–42. In Rosenburg's account of Mississippi's soldiers' home, Beauvoir, he describes Mary Kimbrough as a minor figure in the establishment of the home. In fact, Kimbrough played a key role, working with Varina Davis on a plan to sell her home for the purpose of housing indigent veterans.

15. The UDC was not the only women's organization involved in the care of aging soldiers. LMAs and later the CSMA (founded in 1900) were both dedicated to preserving the memory of "Johnny Reb" by providing for him in his old age.

16. Rutherford, "Confederate Monuments and Cemeteries," *CV* (January 1903), 17. Rutherford's comments about paying tribute to women were made in the context of erecting monuments.

17. *History of the Home for Needy Confederate Women*, 11.

18. Ibid., 41.

19. Ibid., 28; Rosenburg discusses the same sort of paternalism in soldiers' homes (*Living Monuments*, 73–92). Admission qualifications are explained in "The United Daughters of the Confederacy," *CV* (January 1903), 17.

20. *Lost Cause* was published in Louisville, Kentucky, beginning in 1898. It was an illustrated monthly journal similar to *Confederate Veteran*. Ben LaBree was the magazine's original editor, but by 1902 Florence Barlow and Henrietta Mor-

gan Duke (wife of Confederate General Basil Duke) became owners. The two women, especially Barlow, wrote articles and editorials and solicited articles from women in Confederate circles.

21. Barlow, "Three Hundred Confederate Women," *LC* (October 1902), 38.

22. Barlow, "No Home Yet for Widows of Confederate Veterans," *LC* (April 1902), 88. Barlow reminded men that the South was not "poverty stricken." Certainly there was no lack of money for other Lost Cause projects. Men and women had raised $200,000 for the Battle Abbey, a museum to preserve Confederate relics. The fund to build a monument to women, during these same years, was expected to reach $50,000.

23. Ibid., 88.

24. For information on the Texas home, see "A Texas Home for Confederate Women," *CV* (February 1905), 71; "Home for Confederate Women of Texas," *CV* (April 1904), 150; "Home for Wives and Widows in Texas," *CV* (March 1906); "Texas Confederate Woman's Home," *CV* (June 1914), 273. On the North Carolina home, see "Confederate Woman's Home in North Carolina," *CV* (February 1916), 53; McKeithan, *History of the Confederate Woman's Home*. The State of North Carolina funded its Confederate Woman's Home until 1982.

25. Report of the Mississippi Division, *Minutes of the Twelfth Annual Convention*, 164–65.

26. Resolution of Mrs. Faison of North Carolina, *Minutes of the Fourteenth Annual Convention*, 27.

27. "The Women Saved the Day," *Fayetteville Observer*, March 27, 1915.

28. Address of C. Helen Plane, *Minutes of the Seventeenth Annual Convention*, 50–58.

29. Ibid. Information on the Louise Home and William Corcoran from *Dictionary of American Biography*, vol. 4, 440.

30. *Minutes of the Seventh Annual Convention*, 57.

31. Ibid.; Poppenheim, *History of the UDC*, 199.

32. Report of the Relief Committee, *Minutes of the Nineteenth Annual Convention*, 214.

33. Ibid.

34. Report on the Establishment of Departments of History, *Minutes of the Thirteenth Annual Convention*, 218. While Cameron's comments were in regard to the establishment of a department of archives and history, her comments reveal that the UDC was aware of its political influence.

35. Poppenheim, *History of the UDC*, 95, 97.

36. Ibid., 115–17, lists 192 schools and colleges where students received UDC scholarships between 1907 and 1929.

37. Whites, "Rebecca Latimer Felton and the Problem of 'Protection' in the New South," 41–61.

38. "Address Made in Baltimore before UDC National Convention" (1897), Felton Papers, UGA.

39. Address of Mrs. William H. Felton, *Minutes of the Fourth Annual Convention*, 34–37.

40. Untitled handwritten speech, n.d., Felton Papers, UGA. This speech was probably given to the Georgia UDC, but it includes many of the arguments she made at the general convention in Baltimore.

41. Ibid.

42. Poppenheim, *History of the UDC*, 95–127.

43. School reform and anti-illiteracy campaigns in the South are examined in Link, *The Paradox of Southern Progressivism*, 139–42, and Grantham, *Southern Progressivism*, 264.

44. Seth Shepard to the Trustees and Electors of the Southern Industrial Education Association, March 19, 1907, Florence Butler Papers, SHC.

45. Martha S. Gielow, "Daughters of the Confederacy, Confederate Veterans, and People of the South," circular, May 1906, ibid.

46. Ibid.; see also Gielow, "Southern Industrial Education," *CV* (March 1906), 113–14.

47. Gielow, ibid., 114.

48. "To the United Daughters of the Confederacy: Replying to Mrs. Lizzie George Henderson's Letter of May 1906," circular, n.d., Butler Papers, SHC. Henderson's comments derive from this source. In a letter from Florence Butler to Rassie White, Butler tells White that Gielow has asked the UDC to allow her to address them for ten minutes at the 1912 general convention. Butler complained that Gielow "does not know how to speak for ten minutes. If she ever gets the floor, you have to have her taken down by main force" (Florence Butler to Mrs. Alexander White, September 10, 1912, Butler Papers, SHC).

49. Elizabeth Lumpkin Glenn discusses industrial education in "The Land of Our Desire," *CV* (November 1906), 495–96; Varina Davis's original will included turning Beauvoir into an industrial school (Varina Davis Will, August 12, 1901, Varina Davis Papers, Beauvoir). Anne S. Green of Culpepper, Virginia, also submitted an article in support of helping children who were being put to work in "the mills and factories which are springing up in the South," in "Southern Industrial Schools," *CV* (February 1901), 85. Finally, there was also the Berry Industrial School, founded by Martha Berry in Rome, Georgia, in 1902. For more on Berry, see "Berry Industrial School, Rome, GA," *CV* (November 1910), 526, and Martha Berry to Mrs. Morris, October 19, 1920, UDC, Frank A. Montgomery Chapter Papers, MDAH.

50. Message from Caroline Goodlett, *Minutes of the Fifteenth Annual Convention*, 23.

51. Ibid.

52. For additional information on Mary Poppenheim, see Joan Johnson, "'This Wonderful Dream Nation': Black and White South Carolina Women, Race, Place, and Southern Identity in the New South" (Ph.D. diss., University of California, Los Angeles, 1998).

53. Poppenheim, *History of the UDC*, 95–96.

54. J. Foust, president of the North Carolina State Normal and Industrial College, to Ella Brodnax, August 12, 1908, Brodnax Papers, Duke.

55. Mary S. Mauney to Ella Brodnax, June 1, 1908, and Sallie Y. Faison to Ella B. Brodnax, August 12, 1908, ibid.

56. "Peabody College for Teachers," *CV* (December 1906), 568.

Chapter 6. Combating "Wicked Falsehoods"

1. "Address of Miss Adelia Dunovant," *LC* (January 1902), 91–93. The Wilmington race riot is analyzed in a series of essays in Cecelski and Tyson, eds., *Democracy Betrayed*.

2. The objectives of the UDC as set out in its constitution may be found in the *Minutes of the First Annual Convention*, 1–3.

3. Ibid., 2–3. Frederick Douglass sought to preserve a memory of the Civil War that celebrated emancipation and the addition of constitutional amendments granting black men citizenship. He was engaged in a battle for memory of the Civil War that was won by Lost Cause advocates in his own time. See Blight, "For Something Beyond the Battlefield," 1156–78.

4. The Southern Historical Society (SHS) was organized on May 1, 1869, in New Orleans. Its headquarters moved to Richmond in 1873, and publication of its papers began in 1876; see *SHS Papers* (1914), 213; Foster, *Ghosts of the Confederacy*, 54. Historian Gary Gallagher credits Jubal Early's efforts to shape public memory as the reason behind the longevity of the Lost Cause narrative. Early's own crusade was clearly boosted by the efforts of the UDC, a fact Gallagher does not acknowledge in *Lee and His Generals in War and Memory*, 199–216.

5. While the Historical Committee officially represented the UCV, its efforts were primarily directed to the cause of school textbooks. I do not argue that the UCV was insignificant in this area, and in chapter 7, I address the textbook issue thoroughly. In this chapter I focus on the preservation, promotion, and writing of "impartial" history. In this endeavor the UDC did not limit its efforts to school texts, and it proved more creative in preserving Confederate culture, both literary and material, than its male counterparts. On the collection of women's war reminiscences, see Division Reports, *Minutes of the Fifteenth Annual Convention*, 245.

UDC divisions, including the District of Columbia, Kentucky, and Missouri, all reported collecting personal reminiscences of the "women of the sixties"; see also "Work and Spirit of the United Daughters," *CV* (January 1913), 17. In this article Mrs. W. B. Pritchard of the California Division maintains that the Daughters "should record the work of [their] women and what they did during the war and through Reconstruction times."

6. Report of the Historical Committee, *Minutes of the Sixth Annual Convention*, 68–69; "Address of Miss Adelia Dunovant," *LC* (January 1902), 91–93; comments from Waddell in *CV* (November 1901), 486. On the establishment of the committee, see Poppenheim, *History of the UDC*, 135.

7. Address of Francis Nichols, *Minutes of the Ninth Annual Convention*, 10.

8. Henderson, "United Daughters of the Confederacy," *CV* (February 1906), 58; "Historical Report, UDC, 1903," *Minutes of the Tenth Annual Convention*, 122.

9. *Minutes of the Sixth Annual Convention*, 68–69.

10. On the SCV pledge to establish official archives, see "Historical Records to Be Preserved," *CV* (August 1904), 374–75; Resolution of Mrs. Alexander B. White, *Minutes of the Twelfth Annual Convention*, 237.

11. On collecting reminiscences, see *Minutes of the Fourteenth Annual Convention*, 211. The North Carolina Division reported at that convention that its interviews with veterans had been sent to the secretary of state until a Department of Archives and History was "established in fire-proof buildings." Mildred Rutherford quoted from "Requests by the UDC Historian General," *CV* (February 1912), 55.

12. "UDC Building at Jamestown Exposition," *CV* (November 1906), 487.

13. "A Plea for the Richmond Museum," *CV* (August 1897), 416. On the creation of the Confederate Museum, see Coski and Feely, "A Monument to Southern Womanhood," 131–64.

14. "Confederate Relics Hall," *CV* (June 1900), 266.

15. Report of the Mississippi Division, *Minutes of the Seventeenth Annual Convention*, 72; "Texas War Relics to Be Preserved," *CV* (April 1904), 176. On the First White House Association, see "Convention Alabama Division UDC," *CV* (April 1898), 155, and "First White House of the Confederacy," *CV* (January 1904), cover page; Howard, "Alabama Museums," 83–93.

16. Report of the Mississippi Division, *Minutes of the Sixteenth Annual Convention*, 7.

17. "The Restoration of Mississippi's Old Capitol," *Our Heritage: Souvenir Edition* (1952), 12; Report of the Mississippi Division, *Minutes of the Twenty-Third Annual Convention*, 366.

18. *Mississippi Division Minutes* (1914), 86–87; ibid. (1915), 69; Report of the

Mississippi Division, ibid. The Old Capitol currently serves as the home of the state's museum of history.

19. "Our Own Sentiments," *LC* (June 1903), 72; Tennie Pinkerton Dozier, "Southern History: Tennessee," *CV* (May 1908), 201.

20. Cornelia Stone's comments appear in *Minutes of the Eighth Annual Convention*, 71–72.

21. Dunovant's report appears ibid., 125–27.

22. *Richmond Times-Dispatch*, May 28, 1920, CMLS Scrapbook, MOC. Her father was Colonel Charles Stephen Morgan.

23. *Report of the Historian General*, pamphlet, Virginia Morgan Robinson to the General Convention of the UDC, Houston, Texas, October 19, 1909, 4.

24. Virginia Morgan Robinson to Mary Stribling, September 2, 16, 1910, Stribling Papers, Duke.

25. Mrs. J. Enders Robinson to Miss Mary C. Stribling, June 28, 1910, ibid.

26. For an analysis of Mildred Rutherford, see Hale, *Making Whiteness*, 92–113, and Bailey, "Mildred Lewis Rutherford and the Patrician Cult of the Old South," 509–35.

27. Rutherford reported to the Dallas convention that she had written "more than 562 letters, 640 postcards, and has mailed over 51,160 pamphlets" in her Report of the Historian General, *Minutes of the Twenty-Third Convention*, 176–81. Between 1911 and 1916, Rutherford published five of her lengthy speeches to the UDC, including *The South in the Building of the Nation* (1912), *Thirteen Periods of United States History* (1913), *Wrongs of History Righted* (1914), *Historical Sins of Omission and Commission* (1915), and *Civilization of the Old South* (1916).

28. Report of the Historian General, *Minutes of the Twenty-First Annual Convention*, 156–62.

29. Gallagher, *Lee and His Generals in War and Memory*, 222. Gallagher writes that there is no similar literature on Ulysses S. Grant, due, in part, to his personal reputation and the scandals of his presidency.

30. Mildred Rutherford created a program of study for UDC members that asked questions about Confederate history, and suggestions were made for a course of study. "Monthly Programs for UDC Chapter," *CV* (February 1915), 62; "Jefferson Davis," *CV* (July 1898), 295.

31. Hume, "Our 'Black Mammy,'" *CV* (September 1898), 476; Rutherford, "Extract from 'Wrongs of History Righted,'" *CV* (October 1915), 443–44; "Requests by UDC Historian General," *CV* (February 1912), 54–55.

32. Hume, "Our 'Black Mammy,'" ibid.; Rutherford, "The South of Yesterday" (pamphlet), 6.

33. Lost Cause celebrants remembered the Old South as a simpler place and

time, where racial strife and class antagonisms were rarely known to exist. The UDC, like other Confederate organizations, believed there were cultural values associated with the Old South that were useful for the twentieth century. The Daughters wanted to preserve as much of Confederate culture as possible for the New South, which was, in part, a reaction to modernization and social change. Preserving existing cultural values as a reaction to modernization and social change outside the United States is documented in Herf, *Reactionary Modernism*. See also Cornelia Branch Stone, "Vivid Reminiscences of the Old Plantation," *CV* (December 1912), 568–69.

34. Stone, ibid., 569.

35. Rutherford, "Extract from 'Wrongs of History Righted,'" *CV* (October 1915), 443–44.

36. Ibid., 444.

37. Ulrich Bonnell Phillips's *American Negro Slavery* (1918) gave Lost Cause mythology about slavery in the Old South some professional credibility. The Dunning School, in which Phillips trained, had for many years been producing scholarship supporting what Lost Cause advocates perpetuated. Kirby, in *Darkness at the Dawning*, 90–95, writes that Phillips's work had revolutionary effects in the field of history because it defined slavery as a means of racial control. Even without Phillips's writing, the Daughters had proved their effectiveness in promoting the same ideas among children.

38. Mildred Rutherford referred to Reconstruction as "a period of history about which the South still feels sore," in *Historical Sins of Omission and Commission*, 25; see also "Freedman's Bureau," *Our Heritage* (December 14), 1.

39. Higgins, "Reconstruction Period under Military Rule: Infamous Acts of the Year 1867," *Our Heritage* (March 1915), 1; Rutherford, *Historical Sins of Omission and Commission*, 28.

40. Higgins, ibid.; Rutherford, ibid.

41. Foner, *Reconstruction*, 342; Trelease, *White Terror*.

42. "Mrs. S.E.F. Rose," Subject File, MDAH (Rose's essays appeared in the *Confederate Veteran* and were also published as pamphlets); *The Ku Klux Klan or Invisible Empire* (1913) is her primer for children.

43. Rose, "The Ku-Klux Klan and 'The Birth of a Nation,'" *CV* (April 1916), 157–59. Mildred Rutherford added that D. W. Griffith's film *The Birth of a Nation* told only "half of the story" (*Historical Sins of Omission and Commission*, 25).

44. Rose, ibid., 158.

45. Ibid., 159.

46. Rose was not alone in her defense of the Klan of Reconstruction, but her booklet was published widely and used to raise money to build a monument at

her state's soldiers' home in Biloxi. What is striking about Rose is not only her influence in her own state, where her book was adopted as a supplementary reader in the schools, but her influence over a much wider audience, the thousands of UDC members she represented as historian-general in 1916. On the official endorsement of Rose's book, see *Minutes of the Twentieth Annual Convention*, 39. Rutherford writes that Rose is an authority on the subject of the KKK and asks that her book be placed in the public schools; see *Historical Sins of Omission and Commission*, 29.

47. On recording women's role during the Civil War, see article II of the UDC constitution, in *Minutes of the Second Annual Convention*, 10–11; see also "United Daughters of the Confederacy: Origin and Object," *CV* (September 1902), 396–97, for a discussion of the importance of southern women's participation in the Civil War.

48. Taylor, *South Carolina Women*, 5–6.

49. Ibid., 3; Faust, *Mothers of Invention*, 9–29.

50. Taylor, *South Carolina Women*, 389.

51. Ibid., 6.

52. Barlow's comments from editorial, *LC* (June 1903), 70. The journal was the only Lost Cause periodical owned by women. Barlow also supported the South Carolina initiative to publish its book on Confederate women; see "The Women's Book," *LC* (February 1902), 106. An essay sponsored by Laura Martin Rose, for example, is described in "Worthy UDC Worker in Mississippi," *CV* (November 1913), 518.

53. Poppenheim, *History of the UDC*, 226.

54. Kirby, *Darkness at the Dawning*, 94–95; Hall, "'You Must Remember This,'" 453.

55. The Illinois Division helped to set up the scholarship at the University of Chicago to promote "the study and research of the true history of the South" (*Minutes of the Nineteenth Annual Convention*, 24–25). The University of Pennsylvania scholarship was established in 1912; see Poppenheim, *History of the UDC*, 116. The Columbia Teachers' College scholarship was established in 1907.

56. "Something of the San Francisco Convention," *CV* (December 1905), 534–35; Mrs. Livingston Rowe Schuyler, "That Teachers' College Prize Essay," *CV* (January 1909), 39.

57. "Robert E. Lee: A Present Estimate," *CV* (December 1908), 657.

58. Ibid.; see also Schuyler's comments, *CV* (January 1909), 39.

59. "Mrs. J. Enders Robinson's General Circular," *CV* (March 1909), 101.

60. "Wilmington, N.C., Comments," *CV* (March 1909), 102; "Comment by Women of Charleston," *CV* (March 1909), 102; "Protest from the Florida Divi-

sion," *CV* (March 1909), 109; Sue Virginia Tate to Colonel Wharton Green, March 14, 1909, Adeline Davis Green Papers, Duke.

61. "Action Taken by New Orleans Chapter" and "Maryland Daughters Protest against the Prize Essay," *CV* (March 1909), 102–3, 107.

62. "Maryland Daughters Protest," ibid., 107; Cornelia Stone, "The Prize Essay, Columbia University," *CV* (March 1909), 100–101; Lucy Green Yerger, "Historian of the Mississippi Division Comments," *CV* (March 1909), 107; Mrs. D.A.S. Vaught, Committee Report, "The Boyson Essay on Lee," May 4, 1909, LHAC-UDC Papers, Tulane.

63. "Richmond Chapter Condemns It," and "Richmond Chapter Still Displeased," *CV* (March 1909), 107, 137; "Comment by Women of Charleston," *CV* (March 1909), 102.

64. "From the Judges of That Prize Essay," *CV* (March 1909), 101–2.

65. Sue Virginia Tate to Colonel Wharton Green, March 14, 1909, Green Papers, Duke; Mrs. N. V. Randolph to Editor (TS), *New Orleans Times-Dispatch*, November 30, 1909, UDC Collection, MOC.

66. Poppenheim to Janet Randolph, March 2, 1909, UDC Collection, MOC.

67. Schuyler, "That Teachers' College Prize Essay," *CV* (March 1909), 39; Stone, "The Prize Essay," *CV* (March 1909), 100–101; Henderson, "Official Comment on the Boyson Paper," *CV* (April 1909), 180–81; "Another Prize Essay," *CV* (October 1909), 489.

68. Miss Adelia Dunovant to Mrs. Tate, June 4, 1910, UDC Collection, MOC; Dunovant, "Columbia College Scholarships," *CV* (February 1910), 60–61. On the change of scholarships, see "United Daughters of the Confederacy," *CV* (June 1910), 262; Poppenheim, *History of the UDC*, 97–99.

Chapter 7. Confederate Motherhood

1. "Wouldn't Sing 'Marching through Georgia,'" *CV* (July 1902), cover page.

2. "Hearty Tributes to Laura Galt," *CV* (October 1902), 437.

3. The objective "to instruct and instill into the descendants of the people of the South a proper respect . . . for the deeds of their forefathers" appears in the original UDC constitution, printed in *Minutes of the First Annual Convention*, 2–3; "Ritual of the United Daughters of the Confederacy," written by Mrs. J. D. Beale, Montgomery, Alabama, in 1904.

4. For a discussion of republican motherhood, see Linda Kerber, "Daughters of Columbia: Educating Women for the Republic, 1787–1805."

5. I use the term *Confederate motherhood* to describe an ideology similar in purpose to republican motherhood. In the post–Civil War South, southern women were assigned the responsibility of training children to be good southern

citizens. Thus, the term does not refer to women of the Civil War generation but to those women involved in the movement to perpetuate the ideology of the Lost Cause among future generations of white southerners.

6. Handwritten address of Virginia Clay Clopton, n.d., Clay Papers, Duke; Dunovant's quotation from "Principles in Their Relation to Human Action," *Minutes of the Eighth Annual Convention*, 11. Reprinted in *CV* (February 1902), 75.

7. Wilson, *Baptized in Blood*, 140.

8. Dunovant, "Address" (January 1902), 91–93.

9. The UDC waas more proactive in its response to education that UCV Gen. Stephen D. Lee, chairman of the UCV Historical Committee, reported in 1899 that the duty of the committee was "little more than to keep watch upon the histories of the day, and to stimulate to the limited extent of their powers historical research and publication" (*CV* [June 1899], 247).

10. "The Land of Our Desire," *CV* (November 1906), 496. Glenn was speaking to women at the Monteagle Assembly on UDC Day.

11. The terms *pro-southern* and *pro-Confederate* are used interchangeably to indicate those texts whose version of the Civil War interprets the South's cause as a defense of states' rights, not slavery. This version is consistent with the beliefs of Lost Cause advocates as well as scholars of the Dunning School.

12. Historian Fred Bailey has written several articles on the crusade for unbiased histories in various southern states. His essential argument in each article is that the movement was a concerted effort by male and female Confederate organizations. Bailey argues that the SCV and UDC "emulat[ed] the pronouncements of the parent organization" (i.e., the UCV) ("The Textbooks of the 'Lost Cause': Censorship and the Creation of Southern State Histories," 507–33). Bailey is incorrect in stating that the UCV was the parent organization of the UDC. Furthermore, the assumption that the SCV and UDC followed the "pronouncements and policies" of the UCV suggests, incorrectly, that formal pronouncements did not originate with the UDC. The UDC had established "correct" history as one of its objectives in 1894. Moreover, the UCV did not have a monopoly on opinions regarding history. Additional information on southern textbooks appears in Wilson, *Baptized in Blood*, 139–60, and Foster, *Ghosts of the Confederacy*, 115–26 (the quote is on p. 197).

13. Resolution of Helen Millington, *Minutes of the Fourth Annual Convention*, 38.

14. Report of the Mississippi Division, *Minutes of the Eighteenth Annual Convention*, 344.

15. Lee, *A School History of the United States*; Wilson, *Baptized in Blood*, 141; Bailey, "Free Speech and the Lost Cause," 257–58; Katie Daffan, "Text Book Report," *LC* (December 1902), 73.

16. Stories by Thomas Nelson Page, such as *Two Little Confederates, The Old South*, and *De Namin Ob De Twins*, were promoted as appropriate pro-southern material for children. Other popular works included Joel Chandler Harris's *Uncle Remus* and Mary Williamson's *The Life of Robert E. Lee* and *The Life of Stonewall Jackson*. See also Rose, *The Ku Klux Klan*, a primer for children.

17. *The Wrongs of History Righted* (1914) was originally the address Mildred Rutherford gave at the UDC general convention in Atlanta. Rutherford mailed a copy to J. N. Bennett, the principal of the Colored Training and Industrial School in Faison, North Carolina. His response was printed as "Principal of Negro School Writes Miss Rutherford Concerning Book!" dated August 24, 1915, Rutherford Scrapbooks, UGA.

18. Bennett's response was appropriate for a black man writing to a white woman in the Jim Crow South, although his sentiments may have been exaggerated. Rutherford no doubt saw educating blacks via the Lost Cause as another way to maintain the status quo, and she regarded Bennett's response as proof.

19. Elson, *A History of the United States of America;* "Virginians Aroused about False History," *CV* (April 1911), 148–49; "Faculty of Roanoke College 'Defended,'" *CV* (May 1911), 194–95. The Roanoke College controversy over the use of Elson appears in Bailey, "Free Speech and the Lost Cause," 263–65.

20. *Minutes of the Eighteenth Annual Convention*, 29; Report of the Committee on Education, *Minutes of the Twenty-First Annual Convention*, 177.

21. "Virginians Aroused about False History," *CV* (April 1911), 148–49.

22. Bailey, "The Textbooks of the 'Lost Cause,'" 510. He makes the same case for Florida and Texas.

23. Lumpkin, *The Making of a Southerner*, 126–27.

24. Katie Cabell Currie, *Minutes of the Sixth Annual Convention*, 22; on the subject of northern teachers, see "Eternal Vigilance Necessary," *LC* (August 1902), 6.

25. Ava L. P. James to Mrs. [Ella] Brodnax, January 17, 1902, Brodnax Papers, Duke.

26. Lucy Closs Parker to Ella Brodnax, February 7, 1907, ibid.

27. Annie C. Allison to Ella Brodnax, April 13, 1907, ibid. UDC members continued their visits well beyond the period of this study. They were speakers in the classrooms as well as at high school commencements. Elizabeth Bashinsky of Troy, Alabama, for example, traveled her state as a commencement speaker; *Minutes of the Twenty-Fourth Annual Convention*.

28. "Prizes Offered to the Teachers and Pupils of the Public Schools of Scott County, Kentucky," *Minutes of the Eleventh Annual Convention*, 232–34.

29. Louis G. Levile, Rugby Academy, "The Institution of Slavery" (1914), in LHAC-UDC Papers, Tulane.

30. Ibid.

31. Virginia Price, "Our Historical Department," *Our Heritage* (March 1915), 3; Mrs. P. E. "Katie" Smith, interview by author, February 29, 1996, MOHP. In another article appearing in the *Lost Cause*, Price writes that "the principal and school board are not wholly responsible" for what individual teachers do in the classroom.

32. Lizzie George Henderson reported that it would be a wonderful tribute to Lee's life if the "Daughters of the South determine to place in every Southern schoolhouse an engraving of General Lee beside that of the 'Father of his Country,' which the Mt. Vernon Association of women are placing in the public schools!" *CV* (March 1907), 103.

33. Nancy Lewis Greene of Lexington, Kentucky, "United Daughters of the Confederacy," *CV* (July 1901), 326; "Texas UDC Want Five Anniversaries," *CV* (February 1905), 70.

34. Frances Thornton Smith, interview by author, February 14, 1996, MOHP.

35. Edith Royster, "To the Teachers of Wake County," circular, December 18, 1906; "Tribute to Gen. R. E. Lee in Alabama," *CV* (July 1910), 5.

36. Report of the Ohio Division, *Minutes of the Twenty-Second Annual Convention*, 133; "Picture of Gen. R. E. Lee in Montana Schools," *CV* (July 1910), 313.

37. *Minutes of the Eleventh Annual Convention*, 233.

38. Resolutions Presented by Winnie Davis Chapter, *Minutes of the Fourteenth Annual Convention*, 48–50; Report of the Mississippi Division, *Minutes of the Fifteenth Annual Convention*, 315–17, and *Minutes of the Sixteenth Annual Convention;* Cornelia Stone, "To the UDC," *Minutes of the Fifteenth Annual Convention*, 11–12. The Sophie Bibb Chapter in Montgomery, Alabama, placed a portrait of Jefferson Davis in the Carnegie Library and "in each public school in the city" (*Brief History of the Organization*, Daughters of the Confederacy, Alabama, Sophie Bibb Chapter, 1911, 7–8).

39. Report of the President-General (published by UDC, 1908), 4–6.

40. *Minutes of the Seventeenth Annual Convention*, 110–11. Also, Laura Martin Rose suggests that having the ordinances of secession of all states was "useful to students of southern history."

41. Information on the participation of children in Confederate Memorial Day is derived in large part from the author's interviews with women who recalled their own participation in the ceremonies. Regarding children forming a Confederate flag, see "Synopsis of UDC Convention Report," *CV* (January 1912), 4; on children at monument unveilings, see chap. 4.

42. "Our Historical Department," *Our Heritage* (December 1914), 3.

43. Ibid.

44. The history of the Children of the Confederacy appears in Poppenheim, *History of the UDC*, 181–89, and Alvah B. Pritchard, "History of the Children of the Confederacy," *United Daughters of the Confederacy, 1894–1994*, 83. On the creation of the office of third vice-president general, see President-General Rassie White's recommendation, *Minutes of the Twentieth Annual Convention*, 130.

45. Poppenheim, *Minutes of the Twentieth Annual Convention*, 182; *Minutes of the Fourth Annual Convention*, 31.

46. There was much talk at early conventions about whether the children could have representation in the general organization. Although the Daughters believed it was important to work with children, the UDC waited until 1917 to organize the children into an auxiliary organization. See *Minutes of the Fourth Annual Convention*, 31; *Minutes of the Eighth Annual Convention*, 113–14, 128; *Minutes of the Eleventh Annual Convention*, 81; *Minutes of the Twelfth Annual Convention*, 217.

47. *Minutes of the Twelfth Annual Convention*, 217; and *Minutes of the Fourteenth Annual Convention*, 6.

48. Quotation from Mrs. E. J. Ellis, *Our Heritage* (March 1915), 2.

49. Minnie Bell Barnes, interview with author, January 25, 1990. Others interviewed concurred with Barnes about their CofC leaders, including Mildred Youngblood Grant, interview with author, May 14, 1990, and Annie Louise Rogers Wehlitz, interview with author, November 30, 1989, MCF.

50. Pledge of the Children of the Confederacy, CofC Program 1929; on the Charlotte chapter, "United Daughters of the Confederacy," *CV* (December 1901), 539–40; Annie C. Allison to Ella Brodnax, April 9, 1907, Brodnax Papers, Duke.

51. Rutherford, *Monthly Program for Children of the Confederacy* (1915).

52. Ibid.

53. Ibid.

54. Ibid.; the tale of Nancy Hart appears in Rutherford's *Historical Sins of Omission and Commission*, 12, and Faust, *Mothers of Invention*, 203. Helen Keller was also made an honorary member of the UDC.

55. Rutherford, ibid.

56. Stone, *UDC Catechism for Children* (1904). Decca Lamar West, another Texan, wrote a similar catechism, *Catechism on the History of the Confederate States of America*.

57. The author has conducted numerous interviews in North Carolina and Mississippi with women who were once members of the CofC.

58. Helen Foster, interview with author, May 15, 1990, MCF.

59. Mildred Youngblood Grant, interview with author, May 14, 1990, MCF.

Chapter 8. Vindication and Reconciliation

1. Mrs. L. H. Raines to Mrs. M. C. Goodlett, April 29, 1894, Rutherford Scrapbooks, vol. 2, MOC. Historian Nina Silber argues that non-GAR men, even before the Spanish-American War, admired the willingness of southern men to fight and that "it did not matter that he had fought against the Union" (*The Romance of Reunion*, 172).

2. Discussions of sectional reconciliation appear in Wilson, *Baptized in Blood*, 161–82; Foster, *Ghosts of the Confederacy*, 152–53; Silber, *The Romance of Reunion*, 178–85; and Buck, *The Road to Reunion*. Quotation from "Patriotism in the South," *CV* (July 1898), 324–25. The estimated figure of one million southern soldiers' entry into World War I appears in Tindall, *The Emergence of the New South*, 53.

3. Wilson, *Baptized in Blood*, 163; Foster, *Ghosts of the Confederacy*, 145–49; Grantham, *The South in Modern America*, 23–24.

4. "Crisp Resolutions Adopted in Virginia," *CV* (September 1900), 396.

5. Ibid.

6. "The Monument to Captain Henry Wirz," *Southern Historical Society Papers* (1908), 227.

7. "Vicious Partisan Comment on the UDC," *CV* (May 1913), 217.

8. "Daughters of the Confederacy Criticised," *CV* (January 1902), 3–4.

9. Report of the President-General, *Minutes of the Eighteenth Annual Convention*, 96; Mrs. L. Eustace Williams, "Mission of the South's United Daughters," *CV* (September 1912), 440.

10. "The Term 'Nation,'" *CV* (March 1901), 111; "Principles in Relation to Human Action," *CV* (February 1902), 76.

11. "The Term 'Nation,'" ibid.

12. Ibid.

13. Address of Francis Nichols, *Minutes of the Ninth Annual Convention*, 10.

14. Silber, *Romance of Reunion*, 180, 194. Silber also argues that the South's insistence on a sectional identity was attributed directly to the activity of women.

15. Florence Butler to Mrs. Woodrow Wilson, October 29, 1912, Butler Papers, SHC. Butler comments that the convention is the first outside of the South. She also saw the meeting as one intended to "demonstrate to the world that we are a united people." Local press quoted from "United Daughters of Confederacy Gather Here for Big Convention," *Washington Post*, November 10, 1912.

16. Mrs. Alexander B. White to Mrs. Marion Butler, February 17, 1912, Butler Papers, SHC.

17. *Minutes of the Nineteenth Annual Convention*, 82, 88.

18. Address of Virginia Clay Clopton, ibid., 80. White's comments appear on p. 82.

19. Address of William Howard Taft, ibid., 8–9.

20. Ibid.

21. Ibid.

22. "The Confederate Flag in Washington," *CV* (December 1912), 548–49; Isabel Worrell Ball, "The UDC's," *National Tribune*, November 21, 1912.

23. Ball, ibid.

24. James Tanner to Mrs. Marion Butler, November 27, 1912, Butler Papers, SHC.

25. "Laying Cornerstone for UCV Shaft in Arlington," *Washington Post*, November 12, 1912.

26. Scott, *Natural Allies*. Although Scott does not include the UDC in her work, in reality, the Daughters shared many of the same concerns of more progressive-minded women's associations.

27. Mrs. James H. Parker, "Daughters at Peace Congress," *CV* (June 1907), 247; President-General's Report, *Minutes of the Fourteenth Annual Convention*, 73.

28. *Minutes of the Eighteenth Annual Convention*, 91; *CV* (January 1912), 9.

29. *Minutes of the Eighteenth Annual Convention*, 91.

30. *Minutes of the Twenty-First Annual Convention*, 86.

31. Ibid., 104–9.

32. Tindall, *The Emergence of the New South*, 33–39; Grantham, *The South in Modern America*, 80–82; "Annual Convention, UDC," *CV* (December 1914), 539; "An Appeal to the Women of Our Country," *CV* (October 1914), 435.

33. *Minutes of the Twenty-Second Annual Convention*, 64–65.

34. Report of the Committee on Peace, ibid., 85.

35. *Minutes of the Twenty-Third Annual Convention*, 315–20. Mrs. B. B. Ross of Alabama proposed peace resolutions and claimed that "we are startled by so stupendous a manifestation of the spirit of militarism" (*Minutes of the Twenty-First Annual Convention*, 85). On militarism and pro-preparedness in the region, see Tindall, *The Emergence of the New South*, 37–44, and Grantham, *The South in Modern America*, 80–82.

36. *Minutes of the Twenty-Third Annual Convention*, 315–20.

37. Ibid.

38. Ibid.

39. Wilson thanked President General Stevens for "the good will of the mem-

bership" of the UDC in 1914; Woodrow Wilson to Daisy M. Stevens, September 23, 1914, in *Minutes of the Twenty-First Annual Convention*, 105; Odenheimer, "From the President General," *CV* (March 1917), 122–23.

40. Mrs. J. Norment Powell to Cordelia Odenheimer, May 1, 1917, UDC Collection, MOC; "The Mississippi Division," *CV* (July 1917), 329; "Women's Work in War," *CV* (December 1917), 536; "The Louisiana Division," *CV* (August 1917), 379.

41. Odenheimer, "From the President General," *CV* (April 1917), 178, and *CV* (May 1917), 230–31. A North Carolina Daughter also urged the UDC to limit monument building while southern "boys at the front" needed their help (*Minutes of the Twenty-Fourth Annual Convention*, 107).

42. Mrs. J. Norment Powell to Cordelia Odenheimer, May 1, 1917, UDC Collection, MOC.

43. Preston's efforts are described in *CV* (September 1917), 425–26; Prohibition is discussed in *CV* (June 1917), 280–81.

44. Excerpts from the *Town and Country* article appeared in *CV* (December 1917), 535.

45. *Minutes of the Twenty-Fourth Annual Convention*, 107.

46. Ibid.

47. "From the President General," *CV* (February 1918), 86.

48. "From the President General," *CV* (April 1918), 174.

49. *CV* (June 1918), 268, 316–17; *CV* (August 1918), 366–67; *CV* (September 1918), 410–11.

50. Mary Poppenheim to Newton Baker, secretary of war, November 26, 1917; *Minutes of the Executive Board Meeting*, November 19–21, 1918, 9; "War Relief Committee's Work," *CV* (May 1919), 190.

51. Report of the President General, *Minutes of the Twenty-Fifth Annual Convention*, 70–71.

52. Ibid., 70.

53. Poppenheim, "From the President General," *CV* (January 1918), 36.

54. Historian General's Report, *Minutes of the Twenty-Fourth Annual Convention*, 193–96; Report of the President General, 113–15.

55. Blight, *Race and Reunion*, 139, 266.

Epilogue

1. "Dr. McCain Congratulates *Our Heritage* on 46th Anniversary," *Our Heritage: Souvenir Edition* (1906–1952). McCain was director of the Mississippi Division of Archives and History in 1952. He eventually became president of Missis-

sippi Southern College (now the University of Southern Mississippi). He was also a national officer in the SCV.

2. The story of the South Carolina flag controversy received enormous press coverage, much of which can be found online through the World Wide Web. See June Murray Wells, "President General's Statement on the South Carolina Flag Controversy," http://users.erols.com/va-udc/wells.html.

3. Ibid.

4. Dittmer, *Local People,* 12. Interviews conducted by the author revealed that students continued to commemorate Memorial Day in Mississippi until the early 1960s and that their textbooks, until the early 1970s, still contained Reconstruction myths.

5. Dittmer, ibid., 60.

6. Report of the CMLS, *Minutes of the Twenty-Fifth Annual Convention,* 254.

7. Massengill, *Portrait of a Racist.* Massengill is Beckwith's nephew, which raises questions about his objectivity regarding the guilt of his famous uncle.

8. McMillen, *The Citizens' Council,* 11; see also Bartley, *The Rise of Massive Resistance,* 82–107.

9. Bartley, ibid., 240.

10. On constitutionalism, see ibid., 189.

11. Today's SCV, and not today's UDC, is primarily responsible for the defensiveness currently associated with defenders of Confederate heritage. For more information on the UDC, see its official website: http://www.hqudc.org.

Bibliography

Primary Sources

Manuscript Collections

Beauvoir, The Jefferson Davis Shrine, Biloxi, Miss. (Beauvoir)

Kimbrough Papers
Varina Davis Papers

Manuscript Department, William R. Perkins Library, Duke University, Durham, N.C. (Duke)

John Grammar Brodnax Papers
Clement Claiborne Clay Papers
Adeline Ellery (Burr) Davis Green Papers
Hinsdale Family Papers
Charles Edgeworth Jones Papers
John McIntosh Kell Papers
Louisa and Mary Poppenheim Papers
Mary Calvert Stribling Papers
Stone Mountain Confederate Monumental Association Papers
Sara Eliza Ferrebee and Amanda E. (Ferrebee) Welch Papers
Agatha Woodson Papers

Special Collections, Hargrett Library, University of Georgia, Athens, Ga. (UGA)

Nellie P. Black Papers
Rebecca Latimer Felton Papers

Mildred Lewis Rutherford Papers
Mildred Lewis Rutherford Scrapbooks
UDC, Laura Rutherford Chapter Papers

Georgia Division of Archives and History, Atlanta, Ga. (GDAH)

UDC, Lizzie Rutherford Chapter Papers
UDC, Georgia Division Historic Marker Committee Papers
UDC, Atlanta Chapter Scrapbooks, 1895–1939

General Federation of Women's Clubs Archives, Washington, D.C. (GFWC)

Membership Records (Directories), 1890–1910

Eleanor S. Brockenbrough Library, Museum of the Confederacy, Richmond, Va. (MOC)

UDC Collection
Mildred Lewis Rutherford Scrapbooks

Mississippi Department of Archives and History, Jackson, Miss. (MDAH)

Mrs. William B. Colbert Papers
Daughters of Confederate Veterans Papers
Jefferson Davis Collection Papers
Davis (Varina Howell and Margaret Howell D. Hayes) Papers
Department of Education, Biennial Reports (1913–1943)
Department of Education, Social Studies
Hickey Papers
Belle Kearney Papers
Kimbrough (A. McC and Family) Papers
Kimbrough Family Papers
Lyon Papers
McLaurin Scrapbooks
Mississippi Education Association Papers
Mississippi School Curriculum (1926–1931)
Mrs. Dunbar Rowland Papers
Nellie Nugent Somerville Papers (microfilm)
Daisy McLaurin Stevens Papers
UDC Papers, 1896–1954
UDC, General Charles Clark Chapter, Scrapbook
UDC, Frank A. Montgomery Chapter Papers
UDC, Nathan B. Forrest Chapter Papers

North Carolina Department of Archives and History, Raleigh, N.C. (NCDAH)

UDC, General James Johnston Pettigrew Chapter Papers
Jessica Randolph Smith Papers

Southern Historical Collection, Wilson Library, University of North Carolina, Chapel Hill, N.C. (SHC)

Florence F. Butler Papers
Sarah Rebecca Cameron Papers
Elvira E. Moffitt Papers
Eliza Hall Parsley Papers

Manuscript Department, Howard-Tilton Memorial Library, Tulane University, New Orleans, La. (Tulane)

Behan Family Papers
Daisy Hodgson Papers
Louisiana Historical Association Collection
United Daughters of the Confederacy Papers

Virginia Historical Society, Richmond, Va.

Minutes of the Annual Conventions of the United Daughters of the Confederacy, 1895–1919.

Newspapers and Periodicals

Confederate Veteran, Nashville, 1893–1932
Lost Cause, Louisville, 1898–1904
Our Heritage, Mississippi, 1908–1919 (Souvenir Edition, 1952)
Southern Historical Society Papers, Richmond, 1876–1919
Fayetteville Observer, 1908–15
Washington Post, 1907–14

Oral Histories

Mississippi Oral History Program, University of Southern Mississippi (MOHP)

Mrs. P. E. Smith
Berte Houston
Frances Thornton Smith

Museum of the Cape Fear, Fayetteville, N.C. (MCF)

Minnie Bell Barnes
Helen Foster

Mildred Youngblood Grant

Annie Louise Rogers Wehlitz

Secondary Sources

Ayers, Edward. *The Promise of the New South: Life after Reconstruction.* New York: Oxford University Press, 1992.

Bailey, Fred. "Free Speech and the Lost Cause in the Old Dominion." *Virginia Magazine of History and Biography* (April 1994), 237–66.

———. "Mildred Lewis Rutherford and the Patrician Cult of the Old South." *Georgia Historical Quarterly* 77 (Fall 1994), 509–35.

———. "The Textbooks of the 'Lost Cause': Censorship and the Creation of Southern State Histories." *Georgia Historical Quarterly* 75 (1991), 507–33.

Bartley, Numan V. *The Rise of Massive Resistance: Race and Politics in the South during the 1950s.* Baton Rouge: Louisiana State University Press, 1997.

Bederman, Gail. *"Manliness" and Civilization: A Cultural History of Gender and Race in the United States.* Chicago: University of Chicago Press, 1995.

Bercaw, Nancy, ed. *Gender and the Southern Body Politic.* Oxford: University Press of Mississippi, 2000.

Billings, Dwight. *Planters in the Making of a "New South": Class, Politics, and Development in North Carolina.* Chapel Hill: University of North Carolina Press, 1979.

Bishir, Catherine. "Landmarks of Power: Building a Southern Past, 1855–1915." *Southern Cultures* 1 (1993), 5–45.

———. "Landmarks of Power: Building a Southern Past in Raleigh and Wilmington, North Carolina, 1885–1915." In *Where These Memories Grow,* edited by W. Fitzhugh Brundage, 139–68. Chapel Hill: University of North Carolina Press, 2000.

Blair, Karen J. *The Clubwoman as Feminist: True Womanhood Redefined, 1868–1914.* New York: Holmes and Meier Publishers, 1980.

Blight, David. "For Something Beyond the Battlefield: Frederick Douglass and the Struggle for the Memory of the Civil War." *Journal of American History* 75 (1989): 1156–78.

———. *Frederick Douglass' Civil War: Keeping Faith in Jubilee.* Baton Rouge: Louisiana State University Press, 1991.

———. *Race and Reunion: The Civil War in American Memory.* New York: Belknap Press, 2001.

Bodnar, John. *Remaking America: Public Memory, Commemoration, and Patriotism in the Twentieth Century.* Princeton, N.J.: Princeton University Press, 1992.

Brundage, W. Fitzhugh, ed. *Where These Memories Grow.* Chapel Hill: University of North Carolina Press, 2000.

Buck, Paul H. *The Road to Reunion, 1865–1900.* Boston: Little, Brown, 1937.

Cecelski, David S., and Timothy B. Tyson, eds. *Democracy Betrayed: The Wilmington Race Riot of 1898 and Its Legacy.* Chapel Hill: University of North Carolina Press, 1998.

Chafe, William, et al., eds. *Remembering Jim Crow: African Americans Tell about Life in the Segregated South.* New York: New Press, 2001.

Climer, Patricia Faye. "Protectors of the Past: The United Daughters of the Confederacy, Tennessee Division, and the Lost Cause." Master's thesis, Vanderbilt University, 1973.

Clinton, Catherine. *The Plantation Mistress: Woman's World in the Old South.* New York: Pantheon Books, 1982.

Clinton, Catherine, and Nina Silber, eds. *Divided Houses: Gender and the Civil War.* New York: Oxford University Press, 1992.

Clopton, Virginia Clay. *A Belle of the Fifties: Memoirs of Mrs. Clay of Alabama, Covering Social and Political Life in Washington and the South, 1853–1866.* Tuscaloosa: University of Alabama Press, 1999.

Collier, Mrs. Bryan Wells. *Biographies of Representative Women of the South.* College Park [?], Ga.: Published by author, 1920.

Confederate Southern Memorial Association. *History of the Confederate Memorial Associations of the South.* New Orleans: Graham Press, 1904.

Connelly, Thomas L. *The Marble Man: Robert E. Lee and His Image in American Society.* New York: Knopf, 1977.

Connelly, Thomas L., and Barbara Bellows. *God and General Longstreet: The Lost Cause and the Southern Mind.* Baton Rouge: Louisiana State University Press, 1982.

Coski, John M., and Amy R. Feely. "A Monument to Southern Womanhood: The Founding Generation of the Confederate Museum." In *A Woman's War: Southern Women, Civil War, and the Confederate Legacy,* edited by John M. Coski and Amy R. Feely, 131–64. Richmond and Charlottesville: Museum of the Confederacy and University Press of Virginia, 1996.

———, eds. *A Woman's War: Southern Women, Civil War, and the Confederate Legacy.* Richmond and Charlottesville: Museum of the Confederacy and University Press of Virginia, 1996.

Coulter, E. Merton. "The Confederate Monument in Athens, Georgia." *Georgia Historical Quarterly* 20 (September 1956), 230–47.

Cox, Karen L. "The Confederate Monument at Arlington: A Token of Reconciliation." In *Monuments to the Lost Cause: Women, Art, and the Landscape of*

Memory, edited by Pamela Simpson and Cynthia Mills, 199–218. Knoxville: University of Tennessee Press, 2003.

Davies, Wallace Evans. *Patriotism on Parade: The Story of Veterans' and Hereditary Organizations in America, 1783–1900*. Cambridge, Mass.: Harvard University Press, 1955.

Davis, Stephen. "Empty Eyes, Marble Hand: The Confederate Monument and the South." *Journal of Popular Culture* 16 (1982), 2–21.

Dittmer, John. *Local People: The Struggle for Civil Rights in Mississippi*. Urbana: University of Illinois Press, 1994.

Doyle, Don H. *New Men, New Cities, New South: Atlanta, Nashville, Charleston, Mobile, 1860–1910*. Chapel Hill: University of North Carolina Press, 1990.

Durant, Susan S. "The Gently Furled Banner: The Development of the Myth of the Lost Cause." Ph.D. diss., University of North Carolina, 1972.

Elkins, Stanley, and Eric McKitrick, eds. *The Hofstadter Aegis*. New York: Knopf, 1974.

Elson, Henry. *A History of the United States of America*. New York, 1904.

Emerson, Bettie A. C. *Historic Southern Monuments: Representative Memorials of the Heroic Dead of the Southern Confederacy*. New York: Neale, 1911.

Faust, Drew. "Altars of Sacrifice." In *Divided Houses: Gender and the Civil War*, edited by Catherine Clinton and Nina Silber, 177–99. New York: Oxford University Press, 1992.

———. *Mothers of Invention: Women of the Slaveholding South in the American Civil War*. Chapel Hill: University of North Carolina Press, 1996.

Flusche, Michael. "Thomas Nelson Page: The Quandary of a Literary Gentleman." *Virginia Magazine of History and Biography* 84, no. 4 (1976), 464–85.

Foner, Eric. *Reconstruction: America's Unfinished Revolution, 1863–1877*. New York: Harper and Row, 1988.

Foster, Gaines M. *Ghosts of the Confederacy: Defeat, the Lost Cause, and the Emergence of the New South, 1865–1913*. New York: Oxford University Press, 1987.

Fox-Genovese, Elizabeth. *Within the Plantation Household: Black and White Women of the Old South*. Chapel Hill: University of North Carolina Press, 1988.

Gallagher, Gary M. *Lee and His Generals in War and Memory*. Baton Rouge: Louisiana State University Press, 1998.

———. *The Myth of the Lost Cause and Civil War History*. Indianapolis: Indiana University Press, 2000.

Gaston, Paul M. *The New South Creed: A Study in Southern Mythmaking*. New York: Knopf, 1970.

Geertz, Clifford. *The Interpretation of Cultures*. New York: BasicBooks, 1973.

Gilmore, Glenda. *Gender and Jim Crow: Women and the Politics of White Supremacy in North Carolina, 1896–1920*. Chapel Hill: University of North Carolina Press, 1996.

Goodwyn, Lawrence. *Democratic Promise: The Populist Moment in America*. New York: Oxford University Press, 1976.

Grantham, Dewey. *The South in Modern America*. Little Rock: University of Arkansas Press, 1995.

———. *Southern Progressivism: The Reconciliation of Progress and Tradition*. Knoxville: University of Tennessee Press, 1983.

Gulley, H. E. "Women and the Lost Cause: Preserving a Confederate Identity in the American Deep South." *Journal of Historical Geography* 19 (1993), 125–41.

Gutmann, Joseph, and Stanley F. Chyet, eds. *Moses Jacob Ezekiel: Memoirs from the Baths of Diocletian*. Detroit: Wayne State University Press, 1975.

Hale, Grace M. *Making Whiteness: The Culture of Segregation in the South, 1890–1940*. New York: Vintage, 1999.

Hall, Jacquelyn Dowd. "'You Must Remember This': Autobiography as Social Critique." *Journal of American History* 85, no. 2 (1998), 439–65.

Herf, Jeffrey. *Reactionary Modernism: Technology, Culture, and Politics in Weimar and the Third Reich*. New York: Cambridge University Press, 1984.

Hewitt, Nancy, and Suzanne Lebsock, eds. *Visible Women: New Essays on American Activism*. Urbana: University of Illinois Press, 1993.

History of the Arlington Confederate Monument at Arlington, Virginia. United Daughters of the Confederacy, 1914.

History of the Home for Needy Confederate Women, 1900–1904. Richmond, Va.: J. L. Hill, 1904.

A History of the Origin of Memorial Day as Adopted by the Ladies' Memorial Association of Columbus, Georgia. Columbus: Gilbert, 1898.

Hobson, Fred. *Tell about the South: The Southern Rage to Explain*. Baton Rouge: Louisiana State University Press, 1983.

Howard, Milo B., Jr. "Alabama Museums: Early Efforts." *Alabama Review* 35 (1982), 83–93.

Hunter, Lloyd A. "The Sacred South: Postwar Confederates and the Sacralization of Southern Culture." Ph.D. diss., Yale University, 1974.

Jackson, John B. *Discovering the Vernacular Landscape*. New Haven, Conn.: Yale University Press, 1984.

Johnson, Joan. "'Drill into us . . . the Rebel tradition': The Contest over Southern Identity in Black and White Women's Clubs, South Carolina, 1898–1930." *Journal of Southern History* 66, no. 3 (2000), 525–62.

———. "'This Wonderful Dream Nation': Black and White South Carolina

Women, Race, Place, and Southern Identity in the New South." Ph.D. diss., University of California, Los Angeles, 1998.

Kerber, Linda. "Daughters of Columbia: Educating Women for the Republic, 1787–1805." In *The Hofstadter Aegis*, edited by Stanley Elkins and Eric Mc-Kitrick, 36–59. New York: Knopf, 1974.

Kirby, Jack Temple. *Darkness at the Dawning: Race and Reform in the Progressive South*. New York: Lippincott, 1972.

Kubassek, Melody. "'Ask Us Not to Forget': The Lost Cause in Natchez, Mississippi." *Southern Studies* 3, no. 3 (1992), 155–70.

Kyle, Annie. "Incidents of Hospital Life." In *War Days in Fayetteville*, 35–45. 1910; reprint, Fayetteville, N.C.: Williams, 1990.

Lee, Susan P. *A School History of the United States*. Richmond, Va.: B. F. Johnson, 1895.

Link, William A. *The Paradox of Southern Progressivism: 1880–1930*. Chapel Hill: University of North Carolina Press, 1992.

Litwack, Leon. *Been in the Storm So Long: The Aftermath of Slavery*. New York: Knopf, 1979.

Lumpkin, Katherine DuPre. *The Making of a Southerner*. New York: Knopf, 1946.

Massengill, Reed. *Portrait of a Racist: A Revelatory Biography of Byron de la Beckwith*. New York: St. Martin's, 1994.

May, Robert E. "Southern Elite Women, Sectional Extremism, and the Male Political Sphere: The Case of John A. Quitman's Wife and Female Descendants, 1847–1931." *Journal of Mississippi History* 50, no. 4 (1988), 251–95.

McArthur, Judith N. *Creating the New Woman: The Rise of Southern Women's Progressive Culture in Texas, 1893–1918*. Urbana: University of Illinois Press, 1998.

McKeithan, Lulie Biggs. *History of the Confederate Woman's Home*. Published by author, 1950.

McMillen, Neil R. *The Citizens' Council: Organized Resistance to the Second Reconstruction, 1954–1964*. Urbana: University of Illinois Press, 1994.

———. *Dark Journey: Black Mississippians in the Age of Jim Crow*. Urbana: University of Illinois Press, 1989.

Montgomery, Rebecca. *The Politics of Education in the New South: Women and Reform in Georgia, 1890–1930*. Baton Rouge: Louisiana State University Press, forthcoming.

Osterweis, Rollin G. *The Myth of the Lost Cause, 1865–1900*. Hamden, Conn.: Archon, 1973.

Phillips, Ulrich Bonnell. *American Negro Slavery*. New York: D. Appleton, 1918.

Pope, Christine, ed. *Women in the American South: A Multicultural Reader*. New York: New York University Press, 1998.

Poppenheim, Mary B., et al. *The History of the United Daughters of the Confederacy.* Raleigh, N.C.: Edwards and Broughton, 1925.

Pritchard, Alvah B. "History of the Children of the Confederacy." *United Daughters of the Confederacy, 1894–1994.* Special issue (September 1994), 83.

Rable, George. *Civil Wars: Women and the Crisis of Southern Nationalism.* Urbana: University of Illinois Press, 1989.

Radford, John P. "Identity and Tradition in the Post–Civil War South." *Journal of Historical Geography* 18 (1992), 91–103.

Rose, Mrs. S.E.F. *The Ku Klux Klan or Invisible Empire.* West Point, Miss.: West Point Leader Print, 1913.

Rosenburg, R. B. *Living Monuments: Confederate Soldiers' Homes in the New South.* Chapel Hill: University of North Carolina Press, 1993.

Rutherford, Mildred. *Historical Sins of Omission and Commission.* Published by author, 1915.

———. "Address Delivered by Miss Mildred Lewis Rutherford, Historian General, United Daughters of the Confederacy." New Willard Hotel, Washington, D.C. Athens, Ga.: McGregor, 1912.

Savage, Kirk. *Standing Soldiers, Kneeling Slaves: Race, War, and Monument in Nineteenth-Century America.* Princeton, N.J.: Princeton University Press, 1997.

Schama, Simon. *Landscape and Memory.* New York: Vintage, 1995.

Scott, Anne Firor. *Natural Allies: Women's Associations in American History.* Urbana: University of Illinois Press, 1992.

———. *The Southern Lady: From Pedestal to Politics, 1830–1930.* Chicago: University of Chicago Press, 1970.

Silber, Nina. *The Romance of Reunion.* Chapel Hill: University of North Carolina Press, 1995.

Simpson, John A. "The Cult of the 'Lost Cause.'" *Tennessee Historical Quarterly* 34 (Winter 1975), 350–61.

Simpson, Pamela, and Cynthia Mills, eds. *Monuments to the Lost Cause: Women, Art and the Landscape of Memory.* Knoxville: University of Tennessee Press, 2003.

Simpson, Robert R. "The Origin of State Departments of Archives and History in the South." Ph.D. diss., University of Mississippi, 1971.

Sims, Anastatia. *The Power of Femininity in the New South: Women's Organizations and Politics in North Carolina, 1880–1930.* Columbia: University of South Carolina Press, 1997.

Smith, Elsie. "Belle Kinney and the Confederate Women's Monument." *Southern Quarterly* 33 (Summer 1994), 6–31.

Smith, John David. "An Old Creed for the New South: Southern Historians and the Revival of the Proslavery Argument, 1890–1920." *Southern Studies* 18 (Spring 1979), 75–87.

Smith, Stephen A. "The Old South Myth as a Contemporary Southern Commodity." *Journal of Popular Culture* 16 (1982), 22–29.

Stone, Cornelia Branch. *UDC Catechism for Children.* Galveston, Texas, 1904.

Taylor, Mrs. Thomas. *South Carolina Women in the Confederacy.* Columbia, S.C.: State Company, 1903.

Tindall, George B. *The Emergence of the New South, 1913–1945.* A History of the South, vol. 10. Baton Rouge: Louisiana State University Press, 1967.

Trelease, Allen. *White Terror: The Ku Klux Klan Conspiracy and Southern Reconstruction.* New York: Greenwood Publishing Group, 1971.

Turner, Elizabeth Hayes. *Women, Culture, and Community: Religion and Reform in Galveston, 1880–1920.* New York: Oxford University Press, 1997.

Turner, Josephine M. *The Courageous Caroline: Founder of the UDC.* Montgomery, Ala.: Paragon, 1965.

Underwood, J. L. *The Women of the Confederacy.* Published by author, n.d.

War Days in Fayetteville. 1910; reprint, Fayetteville, N.C.: Williams, 1990.

Webster, Gerald R., and Roberta H. Webster. "The Power of an Icon." *Geographical Review* 84 (1994), 131–43.

Wedell, Marsha. *Elite Women and the Reform Impulse in Memphis, 1873–1915.* Knoxville: University of Tennessee Press, 1991.

Wheeler, Marjorie Spruill. *New Women of the New South: The Leaders of the Woman Suffrage Movement in the Southern States.* New York: Oxford University Press, 1993.

Whites, LeeAnn. *The Civil War as a Crisis in Gender: Augusta, Georgia, 1860–1890.* Athens: University of Georgia Press, 1995.

———. "Rebecca Latimer Felton and the Problem of 'Protection' in the New South." In *Visible Women: New Essays on American Activism,* edited by Nancy Hewitt and Suzanne Lebsock, 41–61. Urbana: University of Illinois Press, 1993.

———. "'Stand by Your Man': The Ladies' Memorial Association and the Reconstruction of White Manhood." In *Women of the American South: A Multicultural Reader,* edited by Christine Pope, 133–49. New York: New York University Press, 1998.

Williams, Raymond. *Keywords: A Vocabulary of Culture and Society.* New York: Oxford University Press, 1983.

Wilson, Charles R. *Baptized in Blood: The Religion of the Lost Cause, 1865–1920.* Athens: University of Georgia Press, 1980.

Winberry, John. "'Lest We Forget': The Confederate Monument and the Southern Townscape." *Southeastern Geographer* (November 1983), 107–21.

Women's Christian Temperance Union Convention Minutes for 1900. Chicago: Women's Temperance Publishing Association, 1900.

Wood, W. K. "Rewriting Southern History: U. B. Phillips, the New South, and the Antebellum Past." *Southern Studies* 22 (1983), 217–43.

Woodward, C. Vann. *The Burden of Southern History.* New York: Vintage, 1960.

———. *Origins of the New South, 1877–1913.* A History of the South, vol. 9. Baton Rouge: Louisiana State University Press, 1951.

———. *The Strange Career of Jim Crow.* 3d ed. New York: Oxford University Press, 1989.

Wyatt-Brown, Bertram. *Southern Honor: Ethics and Behavior in the Old South.* New York: Oxford University Press, 1982.

Index

Italicized page numbers indicate figures.

Addams, Jane, 150
advertisements, *51, 109*
African Americans: attitudes toward,
39, 85; disfranchised and oppressed,
14, 160; food conservation lectures for,
155; Lost Cause and, 6, 49, 173n39;
"mammy" monument and, 166n12;
reconciliation's impact on, 158; schoolbooks for, 125, 161; suffrage for, 107;
violence against, 107
agrarian past: idealization of, 4, 37–38, 43;
New South vs., 45–46, 47
Alabama: collecting of documents and artifacts in, 98–99, 117; monuments in,
56, 62–63, 65
Alabama UDC, 157, 189n38
Alderman, Edwin, 113, 115, 116
Alexandria (Va.) CofC chapter, 135
Americanization, 153
American Red Cross, 58–59, 153–54, 155
American Revolution, 122, 137, 145
Andersonville prison, 144
Anglo-Saxonism, cult of: concept of, 5;
educating poor to sustain, 84–86, 87,
91; nationwide emphasis on, 45. *See also*
Confederate culture; Lost Cause; white
supremacy
archives, establishment of, 97–98, 182n11.
See also documents and records
Arkansas UDC, 152, 153

Arlington Confederate Monument Association (ACMA), 53–56, 68
Arlington National Cemetery, Confederate
monument in: cost of, 53, 56, 175n17;
design of, 55–56; fund-raising for, 53–
54, 58–59, 60; illustration of, *69*; national significance of, 6, 68–69, 149; as
symbol of reconciliation, 70–71, 146–
47; as "true" history, 71–72
Athens (Ga.) Ladies' Memorial Association, 39, 103

Ball, Isabel Worrell, 148–49
Baltimore UDC, 114
Barlow, Florence: editorship of, 167n6,
178–79n20; on history studies, 101; on
rehabilitating South, 10; on UDC objectives, 44; women's homes and, 77–78;
on women's role, 111
Battle Abbey (museum), 179n22
Beauvoir (soldiers' home), 79, 82, 89, 98
Beckwith, Byron de la, 162
Behan, Katie, 16, 57–58, 174n2, 174n7
benevolent efforts: achievements of, 91–
92; for Confederate whites only, 74–
75; as objective, 3, 19–20, 82–83;
progressivism's influence on, 73–74,
81, 192n26. *See also* educational efforts;
soldiers' homes; women's homes
Berry, Martha, 180n49

Berry Industrial School (Rome, Ga.),
180n49
Birth of a Nation, The (film), 107–8
Blue and Gray reunions, 70, 144
Boyson, Christine, 112–16
Bryan, William Jennings, 149
Butler, Florence (wife of Marion), 147, 149,
180n48, 191n15
Butler, Marion, 147

Cameron, Rebecca, 83
Campbell-Graves Camp of UCV (Danville,
Va.), 144
Cape Fear UDC (Wilmington, N.C.), 114
career opportunities, 48. *See also* teachers
Carnegie, Andrew, 150
celebrations: children's participation in, 37,
119, 120, 133, 135, 136, 160, 161; of
Davis's and Lee's birthdays, 130–32; memorial efforts vs., 11; monuments as,
66–67; motherhood and, 123; New
Men's absence from, 46–47; Old South
idealized in, 183–84n33; of white supremacy, 13–15; women's leadership in,
12–13, 20–21. *See also* Memorial Day,
Confederate
chapters: Boyson's essay and, 114; CofC
chapters organized by, 136, 137, 158; encouragement of, 30; formation of, 23,
29; history discussions in, 101, 104; in
northern cities, 112; number of, 28;
peace efforts of, 152; SIEA joined by, 87;
textbook campaigns of, 124. *See also*
members; membership
Charleston (S.C.) UDC, 114, 115
children: as celebration participants, 37,
119, 120, 133, 135, 136, 160, 161; educational assistance for, 74; importance
of, 121, 134; indoctrination of, 13–15,
65, 121–22, 127–28, 138–40, 160–62;
KKK primer for, 107, 109–10, 171n19;
misinformation for, 105; monuments'
role in teaching, 68–69; at monument unveilings, 61–65, 66, 70, 136;
representation of, in UDC, 190n46;
role models for, 101; trained for southern citizenship, 122–23. *See also*
schools

Children of the Confederacy (CofC): activities of, 135–36; education via, 136–39;
formation of, 122, 134–35; illustration
of, 134; legacy of, 139–40; role of, 3; as
UDC auxiliary, 157
Christianity, 97, 106
citizenship, 122–23, 145. *See also* patriotism
Clansmen, The (Dixon), 107–8
class differences: in educational efforts,
83–84, 86, 88; in first and second KKK,
171n19. *See also* elites
Clay, Clement C., Jr., 37
Clopton, Virginia Clay, 37, 122–23, 147
CofC. *See* Children of the Confederacy
Colonial Dames, 34, 35, 100
Colored Training and Industrial School
(Faison, N.C.), 125
Columbia Teachers' College/University,
112–16, 185n55
Confederacy: catechisms of, 136, 137, 138–
39, 190n56; defense of, 13, 32, 145,
194n11; seccession of, 133, 137, 189n40;
souvenirs of, 58; White House of, 99.
See also veterans, Confederate; women
"of the 1860s"
Confederate culture: children's importance to, 121, 134; concept of, 1–2; education to promote, 3, 19–20, 75, 83, 91,
120–22, 127–28; feminine ideal in, 41–
45; history's role in transmitting, 3, 19–
20, 95–96, 102; masculine ideal in,
44–47; monuments as continuity of,
67; motherhood in, 122–23, 186–87n5;
preservation of, 7, 37–38, 48, 95–96,
183–84n33; southern honor in, 25, 46–
47, 142–43; values of, 4. *See also* Lost
Cause; slavery; states' rights; white supremacy
Confederated Southern Memorial Association (CSMA): Davis monument
and, 174n7; founding of, 49–50; fund-
raising of, 57–58; members of, 35;
Memorial Day and, 11; soldiers' homes
and, 178n15. *See also* Memorial Day,
Confederate
Confederate Memorial Literary Society
(CMLS), 98, 102, 161

Confederate motherhood, 122–23, 186–87n5

Confederate Museum (Museum of the Confederacy, Richmond), 98, 99, 117

Confederate progressivism: achievements of, 91–92; for Confederate whites only, 74–75; on industrial vs. college education, 83–84, 86, 88–90; as objective, 3, 19–20, 82–83; progressivism's influence on, 73–74, 81, 192n26; use of term, 177–78n6. *See also* education; soldiers' homes; women's homes

Confederate Veteran (magazine): on Boyson's essay, 112, 114; on collecting artifacts, 99; contributors to, 30, 103, 104, 107–8; on fund-raising, 56; on Galt's protest, 118–19; on KKK, 107–8; *Lost Cause* compared with, 178–79n20; on Lumpkin's speaking, 43; North's criticism in, 144; as official organ, 95, 96, 138; SCV criticized by, 46; on UDC founder, 24, 25; on UDC's influence, 126; on WWI, 154

Confederate Veterans' Association (Savannah), Ladies' Auxiliary to, 17

Connor, Bull, 162

cultural memory. *See* public memory

Cunningham, Sumner A., 25, 56, 95, 144

Currie, Katie Cabell, 19, 30, 52, 127–28

Daffan, Katie, 124–25

Dallas (Texas), monument unveiling in, 61–63

Daniels, Addie (wife of Josephus), 154

Daniels, Josephus, 154

"Daughters." *See* Daughters of the Confederacy (DOC); National Association of the Daughters of the Confederacy (NDOC); United Daughters of the Confederacy (UDC)

Daughters of 1812, 34, 100

Daughters of the American Revolution (DAR): building preservation and, 100; members of, 34, 35, 39, 171n14; UDC convention and, 147, 148

Daughters of the Confederacy (DOC): growth of, 16–18; name of, 14–15; objectives of, 2, 15–16; retaining authority of,

in federation, 23. *See also* National Association of the Daughters of the Confederacy (NDOC); United Daughters of the Confederacy (UDC)

Daughters of the Republic of Texas, 34, 35

Davis, Jefferson: Alabama home of, 99; CofC programs on, 137; family of, 62; honoring of, 14–15, 127, 130–32, 156; as martyr, 13; monuments to, 52–53, 56, 57, 61, 62–63, 64, 65; portraits of, 130–32, 160; as role model, 103, 104; writings of, 101, 129

Davis, Jefferson Hayes (grandson), 62–63

Davis, Varina (wife), 89, 99, 178n14

Davis, Winnie (daughter), 14–15, 15

District of Columbia UDC, 53–54, 147, 152

Dixon, Thomas, 107–8, 129

documents and records: collecting, 95–98, 101, 103, 182n11; on women's role, 95, 98, 110–11, 139, 181–82n5

Douglass, Frederick, 181n3

Duke, Henrietta Morgan (wife of Basil), 178–79n20

Duke, Gen. Basil, 178–79n20

Dunning, William, 112

Dunning School, 184n37, 187n11

Dunovant, Adelia, 94; Columbia scholarship and, 116; on history's importance, 93–94, 96, 101; on motherhood, 123; on reconciliation, 145

Early, Jubal, 13, 181n4

Eastland, James O., 162

education: for Confederate whites only, 88; opportunities in, 48; for poor whites, 84–87, 89–91; of president-generals, 38, 39; support for southern, 73–74. *See also* schools

educational efforts: class distinctions in, 83–84, 86, 88; historical efforts linked to, 95; monuments' role in, 68–69; as objective, 3, 19–20, 75, 83, 91, 120–22, 127–28; peace movement and, 150; reformers and, 87–90; school visits as, 127–28, 188n27; success of, 119, 123, 160. *See also* Children of the Confederacy (CofC); essay contests; schools; textbook campaigns

elites: fund-raising and, 11; idealization of, 12, 104–5, 127; interests of, 30–31, 38; as moral guardians, 21, 26–27, 85–86, 122–23; noblesse oblige of, 74; use of term, 5–6; women's home for, 80–81
empire, language of, 45
essay contests: to encourage history studies, 95, 103; on international conciliation, 152; scandal over university, 112–16, 185n55; for schoolchildren, 121–22, 129–30; on women's role, 111
Evans, Clement, 167n3
Exchange Libraries, 102
Ex-Confederate Association, 15–16, 75
Ezekiel, Moses, 55–56, 60

Faison, Sallie, 80, 91
"faithful slave" fiction, 44, 104, 172n36
Fayetteville (N.C.): hospital in, 8; LMA in, 9
Felton, Rebecca Latimer, 37, 84–86, 87
feminine ideal, 41–45. See also Confederate motherhood
First White House Association, 99
flag, Confederate: children as living, 64–65, 66, 133; controversy over, 159–60, 163, 194n2; at monument unveilings, 62, 64–65, 70; role of, 2; in schools, 121–22, 127–28, 130, 133; at UDC convention, 148–49
flag, U.S., 11, 65
Florida, veterans' pensions in, 75
Florida UDC, 114
food conservation, 155
Forrest, Nathan Bedford, 107, 175n19
France, UDC-supported hospital in, 155–57
Franklin (Tenn.): fund-raising in, 56; monument in, 68
Freedman's Bureau, 106–7
fund-raising: for Arlington monument, 53–54, 58–59, 60; by CofC chapters, 136; by CSMA, 57–58; for Davis monument, 52–53, 59–60; for educational efforts, 84; for Lee monument, 13; by LMAs, 9–11; for monuments (general), 51–52; for museum, 179n22; New Men's support for, 46, 47–48; for Shiloh monument, 54–56; for soldiers' homes,

15–16, 75; for women's homes, 76–77. See also government funding

Galt, Laura Talbot, 118–19
Gardner, Gen. Washington, 70
gender differences: educational efforts and, 91; in southern writing, 103–4; in textbook campaigns, 124, 187n12. See also men; women; women's roles
general conventions: Arlington monument and, 53–54; behavior expected at, 33; children's role and, 133, 190n46; education discussed at, 85–86, 90; historian-general's report to, 102–3, 183n27; history's importance discussed at, 93–94, 96, 97–98, 101, 126; hospital funding approved at, 155–56; immigrants discussed at, 153; reconciliation and, 6, 146–49; relief for women discussed at, 79–82; scholarship discussed at, 116; Shiloh monument and, 55; use of term, 170n4
General Federation of Women's Clubs (GFWC), 26, 29
George, James Z., 38, 107
Georgia: monuments in, 50, 53, 174n8; school in, 180n49; veterans' association in, 17
Georgia UDC: appeals to, 84–85; chapters of, 68; educational efforts of, 90; officers of, 39; Stone Mountain memorial and, 174n8; Wirz monument and, 144; women's role documented by, 111
Glenn, Elizabeth Lumpkin, 42; educational efforts and, 89, 123; on southern feminine ideal, 41–43, 48
Goldman, Emma, 144
Goodlett, Caroline Meriwether, 17, 141; activities of, 17, 34–35, 74–75; educational efforts and, 89–90; federation efforts of, 16–17, 18; legacy of, 160; on membership, 19, 22; NDOC constitution and, 21; offices held by, 19; Raines's conflict with, 24–25; on "sacred obligation," 32; on soldiers' homes, 76
Gordon, Maj.-Gen. John B., 14, 58

government funding: for building preservation, 100; for monument building, 57, 175n19; for soldiers' and widows' homes, 74, 75–76, 79, 80; for southern publications, 111; success in attaining, 160, 169n37. *See also* fund-raising

Grady, Henry, 12

Grand Army of the Republic (GAR), 131, 143–44

Grant, Ulysses S., 183n29

graves: children's decoration of, 119–20, 133; reburials in appropriate, 8–9, 53

Griffith, D. W., 107–8

Harris, Joel Chandler, 125

Hattiesburg (Miss.) UDC, 175n19

Hayes, Lucy, 63

Hayes, Margaret Davis (Davis's daughter), 62

Helena (Mont.) UDC, 131

Helms, Jesse, 163

Henderson, Lizzie George, *88*; activities of, 171n16; on educational efforts, 88; on essay contests, 112–13, 115–16; on members' behavior, 33; monument building and, 55; on peace conference, 150; on portraits in schools, 189n32; on SCV, 47–48; status of, 38; on UDC's growth, 28

Henrietta Morgan Duke Chapter (Georgetown, Ky.), 129

Herbert, Col. Hilary, 53–54

Hibbard, Frederick, 56

historian-general office: Boyson's essay and, 114; history programs set by, 104, 137, 183n30; KKK highlighted by, 109–10; reports of, 102–3, 183n27

historical efforts: activities in, 95–96; of CofC chapter leaders, 136–37; Davis and Lee's role in, 130–31; educational efforts linked to, 95; history studies as part of, 101–5; naive approach to, 112–14; North's criticism of, 143–45; as objective, 3, 19–20, 95–96, 102; in schools, 121–22, 127–28, 188n27; success of, 119, 123, 160. *See also* essay contests; textbook campaigns

history writing: by black southerners, 6; monument as "truthful," 71–72; northern bias in, 94, 96–97, 112, 114, 123, 126–27, 143; promotion of "truthful" and "impartial," 39, 93–97, 101–3, 112, 116–17, 144; on Reconstruction, 104, 106, 184n38; on southern women's role in war, 110–11; by white southerners, 4, 102–5, 107–9, 124–25. *See also* textbook campaigns

Hodges, Jim, 159

Home for Aged Confederate Women (regional), 80–81

Home for Needy Confederate Women (Richmond), 76–78

honor, southern, 25, 46–47, 142–43

hospitals, 8, 155–57

Huntsville (Ala.), monument in, 62–63, 65

Illinois UDC, 112, 185n55

illiteracy, 86, 114

immigrants, 153

industrial education, 83–84, 86, 88–90

industrialization, 37–38

J. Z. George UDC (Greenwood, Miss.), 124

Jackson, Mary Anna (wife), 62

Jackson, Gen. Thomas "Stonewall," 4, 38, 62–63, 137

Jamestown Exposition (1907), 98

Jefferson Davis Monument Association (JDMA), 52–53

Jefferson Davis Monument (Richmond): cost of, 56, 175n17; fund-raising for, 52–53, 59–60; placement of, *61*

Johnston, Gen. Albert Sydney, 56, 62–63

Johnston, Gen. Joseph E., 4

Johnston-Pettigrew Chapter (Raleigh, N.C.), 131

Julia Jackson CofC Chapter (Charlotte, N.C.), 136

Keller, Helen, 137, 190n54

Kentucky UDC, 129, 131

King's Daughters, 34

Ku Klux Klan (KKK): children's primer for, 107, 109–10, 171n19; distancing from second, 171n19; reverence for first, 37; white women's writings on, 104, 107–9, 138

Ladies' Memorial Associations (LMAs): children's involvement with, 119; fundraising by, 9–11; legacy of, 16–17, 26, 50; memorial work of, 2, 4, 34, 49, 53; NDOC constitution and, 21–22; objectives of, 19–20; soldiers' homes and, 178n15; urged to join UDC, 30
laws, 14, 142. See also states' rights; white supremacy
leadership: concerns of, 30–31, 38; definitions of, 3; in Lost Cause celebrations, 12–13, 20–21, 52; as public achievement, 35–36; in social welfare, 74–75; in textbook campaigns, 124, 166n9. See also United Daughters of the Confederacy (UDC): power and influence of
Lebanon (Tenn.), monument in, 60
Lee, Ellen Foule (wife of Fitzhugh), 38, 62
Lee, Fitzhugh, 13, 38, 62
Lee, Mary (daughter), 62
Lee, Robert E.: Boyson's essay on, 112–16; CofC programs on, 137; family of, 38, 62; honoring of, 14, 127, 130–31, 161; land of, 54, 69; monuments to, 13, 53, 62–63, 66; portraits of, 2, 58, 130–32, 134, 160, 189n32; as role model, 103, 130
Lee, Susan Pendleton, 124–25
Lee Monument Association, 13
Lee, Col. Robert E. (son), 70
Lee, Gen. Stephen D., 187n9
Leopard's Spots, The (Dixon), 129
liberty bonds, 155
libraries, 102, 138
Lincoln, Abraham, 128, 137
Lost Cause: children indoctrinated with, 13–15, 65, 121–22, 127–28, 138–40, 160–62; early participants in, 2–3; evolution of, 4–7; exemplar of, 43; ideology of, 10–12; as just and heroic, 2, 4, 49, 67, 96, 126–27; leading organization in, 12–13, 20–

21, 52; legacy of, 3, 4, 160–63; narrative of, 44–45, 67, 86, 103–4, 158, 160; politics of, 23, 169n37; scholarship in support of, 184n37; shifts in focus of, 11–12, 16, 25; tradition's link to, 9–10, 44. See also celebrations; vindication efforts
Lost Cause (magazine): description of, 178–79n20; editor of, 167n6; on needy women, 77–78; ownership of, 185n52; on women's role, 111
Louise Home (Washington, D.C.), 80–81
Louisiana: monument in, 64, 65; Public Playgrounds Commission of, 153; soldiers' home in, 75; war support in, 152
Louisiana UDC, 114, 129, 152
Lumpkin, Elizabeth. See Glenn, Elizabeth Lumpkin
Lumpkin, Katherine DuPre, 127

Mary Custis Lee UDC (Alexandria, Va.), 135
Maryland UDC, 82, 114, 155
masculine ideal, 44–47
McKinley, William, 71
McLaurin, Anselm J., 38
McSherry, Virginia, 31, 38, 58, 169n35
members: age of current, 163; as CofC chapter leaders, 136–37; historical writing by, 95–96, 101–5, 107–11, 125, 129, 138, 183n27; northern women as, 30, 112; older generation of, 33–37; as powerful but genteel, 44; as teachers, 86, 129–30; younger generation of, 37–41
membership: advantages of, 29–30; diversity and similarity in, 34; eligibility requirements for, 21–24, 31, 169n35; exclusivity of, 5, 18, 19, 30–31; growth of, 28–32, 50–51, 67, 112; as "sacred obligation," 32
Memorial Continental Hall (Washington, D.C.), 147, 148
Memorial Day, Confederate: children's participation in, 37, 119, 133, 135, 136, 160, 161; CofC programs on, 137; expansion of, 4–5, 20; monuments as focus of early, 66; persistence of, 163; support for, 16; women's role in, 4, 11, 49–50

memorialization: in federation efforts, 18; gender parity in, 24; legacy of, 16, 26; by LMAs, 2, 4, 34, 49, 53; as objective, 2–3, 18–20; rehabilitation as, 9–11; shift in focus of, 66–67; social power in, 12–13; vindication efforts and, 1, 49, 60, 65; women's visibility in, 11, 13–14, 49–50. *See also* graves; monument building; monuments

memory. *See* public memory

men: assumptions about leadership of, 20; educational assistance for, 91; North somewhat respected by, 146; rehabilitation of defeated, 9–10, 41–43, 96; role models for, 103–4, 130; southern ideal for, 44–47. *See also* New Men; soldiers' homes; veterans, Confederate

Mississippi: archives in, 98; artifact collecting in, 99; monument unveiling in, 64; Old State Capitol in, 100; schoolbooks in, 109–10, 124; soldiers' home in, 79, 82, 89, 98; white supremacy's persistence in, 161. *See also* Beauvoir (soldiers' home)

Mississippi Federation of Women's Clubs, 100

Mississippi Plan, 38, 107

Mississippi Textbook Commission, 124

Mississippi UDC: artifact collecting by, 99; chapters of, 124, 131–32, 175n19; Confederate flags and, 133; Davis's centennial and, 131–32; education committee of, 84; fund-raising of, 57; indigent women and, 79. *See also* Beauvoir (soldiers' home)

Missouri, soldiers' home in, 15–16, 75

Missouri UDC, 75, 84

Moffitt, Elvira, 150

Montana UDC chapter, 131

Montgomery (Ala.), monument in, 56, 62

Monumental Association (Raleigh), 57

Monument Association (Nashville), 17, 35

monument building: impetus for, 49–50; by LMAs, 49, 53; marked increase in, 67–68; patriotism evidenced by, 65, 67, 72; questioning money spent on, 87, 90; reward for, 60–61; success in, 160;

UCV and, 52, 58; UDC's growth linked to, 50–51; workforce for, 174n1; WWI's effect on, 155, 157–58. *See also* fund-raising

monuments: children as, 120; cost of, 56; design of, 13, 55–56; education via, 68–69; to Lee, 13, 53, 62–63, 66; symbolism of, 2, 4, 66–72, 146–47; unveiling of, 60–65, 70–71, 133, 136; in vindication efforts, 49, 60, 72; to women, 78, 179n22; women's home as, 77. *See also* Arlington National Cemetery, Confederate monument in; Jefferson Davis Monument (Richmond); Shiloh Monument

moral guardianship, 21, 26–27, 85–86, 122–23

motherhood, Confederate, 122–23, 186–87n5

Mt. Pleasant (Tenn.), monument in, 63

Mt. Vernon, *83*

Museum of the Confederacy (Richmond), 98, 99, 117

museums: buildings for, 98, 99, 100; collecting material culture for, 95–96, 98–99; establishment of, 117; fund-raising for, 179n22

music: child's protest of northern, 118–19; at CofC meetings, 136, 137; at monument unveilings, 64–65

Nashville (Tenn.): college in, 90; fund-raising in, 56; UDC organizational meeting in, 18–19

nation, resistance to term, 145

National Association for the Advancement of Colored People (NAACP), 159, 163

National Association of the Daughters of the Confederacy (NDOC): constitution of, 21–23; members of, 168n27; name change of, 23; objectives of, 19–20; organizational meeting of, 18–19. *See also* United Daughters of the Confederacy (UDC)

nationalism, 45, 145, 151–52

National Peace Congress (NPC), 149–50

National Tribune, 148–49

New Men: characteristics of, 45–46; criticism of, 46–47, 77–78; objectives of, 5; use of term, 173n38

New Orleans: monument in, 64, 65; war support in, 152

New Orleans UDC, 114, 129

New South: economy and exports of, 151–52; illiteracy in, 86, 114; industrialization in, 37–38; influences on, 9–10, 91–92; legacy of Lost Cause in, 3, 4, 160–63; men's roles in, 45–46; monuments' role in, 67; Redeemers of, 107; research on, 165n3; term abhorred, 12; women's dilemmas in, 40–41, 44–45; WWI support in, 151, 152. *See also* Old South

New Women: dilemmas for, 40–41, 44–45; Lumpkin as, 43; tradition wedded to, 10–11, 14, 20–21, 26–27, 44; venue for political expression, 26–27

New York UDC, 149–50

Nichols, Francis, 96, 145–46

North: as conciliatory, 5; history biased by, 94, 96–97, 111–12, 114, 123, 126–27, 143; southern generals celebrated in, 131; South offended by, 143–44. *See also* reconciliation; Reconstruction

North Carolina: archives in, 182n11; CofC chapters in, 136–37; hospital in, 8; LMA in, 9; school in, 125; veterans' pensions in, 75

North Carolina Museum of History, 117

North Carolina State Normal and Industrial College (now UNC-Greensboro), 90–91

North Carolina UDC: chapters of, 114, 131; educational efforts of, 84, 90–91; "mother" of, 21; school visits and, 128; state legislature's cooperation with, 83; war relief work and, 193n41; women's home and, 79, 80; women's role documented by, 111

NPC (National Peace Congress), 149–50

Odenheimer, Cordelia Powell, 154; on northern textbooks, 126; status of, 38; successor to, 156; on Wilson and war, 153–54, 155

Ohio UDC, 131

Old South: idealization of, 2, 12, 37–41, 43, 104–6, 122, 125, 139, 183–84n33; nonsoutherners' beliefs about, 97; preservation of, 7, 37–38, 48, 95–96, 183–84n33. *See also* Confederate culture; Lost Cause; New South; slavery; southern traditions; states' rights; white supremacy

oral history, 95, 98, 139–40, 181–82n5, 182n11

ordinances of seccession, 133, 189n40

Page, Thomas Nelson, 125, 137, 138

Parsley, Eliza Nutt, 21, 23

paternalism, 77, 104, 178n19

patriotism: Confederate flag as symbol of, 133; evidenced by Confederate heroes, 2, 4, 49, 67, 96, 126–27; Lee as exemplar of, 130; monument building as evidence of, 65, 67, 72; monuments' role in teaching, 68–69; northerners' recognition of southern, 142–45, 146, 148; WWI support and, 151–54, 157–58

Peabody Normal College (Nashville), 90

Peace Day, 150

peace movement, 149–53

pensions, 75, 83

Phillips, Ulrich Bonnell, 116, 184n37

Pittsburg (Tenn.) CofC chapter, 134

Plane, Caroline Helen, 80–82, 98

politics and political structure: of historic preservation, 100; of Lost Cause, 23, 169n37; monuments' role in, 66–69; ostensible rejection of, 23, 169n37; possibilities in, 26–27; return of southern control of, 11, 70–71, 142; women's influence in, 29, 53, 57, 72, 83, 123, 160, 179n34. *See also* states' rights; white supremacy

"politics of domestic loss" concept, 9

Poppenheim, Mary B.: on education committee, 90, 115; education of, 116; status of, 38; on "truthful" history, 101–2; war relief work and, 156–57, 158

preservation: of buildings, 98, 100, 117; of documents and records, 97–98, 182n11;

of material culture, 95–96, 98–99. *See also* historical efforts

president-generals: characteristics of, 38–39; power of, 35–36

Price, Virginia Redditt, 32, 129, 133, 189n31

pro-Confederate, use of term, 187n11

progressivism: as influence, 73–74, 81, 192n26; opportunities in, 48; UDC members involved in, 34–37, 41. *See also* Confederate progressivism

Prohibition, 155

pro-southern, use of term, 187n11

public memory: African American, of war, 181n3; Early's influence on, 181n4; gender parity in, 24; KKK in, 110; women's influence on, 72

public roles: context of emerging, 9–10; dilemmas in, 40–41, 44–45; evoked in Lumpkin's traditional woman, 43, 48; tradition wedded to, 10–11, 14, 20–21, 26–27, 44. *See also* politics and political structure

race relations: idealized view of Old South's, 104–6; resentment of interference in, 106–7. *See also* white supremacy

racism: children indoctrinated with, 13–15, 65, 121–22, 127–28, 138–40, 160–62; of Confederate culture, 1–2; justification of, 106; persistence of, 161–63. *See also* slavery

Raines, Anna Davenport, 17; federation efforts of, 16–18; Goodlett's conflict with, 24–25; legacy of, 160; on LMA members, 30; on members' behavior, 33; on membership eligibility, 21–23, 31; offices held by, 19; on sectional reconciliation, 141

Randolph, Janet: on Boyson's essay, 115; monument building and, 13, 52–53, 59–60; on relief committee, 82

rebels and rebellion, resentment of terms, 93, 96, 128, 136, 142, 144

reconciliation: achievement of, 157–58; debate over, 142–43; hindrances to, 111–12, 119, 143–46, 149; Lost Cause origins

and, 4–7; monument as symbol of, 70–71, 146–47; move toward, 149–50; opposition to, 141–42; vindication efforts and, 68–69, 71–72, 142–43

Reconstruction: attitudes toward, 37; KKK's violence in, 107–9; white women's writings on, 104, 106, 184n38

republican motherhood, 122, 123

Richmond (Va.): monuments in, 13, 53, 62, 66; museum in, 98, 99, 117; women's home in, 76–78. *See also* Jefferson Davis Monument (Richmond)

Richmond (Va.) UDC, 115

Robinson, Virginia Morgan, 102–3, 114

Roosevelt, Theodore, 5, 36

Rose, Laura Martin, *108*; as influence, 184–85n46; on KKK, 107–9, 138; KKK primer by, 107, 109–10, 171n19; Old State Capitol preservation and, 100; on ordinances of seccession in schools, 189n40

Rowland, Dunbar, 116

Rowland, Eron, 100, 152

Rowland, Kate Mason, 30

Rutherford, Mildred Lewis, *40*; activities of, 39–41; on black suffrage, 107; as historian-general, 96, 97, 103, 137–38, 183nn27, 30; on LMA members, 30; on peace resolutions, 150; on Reconstruction, 184n38; role models for, 45; on slavery, 104, 105–6; successor to, 109; women's homes and, 80–82; on women's role, 76; writings of, 103, 125, 129, 138, 183n27, 187nn17, 18

San Antonio (Texas), fund-raising in, 56

scholarships: scandal over, 112–16; for studying "true" history of South, 185n55; in support of Lost Cause, 184n37; for teacher training, 73–74, 84, 91, 112, 185n55

schools: citizens' councils on (1960s), 162; Confederate flags and portraits in, 121–22, 127–28, 130–34, 160; essay contests in, 121–22, 129–30; texts sent to black, 125, 161; visits to, 127–28, 188n27. *See also* teachers; textbook campaigns

Schuyler, Leonora Rogers, 112–13, 115–16
seccession, 133, 137, 189n40
sectional identity: flag as symbol of, 149; support for, 141–42, 191n14; Taft's speech on, 148. *See also* reconciliation
self-government, 70–71
Shaw, Gen. Albert D., 143–44
Sherman, William T., 8, 118
Shiloh Chapter (UDC), 54–55
Shiloh Monument: cost of, 53, 56; fund-raising for, 54–56; national significance of, 67–68
Shiloh Monument Committee (SMC), 55, 67–68
slavery: catechism on, 138–39; idealization of, 44, 122, 125, 139, 172n36; justification of, 105–6; paternalism in, 104; revising narratives about, 97; textbooks on, 124–26; as topic in essay contest, 129. *See also* Confederate culture; history writing; Old South; white supremacy
Smith, C. Alphonse, 113, 115
social efforts: for indigent women, 79–82; as objective, 3, 19–20; UDC as leader in, 74–75. *See also* soldiers' homes; women's homes
soldiers, Union, 67–68
soldiers' aid societies, 8–9, 10, 17
soldiers' homes: Beauvoir as, 79, 82, 89, 98; fund-raising for, 15, 75–76; LMAs' and CSMA's role in, 178n15; success in, 160; support for, 73; as symbol, 91–92; women not allowed in, 80
Sons of Confederate Veterans (SCV): building preservation and, 100; defensiveness of current, 194n11; effectiveness of, 166n9; financial support from, 46, 47–48; flag controversy and, 159; founding of, 5, 47; historical efforts of, 97–98; limits of, 123; monument building and, 52; textbook campaign and, 124; UDC compared with, 172–73n37
South Carolina, state flag of, 159–60, 163, 194n2
South Carolina UDC, 84, 110–11, 114, 115
South Carolina Women in the Confederacy (book), 111

Southern Historical Society (SHS), 13, 95, 181n4
Southern Industrial Education Association (SIEA), 87
southern traditions: highlighted in NDOC constitution, 20; idealization of, 41; industry promoted with, 12; Lost Cause linked to, 9–10; monuments as continuity of, 67; preservation of, 26–27, 32–33; suffrage as threat to, 171n13; women's public roles blended with, 10–11, 14, 20–21, 26–27, 44. *See also* Confederate culture; Lost Cause; Old South; slavery
Spanish-American War, 45, 142, 143
St. Louis (Mo.): soldiers' home in, 15–16, 75; World's Fair in, 98
state divisions: appeals to, 87; authority of, 23; CofC chapters organized by, 135; formation of, 29; historical efforts of, 97–99, 101; peace efforts of, 152; relief for indigent women and, 79, 80–83; textbook campaigns of, 124; war relief work of, 155–57. *See also* chapters; *specific states*
states' rights: celebration of, 14; children indoctrinated with, 13–15, 65, 121–22, 127–28, 138–40, 160–62; education to promote, 91; heroes of, 2, 4, 49, 67, 96, 126–27; NDOC as reflective of, 23; North vs. South on, 143; persistent reverence for, 161–63; as reason for war, 12, 96, 138–39, 144–45, 187n11
Stephens, Alexander, 101
Stevens, Daisy McLaurin: on fund-raising, 175n19; illustrations of, 71, 151; at monument unveiling, 70, 71; on peace work, 151–52; status of, 38; Wilson's letter to, 192–93n39
Stone, Cornelia Branch, 36; activities of, 35, 37; age as president-general, 39; appointments by, 84, 86, 90; on Boyson's essay, 114, 115–16; catechism prepared by, 138–39; on CofC chapters, 135; on history studies, 101; Old South idealized by, 105; on portraits in schools, 132; on proposed elite home, 81–82
Stone Mountain memorial (Ga.), 53, 174n8

Stowe, Harriet Beecher, 97
Stuart, Gen. J.E.B., 62
suffrage movement: building preservation and, 100; opposition to, 40–41, 171n13; support for, 34, 37, 41; UDC compared with, 33

Taft, William Howard: Arlington monument and, 54, 71; UDC convention and, 147, 148, 149, 171n17; UDC president hosted by, 5–6, 36
teachers: assistance and scholarships for, 73–74, 84, 86, 91, 112, 185n55; essay contests for, 129; northerners as, 128; UDC members as, 86, 129–30. *See also* schools
Tennessee: archives in, 98; CofC chapter in, 134; fund-raising in, 56; monuments in, 60, 63, 68; soldiers' home in, 17, 35; UDC organizational meeting in, 18–19; widows' and orphans' home in, 35, 74. *See also* Shiloh Monument
Tennessee Confederate Soldiers' Home, Ladies' Auxiliary to, 17, 35
Tennessee UDC: chapters of, 68; educational efforts of, 90; membership of, 169–70n1; Shiloh monument and, 54–55
Texas: college in, 92; fund-raising in, 56; monument unveiling in, 61–63
Texas Federation of Women's Clubs (TXFWC), 35, 37
Texas Home for Confederate Women, 79, 80, 82
Texas UDC: artifact collecting by, 99; on Davis's and Lee's birthdays, 130; essay contest of, 105; membership of, 29, 169–70n1; officers of, 35; women's home and, 79, 80, 82
textbook campaigns: leadership of, 124, 166n9; objective of, 3, 121, 123–27, 187n11; in 1960s, 161, 162; school visits combined with, 127–28, 188n27; success of, 160; UCV's role in, 124, 181–82n5, 187n9
Thurmond, Strom, 162

UDC Catechism for Children, 138–39

Uncle Tom's Cabin (Stowe), 97
United Confederate Veterans (UCV): building preservation and, 100; founding of, 13; Historical Committee of, 95, 181–82n5; limits of, 123; monument building and, 52, 58; on North's attitudes, 144; soldiers' homes and, 75; textbook campaign and, 124, 181–82n5, 187n9; UDC distinguished from, 24, 39; women's auxiliaries to, 16, 30. *See also* Sons of Confederate Veterans (SCV); veterans, Confederate
United Daughters of the Confederacy (UDC): achievements of, 7, 48, 72, 91–92, 117, 139–40, 157–58; appeals to, 84–86, 87; constitution and bylaws of, 21–23, 83–84, 94, 186n3; emergence of, 4–7, 16–17; founding of, 2, 23–25; growth of, 28–32, 50–51, 67, 112; legacy of, 160–63; northerners' criticism of, 144, 148–49; objectives of, 1–3, 27, 73, 86 (*see also* specific objectives); other organizations compared with, 24, 29, 33, 34, 39; power and influence of, 12–13, 53, 57, 72, 126, 157, 179n34; shifts of focus of, 86, 135, 155, 157. *See also* chapters; fund-raising; general conventions; historian-general office; members; membership; president-generals; state divisions

veterans, Confederate: care for aging, 8, 9–10, 17, 35, 74, 75; CofC programs on, 137; as heroes, 2, 4, 49, 67, 96, 126–27; honoring of, 14–15, 127, 156, 161; offended by northerners, 143–44; oral histories of, 98, 182n11; pensions for, 75; rehabilitation of defeated, 9–10, 41–43, 96; reunions of, 13. *See also* soldiers' homes; United Confederate Veterans (UCV)
vindication efforts: by children of veterans and other parents, 37–39; history's link to, 93–96, 101, 103–4; memorialization and, 1, 49, 60, 65; opportunity for, 29; as overarching objective, 3, 5, 27, 32, 97, 146; reconciliation linked to, 68–69, 71–72, 142–43; success of,

vindication efforts—*continued*
142, 158; textbook campaign linked to, 124; "true" history of KKK as part of, 107–9; WWI's effect on, 157–58
Virginia UDC: chapters of, 115; CofC chapters of, 135; illustration of, *83*; textbook campaign of, 126. *See also* Richmond (Va.)

Waddell, Alfred Moore, 93, 96
War between the States: children's understanding of, 128; use of term, 94–95; white women's writings on, 104. *See also* reconciliation; Reconstruction
Washington, George, 128, 130, 160, 189n32
Washington (D.C.): UDC convention in, 146–49; women's home in, 80–81
Weed, Julia, 24–25
Wells, June Murray, 159–60
West, Decca Lamar, *138*, 190n56
West Point (Ga.) UDC, 68
White, Rassie Hoskins, *33*; on membership eligibility, 31, 169n35; on membership numbers, 169–70n1; monument building and, 49, 55, 67–68; on objectives, 32–33, 73; on SCV, 48; on Taft's reception, 147
white supremacy: celebrations of, 13–15; children indoctrinated with, 13–15, 65, 121–22, 127–28, 138–40, 160–62; educating poor to sustain, 84–86, 87, 91; heroes of, 2, 4, 49, 67, 96, 126–27; justification of, 105–6; KKK as heroes of, 107–9; legal enforcement of, 14, 142; monument unveilings reflective of, 61–65; nationwide emphasis on, 45; persistence of, 161–63; reinforcement of, 125, 158; resentment of interference in, 106–7; support for, 1, 4–5, 39, 129, 160
widows' pensions, 83. *See also* women's homes
Williams, John Sharp, 54
Williamson, Mary L., 101, 125, 137–38
Wilmington Race Riot (1898), 93
Wilson, Woodrow: correspondence of, 192–93n39; as essay contest judge, 113; hopes for reconciliation under, 148;

support for, 151, 153–54; UDC president hosted by, 5–6, 36; at unveiling of Confederate monument in Arlington, 70–71
Winnie Davis Chapter (Meridian, Miss.), 131–32
Winnie Davis Memorial Building, 90
Wirz, Capt. Henry, 144
women: dilemmas of, in New South, 40–41, 44–45; education for poor white, 84–86, 89–91; generational differences and, 19, 25, 30; ignored in earlier scholarship, 3; song as affront to, 118–19. *See also* Confederate motherhood; New Women; women's homes; women's roles
women "of the 1860s": caring for, 74, 76–77, 79–82; CofC programs on, 137; official history of, 111; oral histories of, 95, 98, 181–82n5; pensions for, 83; recognizing role of, 10, 110–11; reverence for, 23–24, 38, 43–44, 48, 76; as role models, 154, 174n48; UDC women likened to, 60–61. *See also* women's homes
Women of the South in War Times, The (book), 111
Women's Christian Temperance Union (WCTU), 26, 29, 34, 100
women's homes: campaigns for, 79–82; fund-raising for, 76–77; need for, 77–78; success in, 35, 160; support for, 73; as symbol, 91–92
women's roles: in American Revolution, 122, 137; blending tradition and public in, 10–11, 14, 20–21, 26–27, 44; as caretakers, 77; idealization of plantation mistress's, 39, 41–45, 139–40; in Memorial Days, 4, 11, 49–50; motherhood as, 122–23, 186–87n5; preserving traditional, 26–27, 32–33
World's Fair (St. Louis, 1904), 98
World War I: peace movement and, 149–51; reconciliation after, 157–58; southerners in, 143; UDC's support for, 153–57

Yerger, Lucy, 100, 162
Young, Gen. Bennett, 70
Young Women's Christian Association (YWCA), 34

Karen L. Cox is assistant professor and director of the public history program at the University of North Carolina at Charlotte. *Dixie's Daughters* is her first book.

CPSIA information can be obtained
at www.ICGtesting.com
Printed in the USA
FSOW01n1257031217
41835FS